First World War
and Army of Occupation
War Diary
France, Belgium and Germany

39 DIVISION
Divisional Troops
Royal Army Medical Corps
134 Field Ambulance
6 March 1916 - 12 December 1918

WO95/2579/1

The Naval & Military Press Ltd
www.nmarchive.com
Published in association with The National Archives

Published by

The Naval & Military Press Ltd

Unit 10 Ridgewood Industrial Park,
Uckfield, East Sussex,
TN22 5QE England
Tel: +44 (0) 1825 749494

www.naval-military-press.com

www.nmarchive.com

This diary has been reprinted in facsimile from the original. Any imperfections are inevitably reproduced and the quality may fall short of modern type and cartographic standards.

© **Crown Copyright**
Images reproduced by permission of The National Archives, London, England, 2015.

Contents

Document type	Place/Title	Date From	Date To
Heading	WO95/2579/1 134 Field Ambulance Mar 1916-Dec 1918		
Heading	39th Division Medical 134th Fld Ambulance Mar 1916-Dec 1918 WO95/2579		
Heading	134th Field Ambulance March 1916		
War Diary	Haig Hutments Farnham	06/03/1916	06/03/1916
War Diary	Southampton	06/03/1916	06/03/1916
War Diary	Le Havre	07/03/1916	08/03/1916
War Diary	Abbeville	09/03/1916	09/03/1916
War Diary	Thiennes	09/03/1916	09/03/1916
War Diary	Boesinghem	10/03/1916	10/03/1916
War Diary	Estaires	10/03/1916	27/03/1916
War Diary	Zelobes	27/03/1916	31/03/1916
Heading	134th F. Amb. April 1916 39th Div		
War Diary	Zelobes	01/04/1916	18/04/1916
War Diary	Mesplaux	19/04/1916	30/04/1916
Heading	134th F. Amb. May 1916 39th Div.		
War Diary	Mesplaux	01/05/1916	31/05/1916
Miscellaneous	O.C. 134 F.A. To O i/c A.G.'s. Office Base.	01/04/1916	01/04/1916
Heading	No. 134 F.A. June 1916		
War Diary	Mesplaux	01/06/1916	30/06/1916
Miscellaneous	O.C. 134th Fd. Amb. To A.G. Base.		
Heading	39th Division 134th Field Ambulance July 1916. 39th Division		
War Diary	Mesplaux	01/07/1916	06/07/1916
War Diary	Annezin	07/07/1916	31/07/1916
Miscellaneous	Original To D.A.G. 3rd Echelon August 1916		
War Diary	Annezin E.9.6.28	01/08/1916	10/08/1916
War Diary	L Abbaye Neuville	11/08/1916	22/08/1916
War Diary	Maiziers	23/08/1916	23/08/1916
War Diary	Lucheux	24/08/1916	24/08/1916
War Diary	Bus-Les Artois	25/08/1916	25/08/1916
War Diary	Acheux	26/08/1916	31/08/1916
Heading	39th Div 134th Field Ambulance Sept 1916		
War Diary	Acheux	01/09/1916	30/09/1916
Heading	134th F.A. Oct 1916		
War Diary	Acheux P13.a. 3.3	01/10/1916	04/10/1916
War Diary	Cabstand W. 10 C.u.3	05/10/1916	31/10/1916
Heading	War Diary of 134th Field Ambulance from 1st. November to 30th November 1916 Vol 9		
War Diary	Cabstand W. 10 C43	01/11/1916	14/11/1916
War Diary	Warloy	15/11/1916	16/11/1916
War Diary	Amplier	17/11/1916	17/11/1916
War Diary	Doullens	18/11/1916	18/11/1916
War Diary	Wormhoudt	19/11/1916	30/11/1916
Miscellaneous	IInd Corps Medical Instructions. No. 5 Appendix 1	31/10/1916	31/10/1916
Miscellaneous	Amendment To IInd Corps Medical Instructions No. 5	02/11/1916	02/11/1916
Miscellaneous	Secret and Pressing Appendix 2	01/11/1916	01/11/1916
Operation(al) Order(s)	R.A.M.C. Operation Order No. 15 by Colonel G.W. Brazier-Creagh, C.M.G., A.D.M.S. 39th. Div.	14/11/1916	14/11/1916

Heading	War. Diary. 39th Div Vol 10		
War Diary	Wormhoudt	01/12/1916	12/12/1916
War Diary	A 23. C. 29 Ref Sheet NW. 28/40000	13/12/1916	13/12/1916
War Diary	A. 23.C. 29	14/12/1916	21/12/1916
War Diary	A. 23 c 29 Sheet 28 1/4000	22/12/1916	31/12/1916
Heading	War Diary. Vol XI		
War Diary	A 23.c.2.9. Sheet 28	01/01/1917	13/01/1917
War Diary	Red Farm G.5.0.9.2. Sheets	14/01/1917	31/01/1917
Heading	War Diary. Vol 12		
War Diary	Red. Farm (G.5.d.9.1. Sheet 28).	01/02/1917	12/02/1917
War Diary	Red Farm (G.d.5.9.1.)	13/02/1917	17/02/1917
War Diary	Herzeele (D.10.c.1.7. Sheet 27.)	18/02/1917	23/02/1917
War Diary	Herzeele (D.10.c.1.7)	24/02/1917	27/02/1917
War Diary	Waratah Camp (G.15.a.3.0 Sheet 28)	28/02/1917	28/02/1917
Heading	War Diary of 134th Field Ambulance, From March 1st to March 31st 1917. (Volume 1)		
War Diary	Waratah Camp. (G.15.a.3.0. Sheet 28)	01/03/1917	31/03/1917
Heading	War Diary of 134th Field Ambulance From April 1st. to April 30th 1917. (Volume 14)		
War Diary	Waratah Camp (G.15.a.3.0 Sheet 28)	01/04/1917	16/04/1917
War Diary	Bollezeele (A.24.c Sheet 27)	17/04/1917	28/04/1917
War Diary	Watou (K.4.b. Sheet 27)	29/04/1917	30/04/1917
Heading	War Diary Of 13th Field Ambulance From May 1st To May 31st, 1917. (Volume 15).		
War Diary	Watou (K.4.b.9.5 Sheet 27)	01/05/1917	15/05/1917
War Diary	Poperinghe (G.2.a.2.4. Sheet 28.)	15/05/1917	31/05/1917
Heading	War Diary Of 134th Field Ambulance From 1st June To 30th June, 1917. (Volume 16).		
War Diary	Chateau Rouge Poperinghe (G.2.a.2.4. Sheet 28)	01/06/1917	07/06/1917
War Diary	Red Chateau Poperinghe (G.2.a.2.4 Sheet 28)	08/06/1917	14/06/1917
War Diary	Chateau Rouge Poperinghe (G.2.a.2.4 Sheet 28)	15/06/1917	24/06/1917
War Diary	Chateau Rouge Poperinghe To Gwalia Farm Nr Elverdinghe (A.23.c.2.9. Sheet 28)	25/06/1917	29/06/1917
War Diary	Gwalia Farm Nr Elverdinghe (A.23.c.2.9. Sheet 28.)	30/06/1917	30/06/1917
Miscellaneous	B.E.F. Summary Of Medical War Diaries Of 13th F.A. 39th Div. 18th Corps. 5th Army. (From 10/6/17).	10/06/1917	10/06/1917
Miscellaneous	134th F.A. 39th Div. 18th Corps. 5th Army. Western Front. Officer Commanding-Lt. Col. Hildreth, D.S.O. June 1917		
Miscellaneous	B.E.F. Summary Of Medical War Diaries Of 134th F.A. 39th Div. 18th Corps. 5th Army. (From 10/6/17.)	10/06/1917	10/06/1917
Miscellaneous	134th F.A. 39th Div. 18th Corps. 5th Army. Western Front. Officer Commanding-Lt. Col. Hildreth, D.S.O. June 1917		
Heading	War Diary Of 134th Field Ambulance. From July 1st 1917 To July 31st 1917 (Volume 17.)		
War Diary	Gwalia Farm Nr Elverdinghe (Map Reference A.23.c.2.9. Sheet 28.)	01/07/1917	31/07/1917
Miscellaneous	Summary Of Medical War Diaries Of 134th F.A. 39th Div. 18th Corps 5th Army To 2nd Army Area From August 7th.		
Miscellaneous	134th F.A. 39th Div. 18th Corps. 5th Army. Officer Commanding-Lt. Col. Hildreth, D.S.O. To 2nd Army Area From August 7th.	07/08/1917	07/08/1917
Heading	War Diary Of 134th Field Ambulance From 1st To 31st August, 1917. (Volume 18).		

War Diary	Gwalia Farm A.23.c.2.9. Sheet 28	01/08/1917	07/08/1917
War Diary	W.5.c.3.9. Sheet 27	08/08/1917	13/08/1917
War Diary	I.31.c.4.7. Voormezeele	14/08/1917	17/08/1917
War Diary	Voormezeele I.31.c.4.7 Sheet 28	18/08/1917	27/08/1917
War Diary	Voormezeele I.31.c.4.7	28/08/1917	31/08/1917
Miscellaneous			
Miscellaneous	Summary Of Medical War Diaries Of 134th F.A. 39th Div. 18th Corps. 5th Army.		
Heading	War Diary Of 134th Field Ambulance From 1st. Sept. To 30th Sept. 1917. (Volume 19).		
War Diary	Voormezeele (I.31.c.4.7. Sheet 28.)	01/09/1917	17/09/1917
War Diary	Brasserie N.6.a.2.2. Sheet 28	17/09/1917	23/09/1917
War Diary	Voormezeele (I.31.c.4.7. Sheet 28.)	24/09/1917	27/09/1917
War Diary	Mont Kokereele Farm Sheet 27 R.17.b.5.2	27/09/1917	30/09/1917
Heading	War Diary Of 134th Field Ambulance From Oct. 1st 1917 To Oct. 31st 1917. (Volume 20)		
War Diary	Mount Kokereele (R.17.b.5.2. Sheet 27)	01/10/1917	15/10/1917
War Diary	Keersebrom (S.10.d.5.7 Sheet 28)	16/10/1917	17/10/1917
War Diary	Meteren (X.15.d.3.7. Sheet 27)	18/10/1919	18/10/1919
War Diary	Meteren (X.15.d.3.7. Sheet 27)	19/10/1917	31/10/1917
Heading	War Diary Of 134th Field Ambulance From Nov. 1st 1917. To Nov. 30th 1917. (Volume 21)		
War Diary	Meteren Sheet X.15.d.3.7	01/11/1917	17/11/1917
War Diary	Bailleul 8 Rue Benoit Cortyl	17/11/1917	22/11/1917
War Diary	No 8 Rue Benoit Cortyl Bailleul	23/11/1917	25/11/1917
War Diary	Hilhoek Sheet 27 L.2.0.b.8.8	26/11/1917	30/11/1917
Heading	War Diary of 134th Field Ambulance From Dec 1st 1917. to Dec 31st 1917. (Volume 22.)		
War Diary	Hilhoek L.2.0.b.8.8. Sheet 27	01/12/1917	02/12/1917
War Diary	Hilhoek L.2.0.b.88	03/02/1917	07/02/1917
War Diary	Hillhoek	07/12/1917	10/12/1917
War Diary	Hillhoek L.20.b.88 Sheet 27	10/12/1917	10/12/1917
War Diary	Affringues Sheet 5A Hazebrouck	10/12/1917	10/12/1917
War Diary	Affringues	11/12/1917	29/12/1917
War Diary	Gwalia Farm Sheet 28. A-23-c-2-9	29/12/1917	31/12/1917
Heading	War Diary of 134 Field Ambulance From Jan 1st to 31st 1918 (Volume 23).		
War Diary	Gwalia Farm Sheet 28. A-23-c-2-9	01/01/1918	04/01/1918
War Diary	Gwalia Farm	05/01/1918	21/01/1918
War Diary	Proven	21/01/1918	25/01/1918
War Diary	In train from Proven to Mericourt	25/01/1918	25/01/1918
War Diary	Suzanne (Amiens Sheet)	25/01/1918	28/01/1918
War Diary	Suzanne	29/01/1918	29/01/1918
War Diary	Heudecourt Sheet 57C W.21.b.28	30/01/1918	30/01/1918
War Diary	Heudecourt	31/01/1918	31/01/1918
Heading	War Diary Of 134th Field Ambulance From 1st Feb 1918 To 28th Feb 1918. (Volume 24.)		
War Diary	Heudecourt Map 57C W.21.b.8.2	01/02/1918	28/02/1918
War Diary	39th Division. Defence Scheme. Medical Arrangements Appendix No.		
War Diary	War Diary Of 134 Field Ambulance From March 1st 1918 To March 31st 1918 (Volume 25.)		
War Diary	Heudicourt W.21.b.2.8. Sheet 57	01/03/1918	11/03/1918
War Diary	Heudicourt	11/03/1918	11/03/1918
War Diary	Gurlu Wood Sheet 62c D.28.c.8.6	11/03/1918	21/03/1918
War Diary	Gurlu Wood	21/03/1918	21/03/1918

War Diary	Gurlu Wood Sheet 62c D.28.c.8.6	22/03/1918	22/03/1918
War Diary	Gurlu Wood	22/03/1918	22/03/1918
War Diary	On the Allaines Clery road at "C" in Feuillacourt Amiens 17 Clery	23/03/1918	23/03/1918
War Diary	On Road Between H. 20 & H. 26 Sheet 62 C.	23/03/1918	23/03/1918
War Diary	On Road At Point Between H. 20 & H. 26 (Sheet 62 C)	23/03/1918	23/03/1918
War Diary	G.30.c.8.8. Sheet 62 C	24/03/1918	24/03/1918
War Diary	Point Midnight Between Cappy Bray On Cappy-Bray Road (Arrives)	25/03/1918	25/03/1918
War Diary	L in Chuignes Sheet Amiens 17	25/03/1918	25/03/1918
War Diary	L In Chuignes	25/03/1918	25/03/1918
War Diary	On Road Above the "M" in Mericourt Sur Somme.	26/03/1918	26/03/1918
War Diary	Morcourt	26/03/1918	26/03/1918
War Diary	La Motte	26/03/1918	27/03/1918
War Diary	Villers Bretonneux	27/03/1918	27/03/1918
War Diary	Cachy	28/03/1918	28/03/1918
War Diary	Aubercourt	28/03/1918	28/03/1918
War Diary	Domart	28/03/1918	29/03/1918
War Diary	Berteaucourt.	29/03/1918	30/03/1918
War Diary	Boves	30/03/1918	31/03/1918
War Diary	Guignemicourt	31/03/1918	31/03/1918
Heading	War Diary Of 134th Field Ambulance From 1st April 1918 To 30th April 1918 (Volume 26.)		
War Diary	Guignemicourt	01/04/1918	02/04/1918
War Diary	Hallivilliers	02/04/1918	03/04/1918
War Diary	Fresnoy Andainville	04/04/1918	07/04/1918
War Diary	Dargnies	07/04/1918	08/04/1918
War Diary	Eu	08/04/1918	08/04/1918
War Diary	Arques	09/04/1918	09/04/1918
War Diary	Longueness	09/04/1918	11/04/1918
War Diary	Berthem	11/04/1918	30/04/1918
Heading	War Diary Of No. 134 Field Ambulance. From May 1st, 1918. To May 31st, 1918. (Volume V)		
War Diary	Berthem (Sheet Hazebrouck 5 A	01/05/1918	01/05/1918
War Diary	Berthem	05/05/1918	07/05/1918
War Diary	Berthem (Hazebrouck 5A)	07/05/1918	11/05/1918
War Diary	Berthem	12/05/1918	14/05/1918
War Diary	Pas (Sheet Lens)	15/05/1918	15/05/1918
War Diary	Pas (Sheet Lens 11)	16/05/1918	31/05/1918
Miscellaneous	Report On Training Of 305th Field Ambulance, U.S. Army, By Lieut. Colonel C.M. Drew, Commanding 134th Field Amb. B.E.F. Appendix I.	29/05/1918	29/05/1918
Heading	War Diary of 134th Field Ambulance From 1st June 1918 to 30th June 1918 (Volume 28.)		
War Diary	Pas. (Sheet Lens 11)	01/06/1918	10/06/1918
War Diary	Bertehem Sheet Hazebrouck	10/06/1918	19/06/1918
War Diary	Vieil Moutier (Sheet Calais 13)	19/06/1918	21/06/1918
War Diary	Vieil Moutier.	22/06/1918	27/06/1918
War Diary	Abbeville	27/06/1918	30/06/1918
Heading	War Diary Of 134 Field Ambulance From 1st July 1918, To 31st July, 1918. (Volume 29).		
War Diary	Abbeville	01/07/1918	01/07/1918
War Diary	Etaples	02/07/1918	02/07/1918
War Diary	Bertehem (Sheet Hazebrouck 5A)	02/07/1918	08/07/1918
War Diary	Nine Elms (Sheet 27 L.10.b.3.4.)	09/07/1918	14/07/1918
War Diary	Sheet 27 L.10.b.3.4	15/07/1918	20/07/1918

War Diary	Moynihan Camp 27/L.10.b.3.4	21/07/1918	31/07/1918
Heading	War Diary Of 134th Field Ambulance From 1st Aug. 1918 To 31st Aug. 1918. (Volume 30).		
War Diary	Sheet 27/L.10.b.3.4. Nine Elms.	01/08/1918	12/08/1918
War Diary	Moynihan Camp 27/L.10.b.3.4	13/08/1918	17/08/1918
War Diary	Moore Park 28/S.4.d.7.7	17/08/1918	24/08/1918
War Diary	Moore Park	25/08/1918	31/08/1918
Operation(al) Order(s)	Administrative Order No. 5-30th American Division. Appendix III.		
Heading	War Diary. Of 134th Field Ambulance From:- 1st September 1918. To 30th September 1918. (Volume 31.)		
War Diary	Moore Park 28/S.4.d.7.7	01/09/1918	03/09/1918
War Diary	27/L.10.b.3.4	03/09/1918	06/09/1918
War Diary	27/E.b.d.4.2	06/09/1918	07/09/1918
War Diary	Mesnil St Pol Sheet Lens II	07/09/1918	17/09/1918
War Diary	Lealvillers Sheet Lens II	17/09/1918	24/09/1918
War Diary	Brusle 62C/J.34.b.2.4	24/09/1918	28/09/1918
War Diary	Hervilly 62C K. 2.3. d.10. 6	28/09/1918	28/09/1918
War Diary	Jeancourt	29/09/1918	29/09/1918
War Diary	Jeancourt 62c L.26.d.1.1	29/09/1918	30/09/1918
Heading	War Diary of 134th Field Ambulance. From:- 1st October 1918. to 31st October 1918. (Volume 32.)		
War Diary	Jeancourt 62c L.26.d.1.1	01/10/1918	02/10/1918
War Diary	Asseviller 62c N.13.b Central	02/10/1918	04/10/1918
War Diary	Hamel 62c/K.13.c. Central	05/10/1918	05/10/1918
War Diary	Hamel	06/10/1918	06/10/1918
War Diary	Hargicourt 62/c L.5.d.1.8	07/10/1918	07/10/1918
War Diary	Bellicourt 62B/G.10.a.2.3	07/10/1918	09/10/1918
War Diary	Joncourt 62C/H.8.d.9.10	09/10/1918	12/10/1918
War Diary	Brancourt 62B/C.22.c.1.4	12/10/1918	13/10/1918
War Diary	Brancourt	14/10/1918	15/10/1918
War Diary	Brancourt 62B/C.22.c.1.4	15/10/1918	15/10/1918
War Diary	57B V.17.c.5.6	16/10/1918	16/10/1918
War Diary	Sheet 57B V.17.c.5.6. Busigny	17/10/1918	17/10/1918
War Diary	Busigny V.7.c.5.6./57B.	18/10/1918	18/10/1918
War Diary	Vaux Andigny 57B/W20 Central	18/10/1918	20/10/1918
War Diary	Busigny 57B/V17 C.5.6	20/10/1918	21/10/1918
War Diary	Estrees 62B/H.2.a.6.5	21/10/1918	22/10/1918
War Diary	Marquaix 62C/K.14.C.0.5	22/10/1918	23/10/1918
War Diary	Warloy 57D U.24.d.3.10	24/10/1918	31/10/1918
Heading	War Diary of 134 Field Ambulance From 1st Nov. 1918 to 30th Nov 1918. (Volume 33.)		
War Diary	Warloy 57D U.24.d.3.10	01/11/1918	16/11/1918
War Diary	Picquigny (Amiens No. 17.)	17/11/1918	18/11/1918
War Diary	Abbeville	18/11/1918	30/11/1918
Miscellaneous	Wrapper Indorsement.		
Heading	War Diary of 134th Field Ambulance From December 1st to December 12th Volume 34		
War Diary	Abbeville	02/12/1918	08/12/1918
War Diary	Etaples	09/12/1918	12/12/1918

WO95/2579

134 Field Ambulance

Mar 1916 – Dec 1918

①

39TH DIVISION
MEDICAL

134TH FLD AMBULANCE

MAR 1916 - DEC 1918

WO 95/2579

134th Field Ambulance

March 1916
Nov '16
Dec '18

Army Form C. 2118

Page 1

WAR DIARY
or
INTELLIGENCE SUMMARY
(Erase heading not required.)

134 FIELD AMBULANCE

Instructions regarding War Diaries and Intelligence Summaries are contained in F.S. Regs., Part II. and the Staff Manual respectively. Title Pages will be prepared in manuscript.

Place	Date	Hour	Summary of Events and Information	Remarks and references to Appendices
A14 HUTMENTS FARNHAM	March 6th 1916	6.45 am	First Train party worked to FARNBOROUGH & entrained. Train left at 10.10 a.m.	
		8.45 am	Second Train party entrained at some place & train left at 12.10. Entraining took 35 minutes. Bright day but freezing	
SOUTHAMPTON	6/3/16	12.30 pm	First Train arrived	
		2.15 pm	Second Train arrived. Embarked by 4.0 pm both parties in P.S. GLENARM HEAD. no accommodation. Life R & C. served out. Fitted & worn for flotation. Boat parties told off & paraded alongside each boat. Quite rough in midstream	
		8.0 pm	sailed.	
HAVRE	7/3/16	7.0 am (about)	Dropped anchor outside the harbour.	
		11.0 am	came alongside & started to disembark.	
		4.0 pm	Disembarkation completed. We had both from 12 midday to 1.30 for dinner. March from the boat very steep up to that welcome difficult to disembark	

WAR DIARY or INTELLIGENCE SUMMARY

134 FIELD AMBULANCE

Page 2.

Army Form C. 2118

Place	Date	Hour	Summary of Events and Information	Remarks and references to Appendices
LE HAVRE	7/3/16	4.30 p.m.	Marched to Rest Camp No 1. arrived at 5.30 p.m. S.M. Dees A.S.C. killed by a mule sent to hospital.	
"	8/3/16	7.30 a.m.	Entrained at POINT 3 at 7.30. Train moved off at 10 (about) appointed O.C. 134 on Train by R.T.O. about 290 all ranks of Hutts & Derby on train. An emergency kitchen made of thro' the running Ramp Kettles it was Provided by O.C. 134 Fd Amb	
ABBEVILLE	9/3/16	7.0 a.m.	40 minutes halt for breakfast. This was utilised nearly enough. hotts could be washed. This was the only halt on the journey owing to the late running of the train.	
THIENNES	9/3/16	8.30 p.m.	Detrained & marched to Billet.	
—	—	7.30 p.m.	Men in billets & dinner served	
BOESINGHEM	10/3/16	10.0 a.m.	Arrived. Wagons and all walked in night to fu...	

WAR DIARY or INTELLIGENCE SUMMARY

Army Form C. 2118
Page 3
134 FIELD AMBULANCE

Place	Date	Hour	Summary of Events and Information	Remarks and references to Appendices
ESTAIRES	10/3/13	4:30 P.M.	Frozen to hot blue marsheled onto road 16 mi. march to —	
	11/3/13		Arrive at ESTAIRES. Road muddy & slippery. Pack wagons in courtyard of the PENSIONNAT DES DEMOISELLES. "A" section detailed to form #4 & #5 Field Amb. for instruction. Lt Tutt on No. 6, 4 horse motor to O/c Advance Dressing Station at LAVENTIE. Other officers No. 0, 1 motor, 2 Ford Ambulance to Divisional Collection Station ESTAIRES. 7 motor ambulances (5 Sunbeams & 2 Fords) 1 motorcycle 1 Ford, 1 4 hp & 16 men joined our Column overnight.	
	12/3/13		Lt RACEY. 4 hrly relieved Lt TUTT. Early at the Advance Dressing Station. Inspected Transport & personnel paid.	

Army Form C. 2118

WAR DIARY
or
INTELLIGENCE SUMMARY
(Erase heading not required.)

Page 4
134 FIELD AMBULANCE

Place	Date	Hour	Summary of Events and Information	Remarks and references to Appendices
ESTAIRES	13/3/16		Lt PORTER + party relieved Lt RACEY at Advanced Dressing Station. Inspected by Col SKINNER A.M.S. D.P.M.S. & 2 of his men who remained common half for SCABIES cases. Wired to A.D.M.S. for same.	
	14/3/16		Lt TUTT totally relieved Lt PORTER at Advanced Dressing Station. Arranged with Town Major + the Mairi for men + plans to take to wagons for use of work. Fitted + re-internal to clean + disinfect infantry Hospital + form a 7 gardening dept for Scabies Hospital.	
	15/3/16		Took over Hospital at PENSIONNAT DES DEMOISELLES + 38 trichlorin baths, whole of ground cleaning + rearrangement — Col TUTT. Lt RACEY relieved Lt TUTT.	

WAR DIARY or INTELLIGENCE SUMMARY

Army Form C. 2118

PAGE 5
1/3 4 FIELD AMBULANCE

Place	Date	Hour	Summary of Events and Information	Remarks and references to Appendices
ESTAIRES	16/3/16		Admitted 7. Discharged 4. Remaining 44. All febrile	
	17/3/16		Admitted 12. Discharged 5. Evacuated 2. Remaining 49. The arrangements for treating Scabies consisting of two row of baths, in a canvas boat to hold the eastring & received & drying. The patients located in a small hospital & about 8 baths per hour can be given. No accommodation for Scabies cases.	
	18/3/16		Admitted 165. Scabies from 4 & 5 Bond Watt. "B" Div discharged & Remaining 212. To cope with the outbreak the following arrangements were made. A large motor lorry was obtained & fitted up by the R.E. and with wood heating & water to give 20 Plt. a hour. 12 round iron tubs have been obtained from the Divl. Baths together with 400 suits of underclothing complete. Thurbells tent have been pitched in courtyard of the Q.M. Store & Padlton transferred to monastic hospital in the yard. Owing to the involuntary of the owner of the garden tents cannot be fitted	

WAR DIARY or INTELLIGENCE SUMMARY

Army Form C. 2118
Page 6
134 FIELD AMBULANCE

Place	Date	Hour	Summary of Events and Information	Remarks and references to Appendices
ESTAIRES	18/3/16		to accommodation for 24 patients was borrowed from an Ambulance near.	
	19/3/16		Admitted 3 Discharged 9. Evacuated to Public Hospital MERVILLE 30. Remaining 176. The hot water apparatus is not yet ready for use so only the Estaires cases can be treated unless patients are kept waiting. Such there no can be dealt with - fire - soap - a dirty, awful conditions, they have no funds, there have been no change of underclothing for an unknown time - no soak, no ambulance stripped, dabbed over with refuge [?], afflicted with clean clothing + clean blankets, that been confined to award till his uniform has been disinfected with Thresh.	
	20/3/16		Admitted 2 Discharged 8 Evacuated 1. Remaining 169. Hot water apparatus now just working. Patients bathed + uniform later baked[?]. The double time method	

WAR DIARY or INTELLIGENCE SUMMARY

Army Form C. 2118

134 FIELD AMBULANCE

Place	Date	Hour	Summary of Events and Information	Remarks and references to Appendices
ESTAIRES	20/5/16		is in use, the rear one containing tan dust & fans is used to an incinerator, the first containing running water is a place fit. This place seems to work well. Patients treated with paraffin as they are now no worse off than they have been for some weeks.	
"	21/5/16		admitted 3. Evacuated to trains. Hopital MERVILLE 42. Remaining 130. Watershed in new work now. Water supplied to it from the River LYS by a force pump & hot can put. They 30 baths (about 6 baths 2 patients) one being possible hitherto has been provided & the latter pattern. The advantages as follows has caused or The system of treatment is altered and applied to new cases in found in writer and applied to new wounded. Invaluable to the tout or wout-wing. The morning down to the tout wing during which Death finish is an addition, that afternoon there are done for the walking. The following are taking a very at a time in the forenoon. The following men the bathing room or this ambulance to the go to the washing room +	

WAR DIARY
INTELLIGENCE SUMMARY

Page 5
134 FIELD AMBULANCE

Place	Date	Hour	Summary of Events and Information	Remarks and references to Appendices
ESTAIRES	21/3/16		Thawed, the floor disinfected by sprinkling with formalin & then the tents erected by the working party & put into the baths. At 10a.m. a line of thirty-five underclothing & lather & the disinfector after the bath clean underclothing & blankets supplied to each patient who volunteers to the clean ward. Preliminary arrangements have been made to mount the patients running to settle reinfected. A new hatwood hut has been built at the end of the parade for patients in the tents. The new shower-bath which the bathroom was emptied to be blocked & all built up & to be reconstructed. Also a new urinal complete built for the R.A.M.C. & the old latrine rebuilt. Three lengths of hose so used for the new motor ambulance hospital Rubber doubler moved.	
	22/3/16		Admitted 43 - Remaining 173	

Army Form C. 2118

WAR DIARY
or
INTELLIGENCE SUMMARY
(Erase heading not required.)

Page 9
134 FIELD AMBULANCE

Place	Date	Hour	Summary of Events and Information	Remarks and references to Appendices
ESTAIRES	23/5/16		Admitted 30. Discharged 18. Evacuated 30. Remaining 156.	
	24/5/16		The tonsilitis treatment of patients wanting to undergo this full blot treatment for general light duties and returned same to unit. Modified that out-patients not suffering truly and duty or otherwise to be put on the "sick to light duty" list. Casualties 1 Officer 4.1mm Shrapnel & 12 Remaining 184. Ordered to hold one ambulance cars in readiness. Evacuated 26 wound.	
	25/5/16		Admitted 7. Discharged 5. Evacuated 10. Officer 1 to MALASSISE. Remaining 166. Orders to move to ZELOBES & 7 visit to relieve 141 Fd Amb & 3rd Div att.	
	26/5/16		Advance party 10 Officers & 12 NCOs & Men sent to ZELOBES to take over. B Section complete to remain in charge of the Scabies Hospital at ESTAIRES.	
	27/5/16		The Ambulance less B Section paraded at 8.0 AM & moved off at 8.30 AM marched to ZELOBES arriving at 10.0 AM.	

Army Form C. 2118

WAR DIARY
or
INTELLIGENCE SUMMARY

(Erase heading not required.)

Page 10
134 FIELD AMBULANCE

Place	Date	Hour	Summary of Events and Information	Remarks and references to Appendices
ZELOBES	25/3/16		The hospital is a barn + two canvas huts. Personnel billeted in three small farms with horse lines in a field. The farm in which the Officers have are situated now at about 100 wounded - about 15-20 Officers leaving the present accommodation poor considering Ambulance is for the front line treatment of an action.	
	28/3/16		Admitted 18. Discharged 5. Evacuated 1. Remaining 168. Thirty-five dents stationed in ESTAIRES now a Entirety Hors-line-s barns to billets unaccompany. Residence for trucks, diseases & hurdles to fair trenches. Weather cold + wet. Very high wind.	
	29/3/16		Admitted 2. Discharged 21. Evacuated 4. Remaining 145. Received notification second Lieutenant Churchill 4th Rn Dyke L/Cpl BROWN RAMC 2 NCO + 5 men to LESTREM are coming to join with for duty. Left him Offer to Div. HQ.	
	30/3/16		Admitted 12. Discharged 25. Evacuated 4. Remaining 128. Admitted .13. Discharged 19. Evacuated 34. Remaining 88.	
	31/3/16		Moved half unit to Dm.1 Battn at COULONNE SUR LYS 133rd Ambulance	

R. W. Henry ??
O.C. 134 Fd Amb

39th Div.

134th F. Amb.

April 1916.

WAR DIARY
or
INTELLIGENCE SUMMARY
(Erase heading not required.)

Army Form C. 2118
PAGE 11   Vol 2
134 FIELD AMBULANCE

Place	Date	Hour	Summary of Events and Information	Remarks and references to Appendices
ZELOBES	1/4/16		Admitted 10 Discharged 11 Remaining 60	
	2/4/16		Church Parade 11.15 am in window. Fine day. Admitted 6 Discharged 12 Remaining 54	
	3/4/16		Admitted 11 Discharged 36 Remaining 29 Orders recd to attack each Officer in turn to AT Debilt Park Room, Kitchen & Orderly Room.	
	4/4/16		Admitted 10 Discharged 13 Remaining 26 A Section forward in full marching order with two days rations marched to VIEILLE CHAPELLE to 130 Fd Amb for 7 days instruction. B Section recalled from ESTAIRES rejoined at 2.30 pm. leaving 1 N.C.O. & 1 man in charge of ESTAIRES. The building at ESTAIRES was left quite clean & all the equipment—that is remaining—handed over.	
	5/4/16		ADMITTED 13 Discharged 1 Remaining 32 Orderly round to clean up M. RUSSE – DHAINE'S form which had been left in an insanitary by 119th & 13 Fd Amb. Disinfected the	

Army Form C. 2118

WAR DIARY or INTELLIGENCE SUMMARY
(Erase heading not required.)

134 FIELD AMBULANCE

PAGE 12

Place	Date	Hour	Summary of Events and Information	Remarks and references to Appendices
ZELOBES	5/4/16		Forward party filled in Hun Farm enquir[ies] - a rubbish heap outside the latrines and a latrine bucket rubbish pit of regiment. Burned including an abandoned box containing 20 rounds rattled through the chain in men, Russian the orchard at the end all dwellings. Detailed 1 "BOYER" + 10 men to deal with the matter. Farm too safety too early, men bring from the Ambulance. Reported [ ] to A.D.M.S.	
	6/4/16		Admitted 14. Discharged 11. Remaining 35 - all the filth + manure in that farm removed to the manure pit being cleared by working parties to the field. Received reinf from A.D.M.S. morning O.C. 13 Gds Amb to give A Lectin at VIEILLE CHAPELLE + inspection the clothing of men. Proceeded to join A section + handover Dressing Station + command of B+ E Sections to Lt. TUTT. R.A.M.C.	
	7/4/16		Admitted 8. Discharged 17. Remaining 26. A travel at orderly Room with O.C. 9/130 Fd Amb and noted points in working of Officer Park down a/c 4" Hospital Ratio + 20 new hands to A.D.S. at LA TOURET for instruction.	

Army Form C. 2118

WAR DIARY or INTELLIGENCE SUMMARY

PAGE 13
134 FIELD AMBULANCE

(Erase heading not required.)

Place	Date	Hour	Summary of Events and Information	Remarks and references to Appendices
ZELOBES	8/4/16		Admitted 4 Discharged 9 Remaining 26. Attended at Dressing Station 131 Fd.Amb. & light cases in general emergency. G.J.	
	9/4/16		Admitted 10 Discharged 6 Remaining 25. Church parade at 11.15 — ordered Lt Mitchell & two men for fatigue at A.D.S.	
	10/4/16		Admitted 15 Discharged 14 Remaining 26. Visited A.D.S. Regtl A.D. Posts & trenches with O.C.131 Fd.Amb. Lt Harris + 40 men relieved 3rd party at A.D.S.	
	11/4/16		Admitted 16 Discharged 9. Remaining 33. A section reformed reserve of Fd Amb at ZELOBES, having completed course of instruction.	
	12/4/16		Admitted 8 Discharged 9 Remaining 32. Rearranged duties in the office to enable good substitutes during absence & total (1) Reports of all fatigues in. (2) A & D books & returns & c to keep – (2) Index of all returns & reports in file. (3) A & D books to be kept up to date. (4) Ruff note book of morning sick as in camp Bk. h.	

WAR DIARY or INTELLIGENCE SUMMARY

Army Form C. 2118

PAGE 14
134 FIELD AMBULANCE

Place	Date	Hour	Summary of Events and Information	Remarks and references to Appendices
ZELOBES	13/4/16		Admitted 11 Discharged 5 Remaining 38. Work on RHUSSE D'HAINE to-morrow finished. 5.3 looker harness mended & front of litter. Lowest of the dug out being thin & below the level of the pit 20 loads of clay were tipped into it & beaten down to form a good cover. Tomorrow intend to make use from a good offensive.	
	14/4/16		Admitted 11 Discharged 3 Remaining 46 one officer sick. Nothing to note. Got helve installed. Two wagons found S.S.S. equipment tried & alleged.	
	15/4/16		Admitted 5 Discharged 12 Remaining 39. Orders received to take over Dressing Station at MESPLAUX + A.D.S. at the TUNING FORK from 130 Fd Amb.	
	16/4/16		Admitted 12 Discharged 13 Remaining 38. An Advance party of two officers & 4 boyers in command of Lt RACEY + 1 officid duty Lt Myttrap. Dispensing bt 2 cooks, 1 water cart orderly + 1 mule with 2 S.S. wagons & 1 lock cart + 1 water cart + tentless detail, two of horses	

WAR DIARY or INTELLIGENCE SUMMARY

Army Form C. 2118

Page 15 — 134 Field Ambulance

Place	Date	Hour	Summary of Events and Information	Remarks and references to Appendices
ZILLEBEKE	16/4/16	9.0 am	Changes & bathers to our protegs but prevented to the ADS to take over from 130 Fd Amb. This fort was worked at 9 am & took over the 3 days rations received & fryg Parmer Field Engineers Rowel, & wounded. The G.S. & Hussar wagons returned to H.Q. 2.T. when unloaded.	
		2 pm	An advance party of our Bearers 1 officer & 8 men with our Med. Equipt & 2 large fountains proceeded to MESPLAUX to take over the Bearing Station there.	
	17/4/16		Admitted 5 OR wounded & 1 Russian 8.34 Lt Huggins RAMC Officer Posted equipment ready for move tomorrow.	
	18/4/16		Reveille at 5 am. All wagons packed by 8 am. Breakfast at 8 am. Unit moved off at 9.0 am. Arrived at 11.0. All parties at ZILLEBEKE unable to reach the Division were transferred and to arrive at MESPLAUX 2.3 cars belonging to 39 Ch Amb. left by turning 1st Fd Ambulance & 10 Other Returning own 56 & 7 Ch Ambulance & Officers 2	

WAR DIARY or INTELLIGENCE SUMMARY

PAGE 16

134 FIELD AMBULANCE

Place	Date	Hour	Summary of Events and Information	Remarks and references to Appendices
MESPLAUX	19/9/16		Admitted 17 Discharged 9 Remaining 64 Officers — 2 — 2 Lt. HILL T.M.B. Injured Discharged Lt. HODGINGHAM to duty Lt. BROWN 17 K.R.R. Injured Lt. BROWN K.R.R. SCABIES This Farm is unusually large for this part of France & well adapted about 105 patients & 100 officers can now be in it. There is available pits & one should be in — the enclosed farmyard. This water cannot be used — in that bed & will up in about 2 days also the water round the farm stagnant & the water would need [illegible] that	
	20/9/16		Admitted 10 Discharged 4 Remaining 70 Visited A.D.S. in a well farm building not damaged but there was still down & but troops Lt. Brown has received traced with toothache [illegible] him from his Regt Aid Post (with artillery) to A.D.S. but in state of exhaustion.	

WAR DIARY or INTELLIGENCE SUMMARY

Army Form C. 2118

PAGE 17

134 FIELD AMBULANCE

Place	Date	Hour	Summary of Events and Information	Remarks and references to Appendices
MES PLAUX	21/4/16		Admitted 5 Discharged 11 Remaining 64. Marial Comfort Bags at BETHUNE and supply parcel of things were filled but luckily no callers for any further details to trouble the nurses.	
	22/4/16		Admitted 3 Discharged 48 Remaining 39. Officers — 1 — — 2 — 1. Rented A.D.S. was now started at the Relay Station at FESTUBERT. The horses have been very unlucky lately, the dugouts having been hit and 2 tons out of the horse dugouts have been withdrawn. Buses carried by Lt HARRIS + 40 other ranks. The work can only be done at night.	
	23/4/16		Admitted 18 Discharged 15 Remaining 42. Officers — 2 — — 2 — 1. Church parade in Esquerdal Wood.	
	24/4/16		Admitted 2 Discharged 3 Remaining 42 Remaining 43. Officers — 1 — — 2 — 1. G.O.C. Division inspected the Dressing Station during the morning. Aeroplane activity.	

WAR DIARY or INTELLIGENCE SUMMARY

Army Form C. 2118

Page 18

134 Field Ambulance

Place	Date	Hour	Summary of Events and Information	Remarks and references to Appendices
MESPLAUX	25/4/16		Admitted 9 Discharged 14 Remaining 37. Officers 1 — 0. Visited A.D.S. all correct. Two stretchers were obtained from the farm & cleaned out & established in a new loose box for walking cases in an over-population 25.	
	26/4/16		Admitted 11 Discharged 10 Remaining 38.	
	27/4/16		Admitted 6 Discharged 9 Remaining 35. A French soldier 1720 PHILBERT ALFRED Bn. 15 Chltravailleurs admitted suffering from slight pontoning wound recd. at 8.45 last night to left jaw at attack, & eye. Dressed by with painkiller & instructions & sent to nearby the returning train. Remained overnight. Reported the during station that found & informed the lieut. there a Rthul.	
	28/4/16		Admitted 8 Discharged 7 Remaining 36. Found on man admitted PRATS FRANCOIS XAVIER suffering from Bad compound fracture Tib. & Fib. of Rt tibia.	

Army Form C. 2118

WAR DIARY
or
INTELLIGENCE SUMMARY

PAGE 19

134 FIELD AMBULANCE

(Erase heading not required.)

Place	Date	Hour	Summary of Events and Information	Remarks and references to Appendices
MESPLAUX	28/4/16		carried by wounded from a bomb dropped by an aeroplane in a field where he was working.	
	29/4/16		Admitted 22. Discharged 19. Remaining 39. The Revd. J. Cleim having recovered & having re-assumed by a Revd Medical Officer was returned to duty. The division was removed to the French Civil Hospital at BETHUNE. His leg is now septic & there appears to be little chance of saving it.	
	30/4/16		Admitted 14. Discharged 11. Remaining 42. Church Parade in Surgical Ward.	

V.C. Humphreys
Major
Commanding
134 Fd Ambce

39th Div.

134 F. Amb.

May 1916.

COMMITTEE FOR THE
MEDICAL HISTORY OF THE WAR
Date 26 JUN 1916

Army Form C. 2118

WAR DIARY or INTELLIGENCE SUMMARY

(Erase heading not required.)

Vol 3
PAGE 20
134 FIELD AMBULANCE

Place	Date	Hour	Summary of Events and Information	Remarks and references to Appendices
MESPLAUX	1/5/16		Admitted 14 Evacuated 11 Remaining 42. No 69007 Pte P. Lee attached to ADMS staff for shorthand duties from 1.5.16 until further orders. Pte Rillitts and returned to duty. Also paid these. Cpl H. Booth granted special leave to England on account of illness of father 4/5/16 – 11/5/16 –	
	2/5/16		Admitted 22 Evacuated 16 Remained 48	
	3/5/16		Admitted 25 Evacuated 15 Remained 58	
	4/5/16		Admitted 18 Evacuated 14 Remained 54. Capt. G.D. ROBERTSON RAMC att 164 Bde. R.F.A. Catarrhus Jaundice. Officers " 1. Remained " 1.	
	5/5/16		Admitted 24 Evacuated 27 Remained 51. A bathing post is being constructed in the small stream in rear of the farm buildings – for the use of all ranks.	
	6/5/16		Admitted 3 Evacuated 13 Remained 41	
	7/5/16	9.30 AM	Lt Tutt and 32 other ranks left the dressing station for duty at A.D.S. Bathing place opened. Lt Bonser & 29 other ranks returned from ADS to dressing station. Admitted 8 Evacuated 13 Remained 26. BEAN. R.W. 2 N.W. Bde. R.Z.A. att 164 R.Z.A. Trench Fever. Officers " 1. — 2. Capt. Cpl. D. Cox and 8 men returned from A.D.S	
	8/5/16		Admitted 5 Evacuated 3 Remained 38. 1. 2. Lt G.W. RACEY RAMC. 134 Fld Amb Acute Tonsilitis Officers " " Capt BEAN. R.W. evacuated to 33 C.C.S BETHUNE.	
	9/5/16		Admitted 11 Evacuated 11 Remained 38 Lt. J.H. PORTER RAMC attached to Pt CAMBRIDGESHIRE Reg as temporary Medical Officer.	
	10/5/16		Admitted 13 Evacuated 10 Remained 41. L/Cpl H. FACER and ten men commenced fatigue work at divisional baths LE Q BESNOY.	

Army Form C. 2118

WAR DIARY or INTELLIGENCE SUMMARY
(Erase heading not required.)

Page 21
134 FIELD AMBULANCE

Place	Date	Hour	Summary of Events and Information	Remarks and references to Appendices
MESPLAUX	11/5/16		Admitted 6 Evacuated 5 Remained 42. Officers 1. 1. Major Willis A. 179 R.F.A. Neuras Kenia. Evacuated 11/5/16. 2. Pte. Calitaro J. Cullen J. Dalley F.S. Dunn A. transferred from Base to 134 Fd Amb. arrangements being made to take a long time bath being constructed in an alcove of the courtyard of the Ballroom for bathing patients and all ranks – walls on two sides are of canvas –	
	12/5/16		Admitted 18 Evacuated 11 Remained 49. Officers 1. 1. 2 Capt. Edwards G. R.E. 254 Tunnelling Cy Synovitis left knee & shown caused by fall – Cpl. W. Butter returned from leave –	
	13/5/16		Admitted 17 Evacuated 19 Remained 47. Officers 2. 2 Lt Arkcott. 12 Rl Sussex Influenza. Sgt C. Sanders and 9 other ranks returned from A.D.S. after completion of work at dug outs – Capt. N. Butler sent to A.D.S to join "B" Section Lt. Brown returned from A.D.S to Dressing Station and Lt. Huggins replaced him at A.D.S	
	14/5/16		Admitted 6 Evacuated 17 Remained 36. Officers 2 Lt Mitchell relieved Lt Tutt as o/c A.D.S Lt Tutt relieves Lt Potts as temp M.O. 1st Can. B.S. Reg. Lt Potts returned to Dressing Station Capt J & Robertson put on light duty and placed i/c Medical Wards 1 and 2.	
	15/5/16		Admitted 15 Evacuated 12 Remained 39. 2nd Lt. Caldecott. R.G. 12 Rl Sussex. G.S.W. Back & chest. Officers 1. Lt. Potts reported to A.D.M.S. office 39 Div. for duty O.C. 134 Fd Amb visited A.D.S & found all correct.	
	16/5/16		Admitted 16 Evacuated 15 Remained 27. 2nd Lt Barnes. HQC Atravin St Kerne. Officers 2. 2nd Lt King. L.F. R.E. 254 Tunnelling Coy. Fractured clavicle. contused wounds head Zaccidental. Lt. J.H Potts promoted to Rank of Captain. Lt & Qr M Johnson placed i/c cookhouse, catering arrangements & ballroom – Bathroom completed & ready for use – very satisfactory	

WAR DIARY or INTELLIGENCE SUMMARY

Army Form C. 2118
Page 22
13 Field Ambulance

Place	Date	Hour	Summary of Events and Information	Remarks and references to Appendices
MESPLAUX	17/5/16		Admitted 20. Evacuated 16. Remained 41.	
	18/5/16		Admitted 16. Evacuated 7. Remained 40 Officer. 1.	
			Capt. NICHOLS. A.S.C. Neuralgia —	
			Surgeon General. Sir W. PIKE DMS "1st" Army accompanied by A.D.M.S. 29 Div visited the Dressing Station and made a tour of inspection and expressed his satisfaction with the work — He then went on to the A.D.S. arriving there about 12.30 p.m. and inspected same. He seemed perfectly satisfied with the condition of everything he saw, except the niessin and urinal. It was some minuted that the condition altered — A note was taken of requirements and the work proceeded with —	
	19/5/16		Admitted 10. Evacuated 15. Remained 35.	
			1. 2nd Lt. HORDER M. L. 186. R.F.A. Nervous debility N.Y.D.	
	20/5/16		Admitted 10. Evacuated 8. Remained 37. Capt. TERRY. C.F.A. n/r Rl. Sussex asst Staff Capt. 116. Bde. Duty. N.Y.D. Officer. 1.	
			1. Capt. TRUMBLER A.S.C. Fractured acromion process (accidental)	
			The G.O.C. x1st Army Corps (Lt. Genl. Sir R.C.B. HAKING) & Staff accompanied by A.D.M.S. 29 Div. visited the Dressing Station about 2 p.m. & inspected all portions. He appeared very satisfied and remarked to the Officer commanding the Ambulance that it was the best Field Ambulance he had visited in the XI Army Corps. He did not visit the A.D.S.	
	21/5/16		Admitted 16. Evacuated 13. Remained 40. 1st Lt. ELLIOT G.E. 13 Rl. Sussex. G.S.W. Head, Hernia Cerebri. Officer. 2. 2nd Lt. CROCKFORD A.L. 1/3 GLOSTERS. G.S.W. Elbow.	
			Major General BARNARDISTON Commanding 39. Div. accompanied by A.D.M.S. 39. Div. visited the Dressing Station making only a brief stay — He was pleased with all he saw & expressed his satisfaction —	
	22/5/16		Admitted 16. Evacuated 17. Remained 39. 2nd Lt. ROBERTS. N+P. 13 Rl. Sussex — Scabies — Officer. 3.	
			Lt. W. R. TUFF posted as Medical Officer i/c 1st CAMBS. REGT. and struck off the Strength of this unit. Capt. T. G. HUNT r D. Jodar returned to 267 Coy 39 Div train along with 2 horses + one mule —	

WAR DIARY or INTELLIGENCE SUMMARY

Army Form C. 2118

Page. 23

134 FIELD AMBULANCE

Place	Date	Hour	Summary of Events and Information	Remarks and references to Appendices
DERNESPLAUX	22/5/16		1 motor cycle returned to 39 Div. Supply Column. Pte Craigo M.T.A.S.C. returned from A.D.M.S. Office. — Improvements to trench & incinerator at A.D.S. suggested by the Surgeon General 16th in'st have now been completed. The new incinerator is built of brick & is satisfactory. —	
	23/5/16		Admitted 11 Evacuated 11 Remained 39. 2nd Lt. CORNWALL 13 R't SUSSEX for inoculation and exposed officers. 1. & vaccination.	
	24/5/16		Admitted 12 Evacuated 10 Remained 41 Capt. ROBERTSON R.A.M.C. discharged to duty, & to report to O.C. 133 others. 2. for duty.	
	25/5/16		Admitted 11 Evacuated 9 Remained 43. others. 1.	
		3 p.m.	A.D.M.S. 39 F.W. arrived at A.D.S. and inspected the local Railway with a view to improving it so as to be able to evacuate wounded from the trenches by this means. — He was accompanied by Lt. HUGGINS. A small fire occurred about 4.15 p.m. in some Ampts built with the rain over sandbags. Two minutes after the outbreak was reported the men had fallen in & worked	
	26/5/16		Admitted 16 Evacuated 12 Remained 47 his outbreak - they showed great smartness all round - no damage done - Pte. J't Lloyd — H.Q Mess & Sgn McConnel transferred from base details as reinforcements to 134 Field Ambulance —	
	27/5/16		Admitted 7 Evacuated 14 Remained 40. Major V.C. HONEYBOURNE R.A.M.C. O.C. 134 F'd Amb - Colitis - (Evacuated) officers. 2. 2nd Lt. FOSTER 6th CHESHIRES Multiple wounds (Sh. leg r't hip Capt. C.D. ROBERTSON R.A.M.C. 133 F'd Amb took over command of 134 F'd Ambulance R't r. leg & Br'bh. Evacuated to 32 C.C.S. vice Major V.C. Honeybourne. N.C.W RACEY S/sgt Sanden Sgt Male & 29 Other ranks and Officers between left dressing station for duty at A.D.S Lt. G.W Huggins, Sgt Cox & 19 o'r ranks returned from A.D.S.	
	28/5/16		Admitted 16 Evacuated 17 Remained 39	

WAR DIARY or INTELLIGENCE SUMMARY

Army Form C. 2118

Page 24.

134 FIELD AMBULANCE.

Place	Date	Hour	Summary of Events and Information	Remarks and references to Appendices
MESPLAUX	28/5/16		Lt. W.T. BROWN. R.A.M.C. appointed Medical Officer to 13 GLOUCESTER REGT and is struck off the strength of this unit. Cpl. Martin and 7 other ranks returned from A.D.S.	
	29/5/16		Admitted 4. Evacuated 7 Remained 26. 2nd Lt. ODOM G.C. M.G.C. 118 Bde. G.S.W. Thigh - Officers. 6 men of 106 Fd. Amb. attached to A.D.S. & returned by 134 Field Ambulance from 29.5.16.	
	30/5/16		Admitted 9 Evacuated 0 Remained 45. Officers. Major G.C. Honeybourne R.A.M.C. arrived from 33 C.C.S. & handed over cash, maps & consumption and other documents to Capt. G.D. Robertson and returned to C.C.S. Instructions to the Bearer Subs. are being put up in the field adjacent to the home farm to accommodate the A Section 2/3 Field Ambulance coming in on June 3rd for instruction - Premier also residence & latrines are being erected for their use — Lt. D. Munster sprained his ankle & was placed on the sick list.	
	31/5/16		Admitted 8. Evacuated 0. Remained 44. 2nd Lt. CRAIG. 17. R.Scots. G.S.W. abdomen & R arms (Evac 33 CCS) Officers. 2 Midday Efforts being made to empty the courtyard of the farm. Progress slow	

G.D. Robertson
Captain R.A.M.C.
Commanding
134 Field Ambulance

O.C. 134 F.A.

To. o/c A.G's Office,
Base.

1-4-16.

Herewith first portion War Diary of No. 134. F.A.

V E Honeybourne

Capt. R.A.M.C.
O.C. 164th FIELD AMBULANCE.

No. 134 F.A.

June 1916.

COMMITTEE FOR THE
MEDICAL HISTORY OF THE WAR
5 AUG. 1916
Date

June
Army Form C. 2118

WAR DIARY
or
INTELLIGENCE SUMMARY
(Erase heading not required.)

134. F Amb

Vol 4

Place	Date	Hour	Summary of Events and Information	Remarks and references to Appendices
MES PLAUX	1.2.16		Remained. Admd 1 Off 43 OR. – Admitted 2 Off 76. J OR. Evac. 1 J. Remaining 2.44. 1810. Routine Parade	Rf. Maries & os.
"	2.6.16		No. of Can remain 7. 2 Officers v 44 ORanks. Admn ovq 41 Evacuation 14 – Major A.C. HILDRETH R A M C joined this unit to assume command vice Major HONEYBOURNE V.C. R A M C.	16. C.H. dredith 2 of RAC
"	3.6.16		Remained Officers 2. OR. 44. Admns 6 Evacuation 9. Remaining 2 Officers OR 44. Ambulance 9 Ike 2/3 J Ambulance – 4 off ans v 62 men arrived for training.	HCH
"	4.6.16		Visit 16 A.D.S. v Relay Post one Officer v 20 ORs. detailed from 2/3 J Ambulance for further at A.D.S. Lieut MITCHELL R.A.M.C. return'd by Major MOXEY. Remand at 1K A.D.S. Remaining O 2. OR 41. Admns O1. O.R 6. Evacuees 14 (130R 10)	HCH
"	5.6.16		Remained 2. v 36 OR. Admns 6 OR Evacuation 3. Remaining 2 Officers v 37 Men. – Shared orderlies 4 Gunners to this unit v allocated last one Corporal orderlies from 1/6 Ch. Amb at GORRE.	HCH
"	6.6.16		Remained 2.0. 37 OR. Admtd 18. OR. Evacuation 14. Relieving party 9/ Officers v 6 other ranks 1/5 A D S to instalation front parts returned. Lieut S W BURRELL R.A.M.C. reported for duty.	HCH
"	7.6.16		Remained 2.0 41. OR. Admitted 5. Evacuees 8. Remaining 2.8 38 OR. Lieut ODOM M Q O 118 "O D" Durham M S. Unit 200 M S XI Corps. Shown round Coll PORTER R A M C. Unit 16 Brig R A M – And Post v A.D.S. And HOBBS 12 Royl Sussex admtd Ike 1/5 Ad Post v A.D.S. Admn OR ? Evacuees 4. 2 officers 44 OR remained. Unit 1/5 D. DLS v 1/5 A DLS (2 ratm O.C.)	HCH
"	8.6.16		Received the Officers of 1/5 and on Adm instln Da am S Confe	HCH

1875 Wt. W 593/826 1,000,000 4/15 J.B.C. & A. A.D.S.S./Forms/C. 2118.

WAR DIARY
or
INTELLIGENCE SUMMARY

(Erase heading not required.) 134 Field Ambulance

Army Form C. 2118

Place	Date	Hour	Summary of Events and Information	Remarks and references to Appendices
MESPLAUX	10.6.15	9.15	Removed 2 Off 44 O.R. Admsn 16 - Evacns 15 Remg 2 Off 44 O.R. Lieut BURRELL R.A.M.C. proceeded to A.D.S.	1st Nch entr Super Rev
"	11.6.15		Relief of 2/1 S.M. Ambulance left. 15 pers fm A.D.S. Civilly public comm g intole. Capt PORTER left for A.D.S. Remg 2 Off 45 O.R. Evacns 6.	HEH
"	11.6.15		Admsn 11. Evacns 9. Others 2 & 1 O.R. A.B.n.S. invited the Wind Russell - RACEY relief fm Aid Posts	HCH
"	12.6.15		Bn advct inspect of units. Engineer organisation & Car'y of R2 & Wd'd in Car'y of Relatives in Car'y of a Rush of Wounded. RE. 2 W.O.R. A.S.E. 17. Renard 2 Of 32 O.R. Confer with Officer re organisatn of Relatives.	HCH
"	13.6.15		Visit 15. GDSP + Relay Post. Readmst of army Kennel. Report 15 A B n S re accommodation Aid Post & Lyy Cars. Relay Post 20. A.D.Y. 50. 2. Army Staten 500 - additional 100 cots - beds. Remg 20. 32 O.R. Admsn 20. E 7. Remg 104. 46 ten.	1 SCH
"	14.6.15		Remand 1 Off 46 Men. Admsn 2 Off + 21 O.R. Evacn 15. 19. Brig 3. Remg 3 Of 44 O.R. Remg 3 Off 44 O.R. Lieut HARRIS + 10 men detailed for A.D.S. 15 A.D.S. 15 Rue DE BOIS. Admsn 30 frm 18 O.R. Evacn 10 Ps. 2st O.R. 4 O.R. to Duty 5 Of + 34 O.R. Remg	HCH
"	15.6.15		Party of 1 NCO + 2 from 16 Bn admd 107 Men 5 O'br Tanks 16 XI Cav Rn 2 bu then 16 Men & Recruit for Brig. Remand 5 Of + 34 O.R. Admsn 19 E 30. Remg 1 Of + 27 O.R.	1 SCH
"	17.6.15		Lieut HARRIS + body return to Hea Quarters. announ order of A.B.n.S. which he is keen	HCH

Army Form C. 2118

WAR DIARY
or
INTELLIGENCE SUMMARY
(Erase heading not required.)

Instructions regarding War Diaries and Intelligence Summaries are contained in F. S. Regs., Part II. and the Staff Manual respectively. Title Pages will be prepared in manuscript.

Place	Date	Hour	Summary of Events and Information	Remarks and references to Appendices
NESPLAN	17.6.16		Remains 1 Off. 27 OR. A 16. E 12. Remay 17 v. 31. Party from BOIS DE PÉCAUT.	Helehalt Ingu Rais
"	18.6.16		Visit 16 A.DS. Admitted 16. E 11. 1 Bus letter Retry, A.DS R 19. 3 OR. V.i.d. by G.O.C 39 Divn.	H.C.H.
"	19.6.16		Admission 1 Off W 17 OR. E 5. Bus Pt. Remay 2 Officer 42 OR. Lieut HARRIS invaded to A.DS.	H.C.H.
"	20.6.16		Admission 17 OR. 2 Off v 22 OR. Evacuates 8 16 Buspt. 37 OR. LIEUT BURRELL reported for duty to 30 C.C.S. Capt FOTHERGILL reports for duty. Pte PEEL 17 Rotts v Duty sent to BUSNES Hospital	H.C.H H.C.H
"	21.6.16		Capt. FOTHERGILL sichs. LIEUT HARRIS at A.DS. Remay 37. Admitted 14 Evacu 23. Remay 28. Visit into Ba Offs. to A.DS as near Relay Post.	H.C.H.
"	22.6.16		Remains 28 Admitted 13. Evacuates 11. Remay 32. Conference at A.D.D.S. Office. No advance to attack.	H.C.H.
"	23.6.16		Remains 32. Admitted 24. Evac 25. 21 Remay 35.	H.C.H.
"	24.6.16		Remains 35. Admin 1 Off. 2er 0 OR. E 1 Off. 22 OR. Remay 37. V.i.d. 16 A.DS. an an guard. H. O. heavy Refreshment stall at FESTUBERT.	H.C.H
"	25.6.16		Remains 37. A 15. E 18. Remay 34. Routini work.	H.C.H
"	26.6.16		Remains 34. A 14. E 19. Remay 29. Routini work. Completed near Sunday Pickets.	H.C.H.

WAR DIARY or INTELLIGENCE SUMMARY

Army Form C. 2118

Instructions regarding War Diaries and Intelligence Summaries are contained in F.S. Regs., Part II. and the Staff Manual respectively. Title Pages will be prepared in manuscript.

(Erase heading not required.)

Place	Date	Hour	Summary of Events and Information	Remarks and references to Appendices
MESPLAUX	27.6.16		Remained 29. Arrivals 1 Officer 13 OR. E 19. 8 OR. Remany 34. Visit to ADS re Scheme of Evacuation & Relay. Divisional Scheme carried out last night – Scheme to be tried next Sunday Tonight.	He returns Byr Reserve
"	28.6.16		Remained 34. A 19. 18 OR. E 22. R 19. 30 OR. Visit to ADS v Adv. Post-	NCH
"	29.6.16		Self reported Can. Seg. WEBSTER sent to Busnes Cas. Ht. officers at Rte La TOURET. Remained 19.30 Ad. 137 OR E 2 OR. 27 OR. Remany 40.	HCN
"	30.6.16		Remained 40. Arrivals 1 Off. 24 OR. E 30. Remany 1 Off. 34 OR. Three Officers v Bearers sent to sent out to Amient 132 2d Aust. Lieut RACEY & Lieut HIGGINS arriving at ADS at 9.132. Lieut MITCHELL to R.A.P. PLUM STREET. Arrivals during the week: 13 OR. 436 OR. 7 thru' Junior Battle Casualties amongst Officers v 116 OR. Injuries, General 6. Rankins 16. CCS 12 Off. 222 OR. Cap. Ross Walker 109. To Brig. 57. Died of Wounds 2 on being conveyed to advanced dressing Station.	HCN He returns 2 yr Reserve

O.C. 134th Fd. Amb.
To A.G., Base.

Herewith War Diary of this Unit for month of June please.

[stamp: 134th FIELD AMBULANCE 2 JUL 1916]

[signature]
Major. R.A.M.C.
O.C. 134th FIELD AMBULANCE.

July 1916.

39th Division

134th Field Ambulance

WAR DIARY
or
INTELLIGENCE SUMMARY

(Erase heading not required.)

Army Form C. 2118

134 Field Ambulance. 39th Division

July 39 Vol 5

Place	Date	Hour	Summary of Events and Information	Remarks and references to Appendices
MESPLAUX	1.7.16		The three Sections had 3 Bearer Sub Division Cpt 16/132 Fd Amb. rejoined unit. Remand 1 Off. 34 OR. Admitted 9. Evacuated 79. To Evg 9. Opened OR. 15 Remaing	Remand App. Rainc
"	2.7.16		Remand 1 Off. 15 OR. Admitted 34. Evacuated 23. Died 2. Remaing 1 Off. 25 OR. Remainder of Bearer Division rejoined unit. Practice hand to a unit of pioneers. Ambulance – Setruin trapped workers adormly	NCH
"	3.7.16		Remand 1 Off 23. Admitted 21. Evac. 17. 26 OR. Remaind 20. Raid 5 wound in the order. Captains at a. om. place.	HeH
"	4.7.16		Casualties arrived abt 4.3 am. Total number handed thru 4 Ambulance 87. 59 thru Main S. Dressing 23 cm. Duck Summer to C.C.S. whole y 2 Hann. Ambulance Cart & sherund hollow effort handeiled to a dm s. the had prepared his shelters wounded f hollow waters assembly. - Remaing 20. Admin S. 7 OR. Evacuat S. 1.3 Off. Remaing 4. Off. 65 R. - All little casualty new evacuated 9.12.30 intercepted 9 am 5.7.14 troubled – suspendently return A 2.27. Evacuated 2.26 Remaining 1.	HeH
"	5.7.16		Remaind 4 Off 66. Admin 9. 17 OR. 15 CCS 3v 57 CRSI. Remaing 1v 20 OR. Remaind 1 20 OR. A 1 Off 22 OR. Evacuated 16. Remaing 2 Off 26 OR. 2 cases cam to Ls helpers to move to ANNEZIN the evening 97	He.H.
"	6.7.16			
ANNEZIN	7.7.16		Remaing 2 Off 26 OR. Admitted 27 OR. E 15 OR 10 Off. Remaing 1 Off 38 OR. 2 med ANNEZIN v took our Briv Rest Station from 101 Fd Amb. with Patients. wrote in a DS at LONE FARM also Div Laundy v Baths ANNEZIN v Baths BETHUNE v Baths ANNEQUIN	

134th FIELD AMBULANCE
-1 AUG 1916

Army Form C. 2118

WAR DIARY
or
INTELLIGENCE SUMMARY
(Erase heading not required.)

Instructions regarding War Diaries and Intelligence Summaries are contained in F.S. Regs., Part II. and the Staff Manual respectively. Title Pages will be prepared in manuscript.

Place	Date	Hour	Summary of Events and Information	Remarks and references to Appendices
ANNEZIN	7.9.16		Capt PORTER & Lieut HARRIS took one LONE FARM A.D.S. Capt PORTER at ADS MARRAIS. Took on 67 Patients 1 23 Leti.	HCH
"	8.7.16		Sent to Hosp. highway & Railway Received 1.38 Casualties 90 O.R. CCS 13 Officer 1 Railway 1 O.R. 114 O.R. Received 2 Leti.	HCH
"	9.7.16		Received 1 114 O.R. Casualties R.O.R. E.8. Railway 1 Off. 118 O.R. Casualties at ADS thro'	NCH
"	10.7.16		Received 1. Off. 118 O.R. A.B. O.R. E. 18. Railway 1 Off. 113 O.R.	NCH
"	11.7.16		Visit to A. D.m.S. Thus — informed of losses faster FESTUBERT Side. Sent to C. WT 24 Reinforced: and 29 Men believing 2 7 Off. 2 little two chaus. 2 12 men of Battery Case out ft. Lying Down. Sybil Sondes betd. Alt Suffer on Rtn Sorted by Battery Slept. 7th Sergeant at A Bg MARRAIS & Regained Officers. 7 casualties R 1 Off. 113 O.R. A. 1.45 O.R. E 32. Railway 1 Off. 131 O.R.	HCH
"	12.7.16		Received 1 Off. 131 O.R. A. 48 E 45 Railway 1 Off. 130 O.R. D.D.m.S. & Capt. Visits Brig. Rgt. 2/Pat'n Capt. PORTER Evac. to 1. C.C.S. Ambulance 2 times - 3 days in the trenches here.	HCH
"	13.7.16		R. 1 Off. 134 O.R. Casualties 1 Off. 22 O.R. E 1 Off. 39 O.R. 1 Off. 116 O.R. Sent to ADS. Received notice Lieut D.R. Scott Came on the 15th July.	HCH
ANNEZIN	14.7.16		Received 1 Off. 116 O.R. Casualties 55 O.R. E 32 O.R. 1 Off. Railway 139 O.R.	NCH

WAR DIARY or INTELLIGENCE SUMMARY

Army Form C. 2118

(Erase heading not required.)

134 Fd Ambulance

Place	Date	Hour	Summary of Events and Information	Remarks and references to Appendices
	15.7.16		Remains 13 OR + Aid Posts arranged for Bttns & Aid Posts. Advance dressing stn + Car Posts as before. Remains 105 OR. G.2.B.E.22. Admits 21 OR. E.55. Remains 105 OR. Vide 10 ADS Lone Farm - Divisional Rest-Station also - 15 sit and Minor ailments received here.	He H.
	16.7.16	"	Remains 105 OR. Remains ? Ill. Routine orders.	NCH
	17.7.16	"	Remains 111 OR. A.3 OR. 18 OR. E.19 A.10 OR. Remains 2 OR 111 OR.	NCH
	18.7.16		Remains 2 OR 111 OR. A.3 OR. E.29 A.3 OR. Remains 99 OR.	NCH
	19.7.16		Remains 99 OR. A.10 A.26 OR. E.17.26 OR. Remains 97. Today the white L.v.R Aid Post joined up FESTUBERT ordered. B.shurst Ambulance divides to take up at MARRAIS Y LONG FARM to R.O.C. 118. I BDC Field Amb. 16 to 2 h.50 from FAUQUILLRIDGE to LONG FARM. 20 Men Debet up for Fatigue party to Engineers.	NCH
	20.7.16		Remains 97 OR. Admits 30 OR 40 N. E.25 OR. 10 H. Remains Gain 30 OR. 10.30 R. 30 beds Casualty Bury Ri. August 19/20. 30 R. 27 OR. Lieut HIGGINS sent to LONE FARM to relieve Lieut HARRIS for the night who took over Reserved Aid Post - from two I Cawl Rgr. Brt Open v 16 OR. v 12 other Ambulance beans from 1832 Fd Awk for this Regent to Cav. g. Emergency.	He 4.
	21.7.16		Remains 3 OR 103 OR. Admits 3 OR 20 OR. E.4 OR. 34 OR. Remains 26 OR 87 OR. Some of the personnel sent through for chaths.	17 X
	22.7.16		Remains 2 OR 89 OR. Admits 21 OR. E.16 A.33 OR. Remains 10 A.77 OR. Exhibit of Gas Horns. Vide 15 G Boy MARRAIS	16 ce

Place	Date	Hour	Summary of Events and Information	Remarks and references to Appendices
	23.7.16.		Remand 10A 77 OR. AOR 10A 370R. Evand 5 340R R 20A 00 OR - Broken second lieut - LONE FARM ADJ. needs be taken on as OC 133 70 and in dir. arrangements made with OC 133 70 and relieves tonight - he remains chug. MG. coverg 24/25 2 night Lieut HARRIS + 20 OR beyond hedge garden chug. the night	16A
	24.7.16		Remand 2 OA. 200R. AOR 16. 1 OA 150R E & Draft. 10A. 240R Remay 2 Offrs & 71 OR. Leclin a tui and Tui & Lieut HUGGINS 16 Schowly 2 section at OR School of 2 section 2 night 5:30 hr. Handed over ADS LONE FARM to 133 FG and went through GO.S. Chember.	16A, 14A
	25.7.16		Remand 26A 710R. AOR 15. 130R E 350R R 20A. 490R. 38 OR. the personnel	15A, 14A, 14A
	26.7.16		Remain 20A. 290R. AOR 15 2A 150R E 10A 110R. Remay 30A 5T OR	14A
	27.7.16		Remain 34A5T0R. AOR15. 15OR E 10OR R 30A 530R AOrs to hinders Ambulance	
	28.7.16		Remain 30A 530R AO 19A 160R E 24 Remay 40A 450R. Pte CUNNINGHAM T chu at 33 C.C.S. sundry bruing shock by Pte CULLEN R.M. C.	
	29.7.16		Remain 40A 45T 40R. AOR 15 210R E 180R 10A. 10A in - Court harhel "personal" held 15 AOR a have lay the charge against Pte CULLENS R a.m. C. when on Bearer guard to person of Lieut LACEY, Lieut ANDERSON (T) R.a.m.C. 2 parts the Dept Lieut MITCHELL reports attaction 15 - 10 in RE	14A

Place	Date	Hour	Summary of Events and Information	Remarks and references to Appendices
	31.7.16		Remaining 19 offs. 33 ORs. Admitted 2 offs. 17 ORs. E. 8 OR. Remaining 3 offs 42 ORs. Total number of cases pass through Ambulance 844. Of the number 252 were transfers from 101 F.A. Amb. 368 Battle Casualties. 465 were sent to C.C.S. 331 to Divs. v. Corps. R.S. Ran a funeral. 19 cases were interred during the week. 10 of whom were brought to C.C.S. 5 Cars of Infantry sheenie 2 Roads, 1 Orphans + 2 Futures of slung items through the Ambulances by 1 Car of Armd. S/Capt Curr. The Ambulances. We to 2 A.D.S. Marais, Lone Farm, dug outs with — Barran'd Rest Station — Brussel Laundry Belts. The employment during Pte. Cunningham & 7. 28. Cav. on full Casualty of the matter. The G.O.C. of the Divin accomp. by the A.D.S. 3.S. An inspected the Ambulances + furnish satisfactory with the condition. A Small raid on camp in our sector aught 30/31. out 14 Casualties.	14 cas

H.C. Hitchcock
2 Lt 70 Ambulance
O.C. F.M. 70 Amb.

Army Form C. 2118

WAR DIARY
or
INTELLIGENCE SUMMARY

(Erase heading not required.)

134th R.A.M.C.
134th FIELD AMBULANCE.

39/Vol. 6

Instructions regarding War Diaries and Intelligence Summaries are contained in F. S. Regs., Part II. and the Staff Manual respectively. Title Pages will be prepared in manuscript.

Place	Date	Hour	Summary of Events and Information	Remarks and references to Appendices
October 1916			Original :— To D.A.h., 3rd Echelon.	

[Stamp: 134th FIELD AMBULANCE 1 SEP 1916]

[Stamp: COMMITTEE FOR THE MEDICAL HISTORY OF THE WAR Date -9 OCT 1916]

Army Form C. 2118

WAR DIARY
or
INTELLIGENCE SUMMARY
(Erase heading not required.)

R.A.M.C.
134th FIELD AMBULANCE.

Instructions regarding War Diaries and Intelligence Summaries are contained in F.S. Regs., Part II and the Staff Manual respectively. Title Pages will be prepared in manuscript.

[Stamp: 134th FIELD AMBULANCE 1 SEP 1916]

Place	Date	Hour	Summary of Events and Information	Remarks and references to Appendices
ANNEZIN E.9.6.28	1/8/16	10am	Remained 3 Of, 42 OR. Admitted 9 OR. E.170R. Remaining 10 Of, 340 OR. Routine as usual. 3 G. personnel unit through Gas Chamber. Visit from Col Galloway. Indented abroin to First Army.	Helmut bagn Room
"	2/8/16	7hrs	Remained 10 Of, 340 OR. Admitted 10 R. E.40 OR. Remaining 10 Of, 40 OR. Visit to A.D.S. at 12.30 hrs - also Cognuse at A.Dns. Place re time & other details. Weather cloudy.	1 B.C.H.
"	3/8/16	7hrs	Remained 1 Of, 29 OR. Admitted 14 OR. E.170 R. Remaining 10 Of, 26 OR. 1 - Routine work.	1 B.C.H.
"	4/8/16	7hrs	Remained 10 Of, 33 OR. Admitted 11 OR. E.15 OR. R. 10 Of, 29 OR. Routine work.	H.C.H.
"	5/8/16	7hrs	Remained 10 Of, 29 OR. Admitted 14 OR. E.17 OR. Remaining 10 Of, 26 OR. Routine work.	1 B.C.H. H.C.H.
"	6/8/16		Remained 10 Of, 26 OR. Admitted 12 OR. E.16 OR. Remaining 22 OR. Routine work. 10 Of, 22 OR. Attended memorial service in Square BETHUNE	H.C.H.
"	7/8/16	10.30 am	R. 10 Of, 26 OR. Admitted 10 Of, 14 OR. E.18 OR. Remaining 2 Of, 18 OR. Weather cloudy & colder. BETHUNE shelled 133 H.A. & 91" R.A. Brandies came here. The form 62 the adjoining school was required by the Ambulance at 7.30 hrs. to ALLOUAGNE. Cases had in the billet behind Ambulance on Sunday shall visit A.D.S. & M/Os Ambulance at 5 hrs. 3 Pencil contain wounded who hand's to this Ambulance being wheel died. Three cases were hopeless Lieut. to the Corps & Divisional Hospital. One Italian polish arrived dead	H.C.H.

Army Form C. 2

R.A.M.C.
134th FIELD AMBULANCE

134 Fd Ambulance

WAR DIARY
or
INTELLIGENCE SUMMARY
(Erase heading not required.)

Instructions regarding War Diaries and Intelligence Summaries are contained in F.S. Regs., Part II. and the Staff Manual respectively. Title Pages will be prepared in manuscript.

134th FIELD AMBULANCE
1 SEP 1916

Place	Date	Hour	Summary of Events and Information	Remarks and references to Appendices
ANNEZIN	7.8.16		Cases admitted followin 3 + 6 h.m. Total no. g wounded in Shelling St. Kellis. Their Corps been the onf evacuees in this Ambulance. heads the 3 Captain the remainder were ordinary sick wounded to Ambulance.	156/returns
"	8.8.16	9am	Received 2.0 p.m. 18 o/R. Admitted - Armentls 68 o/R. 62 g which are transfer. E 2 o/R 20 o/R. Remaining 62 o.R. Admitted 1. and g 97". 2nd Cavl. arrived at 6.0 f. Lieut. Bays 128 exposed.	142 L
"	9.8.16	4h.m	Received 63 o/R. Q. Bruille, 104, 157 o/R. E/16 o/R. Remaining 104 62 o/R. Admitted hard g 97". 2nd Cavl. arrived 12 h.r. Sgt. 97 9d sick. 1m 3 hours senior the Ambulance. D.S. & Capt. riches. did in search for these Insurance Pte Cullen R.A.M.C. a casualty of last fight. J. 2 G. Ch. The him moved from Capt to 1. 2 taken to ground wards - Lieut. MITCHELL R.A.M.C. relieved Lieut. Hanson our A.D.S. MARAIS & Buissy at ANNEZIN 4th 97th 2d Aut. Hardest out.	156 R
"	10.8.16	9am	D ANNEZIN at 3.30 p.m. arrived at one field. RAIMBERT at 5 o'm. very hot + living heat. The hand has appreciated & played E route to carabin.	156 R
L'ABBAYE NEUVILLE Farm	11.8.16	10 p.m.	left RAIMBERT at 3.30 p.m. arrived L'ABBAYE NEUVILLE Farm 8.30 p. bitter + lofty at 9 a.m. 20 Cavalier in route 2 and 2nd 20 h.t. h.m.y Remained and advanced 5. E 5° lies g the air.	6 C M
"	12.8.16	4.30h	Eric's Camp for pursuant. Searches barns & farm. Scarcity g water for horses about 12 hrd Anf g made.	142 L

Wt. W593/826 1,000,000 4/15 J.B.C. & A. A.D.S.S./Forms/C. 2118.

WAR DIARY or INTELLIGENCE SUMMARY

Army Form C. 2118

134th FIELD AMBULANCE R.A.M.C.

(Erase heading not required.) 134 Fd Ambulance

Place	Date	Hour	Summary of Events and Information	Remarks and references to Appendices
LA BAYE NEUVILLE	13.8.16	11 am	Remained until A.30 when E1 R Mid A orders until march 6-7 am. A Coys S.W.ds & Watnedts Coys. 12.30 Noon D & C orders until march 7.0-8 km. General fatigues during the day & Candle with Creek.	HCH
"	14.8.16	11 am	Remained Coms E.R. Mid. Doctrin until march 7.0 am A v C 7 to 8 km. Lectin on Haversack guns & orders Given 10 Min orders 2-3 km. Rainy	HCH
"	15.8.16	11 am	R Mid A. 7 OR E 7 OR R Mid C orders until march 6.30-7.30 A v B guns orders march lectin & orders Given on orderlies. Rainy weather	HCH
"	16.8.16	11 am	Remained until A. 8 OR E 7 OR R 10 PR. Ambulance. Raining & Evening. Demonstration on how to lift wounded & attendance & rifle drill. Unit of OOR S.V. Coys & Officers & men S. 3 OR. Dr 3.15 pm. Weather showery. 13 Reinforcements arrived last Evening of personnel. 3 Mid. Side addition. 13 buffer Nor 7 guns.	HCH
"	17.8.16	7.30 pm	Remained R Orderlies 10 OR (& Transport) Branch Orders R. 30 R very wet day. Ordinary fatigues. Rd & horseshoe. Rd & Enable. Carried out ordry fatigues	HCH
"	18.8.16	8 pm	Remained 3 OR A. 3 OR E. 6. R. Mid. knowing Rnds march. Fatigue. & Red horseshoes very wet day. fieldomstin with kindle the Train Unedo	HCH
"	19.8.16	6 pm	Remained until A 10 R 10 OR E 19 R/100 R Rent. Rnds Trans. & Fatigue. Showery weather	HCH
"	20.8.16		Remained 1 OR A 10 R 8 OR E 10 R 8 OR R 1 OR Church parade held in Pardy wheat. Fatigues Weather Showery.	HCH

WAR DIARY
or
INTELLIGENCE SUMMARY
(Erase heading not required.)

Army Form C. 2118.
R.A.M.C.
134th FIELD AMBULANCE.

OC 134 Fd Ambulance

Place	Date	Hour	Summary of Events and Information	Remarks and references to Appendices
ABBAYE NEUVILLE	21.8.16	4 pm	Unit proceeds to 1st Pal to Bath removing personal kit & Camp Kit. RIOR & 70R EOOR RMC Huthir bright no rain. Camp which Luncheon to move.	See details Appendix
"	22.8.16	6 pm	Remaining A 2 O R E 2 RMC Remainder to move - left billet at 8.30 am to MAIZERES	See 4
MAIZIERS	23.8.16	11 am	Remaining A 3 E 3 RMC Left billet 9 am & arrived at new billet 7.45 am no billets in town - no Cresselin in order that kit not cleaned 9 am	See 4
LUCHEAUX	24.8.16	6 pm	Remained at Admells 27 E 24 Remains 3 OR marches out & billet & arrived at LUCHEAUX 12.3 p.m - No Casualties & weed - very hot & trying march	NC4
BUS-LES- ARTOIS	25.8.16	7 pm	Left billet 6.30 am marches to BUS LES ARTOIS arrives 1pm Orders OC 107 Fd Amb send with 6.30 am view to taking over Ambulance Corps Collecting Stahn & ADS MESNIL Capt FOTHERGILL 1/c & B Section took on a DS MESNIL at 7 pm - Lieut HUGGINS took on Corps Collect. Stahn ACHEEUX R.S. Ad 43 E 46 R Ml	See 4
ACHEEUX	26.8.16	9.30 pm	Left rest billet 9 am arrive ACHEEUX - 11 am took on new Dressing Stahn & Corps Collecting Stahn from 107 Fd Amb who handed a Corps Collecting area 12 Mil Ad 104 12 on E 104 12 OTO Remaining rest	NC4
"	27.8.16		Remaining rest Admells 55 (9 from 12 RNB Thanks from 107 O Amd 42 hrs Admission Evil - Remaining 5.55 DS.ds a DS MESNIL & and took autumn from a DMS to Admit to QBS at Easton Lieut HARRIS in relation to Corps Quarry Sergent The captain of luiday the PORTERS as a Collectly Station and y in MCCath. In all the system Carries and of horseman Ambulance Cases	See 4

1 SEP 1916
134th FIELD AMBULANCE

WAR DIARY or INTELLIGENCE SUMMARY

Army Form C. 2118
R.A.M.C.
134th FIELD AMBULANCE

O C 134 Fd Ambulance

Place	Date	Hour	Summary of Events and Information	Remarks and references to Appendices
ACHEUX	27.8.16		Keen winds. Sent M.O. in Ambulance him & back to MESNIL for hircharel ambulance & accoutrements from MESNIL Rain here rest - to M D Station. There a Dist B appended by Operation was not conduct favourable.	ACH
"	28.8.16	9a	R.5.OR. A.3, E.37, R.49. Capt. R.H. FOTHERGILL returned to Hqrs. Question moved - G.S.W. Legt. Hand - 4 on Stretchers.	ACH
"	29.8.16	10a	Division g Indian g Rnn g Inf. go & Inflicts knchin Built central Record under Bullets front line trenches. A Bn's & Divns Bn's Bn's holds Ambulance.	ACH
"	30.8.16	10a	R.49. R.27R. 29. Buis 16.4R. 2 OR. R.35. Returned for Relieving Standin Receive Ambulance A Bn's 2 Bn's Horses Horses & Lorry g 13 D R's Band arrived R. Renaux 33. B.D. Mt. 29. E.49. Renaux. 13. A.D.M.s bodies renned. Returned G Civil. Entering Station & Annexes for Ordinans about 8 pm new lost.	10 CH
"	31.8.16	10a	12 13 Or R. Q.35. Buis E 37 R.10. Shell hit Whole Dry & Regimental Dump the ninth 3502 Case hand Turns to the Ambulance. 420 admissions & 74 hamfas Bullets Casualty 99. Sigr & Pact 1. Ac.ass hit Engineer 7 Sect. 305. No officers there offices 5 Seed. Both Casualty 2 The wind during the stay at ANNEZIN acted to a Heavy Ambulance Clearing the bombardment of BETHUNE & round. Bands from the Ambulance helm & round 200 Cases acting on the enemy get in g the A D M S & Able. Chateau for the Damang g was accommodated Ready & also the Case received wound station the whole lot has half DM g the Ambulance was all to Renaux the Cross Bali in the Swamp of another offr	15 CH

134th FIELD AMBULANCE SEP 1916

WAR DIARY or **INTELLIGENCE SUMMARY**

Army Form C. 2118

R.A.M.C.
134th FIELD AMBULANCE

134 Fd Ambulance

Place	Date	Hour	Summary of Events and Information	Remarks and references to Appendices
ACHEUX	31.8.16		Coming on the Bus just as we were leaving to go to bivouacs of the Ambulance which was 200 yds North of road. N.C. 6 and 9 arrived delayed by roads & fumes this I attribute largely to the old & run of horses. The remnant of cookers with a Fd Ambulance marching behind a Brigade on a bye lane in bright sun ask too much of supply. The bu. was too far & too hard when on 28/7 at INGOUVILLE the Remy N.C. had been under Canvas & horses a shelter this time & first known a route march. The Radl. horse useful on coming into our present billet 48 hours previously. Blown shouting as below. The Divisn reached here standing up then on wheeled stretchers – he 24 hrs deployment advanced to Louvencourt station & came ns/ores. The Achieving had rested enroute, & hearty. We the cookers up to any at the Coyst. Externally, the the understory before we sheltered they had only eating. The Regiment 4 miles far to remay infact a stationary mud for to Regiment halts for to Remay infact a number of runcold Ings wards. I think he treleade us under & welcome) & the Bivouac & a well as we have captured into Store Regults – hand blown the Regiment long. Jackl 3 by a Bn S & Bn S E Cooks invites the and	18 Co.s

1 S Oldland
Lt Col R.a.m.c.
o.c. 134 Fd Aml.

134. F.Amb.

140/134 / 39

39th Div.

COMMITTEE FOR THE
MEDICAL HISTORY OF THE WAR
Date 30 OCT. 1916

134th Field Ambulance

WAR DIARY or INTELLIGENCE SUMMARY

134th FIELD AMBULANCE
Army Form C. 2118

134 Field — Central one

Place	Date	Hour	Summary of Events and Information	Remarks and references to Appendices
Acheux	1.9.16	8/11	Remains OR 10 Admissions 10½ 23 OR E 19/24 OR Remaining 4 OR LIEUT MACRAE. Remaining held 3/10 134 FA and I found the unit. Was preparing to head for operations by the BDivision as well as Corps Collecting Station organized as a Main Dressing Station for the BDivision as well as Corps Collecting for the E Corps Posted by A Dns S. Two rows of tents pitched as aide for Stretcher cases. This for walking Cases. The erection of a latrine and placed tins and all arrangements for a hospital made in hand. Light of the tent width.	HQ Wolvrell Wood
"	2.9.16	11/11.	Remains OR 4 Admissions 6½ 3 OR 29. E 9½ 3 OR 26 Remaining 7 Lieut MACNEIL reported arrival and discharge with Lieut SIMPSON who reported Head Quarters from MESNIL. Arrangements for operation on following morning completed - Capt. HUNTER took over A.D.J Cookers + Capt. ROBERTSON A.D.J MESNIL. The Ambulance of the Division was hooked and arranged 20 hour dues of 134 FA Ambulance on the line from Beau A.D.S + Mc Cars 9 132 FA Amb. on the MESNIL Road whilst 133 was at Mc COSKERS Run. The A.D.J at which were Bearers Squads from Lieut NAPARRA 5 Field Amb reported for temporary duty at Head Quarters Lieut 15 A.D.J COOKERS + MESNIL Weather fair.	HQH
"	3.9.16		Operation Commenced at 5.10 am Casualties arrived at D Station about 8.30 am It was always taken away as Congestion Behaved things. Mesnil many 10 shillings The Convoy worked all without any Casualties Lieut MITCHELL was wounded - 5 OR killed + 24 wounded. The Number of Casualties passing through the C.C. Station & L.B Station during the 24 hours afterwards 1580 of which 412 famous	HQB

Army Form C. 2118

134th FIELD AMBULANCE

WAR DIARY or INTELLIGENCE SUMMARY

(Erase heading not required.)

134 F.d

Place	Date	Hour	Summary of Events and Information	Remarks and references to Appendices
A.Q. HEUX	3.9.16	9 am	Through 15 & am Drum'y Station. There were all attd dis 16 sect 4 Brigades 4.5 am. The fullowing moved 4 Brandhurne to army Tram a with a 5 ha C for military care. Ng Congston Buchtes duties, ad Head Quarters & any when also 7 the Bane. Thead Quartin ma. duties prepared by the B.19-15 & dining the afternoon by the Bne 5 19.Dr.5 & duty. Lieut MacPHERSON Remand 7 As wells 5.Sept 21 oR E.3 M. 42 orR. Remang 2 oR 36 oR (noon) (759 kC ammum plus butts Canaller)	He Ind ut dist
ACHEUX	4.9.16	6 hm	Open Comp Conn? & Start asmd 2 am. R 27R 385R A Dr wls 25oR 324 HR E 27R 378M Dis 2 R oR 2 Lieut NAVARRE ngoind this unit. Rened this buty both at A Dg & Head Quartin (309 g amum plus butts Canaller). A.B.A.S walls Head Qu wls ad R or 2. A D wels 0/8 2 ok R 2/6. E 179. Dis 10 Remang 2 oR 29 ob. General cluring up & Conf? & Evacuation Con tued (209 g ammum plus butts Canaller)	He H.
"	5.9.16	4 hm		He 15
"	6.9.16	7 hm	Rem amd 2 oR 29 oR. Adr wls 7 oR 1210R. E 9 oR 146 oR. Brig 3 Remang 1. Lieut Boyess attached Informing on h.o 1/st Hccl. Lieut ANDERSON posted as 2 o 15. 16 " R Cot. 7 Respourts arr ved (54 g amum. Butts Canaller). ACHEUX shelled with San shells. no dam. age done.	He 18.
"	7.9.16		Capt W J T D SMYTHE & Lieut J L HENDRY reported for duty. Remang? Or 1. AD wls? 87 15 = OR 34 E 0/9 11 5 oR 47. Remang 28 (222 HC ammum plus Battle Canaller) Und 4 U B HS v ADMS.	14C H
"	8.9.16		Lieut G W RACEY pontes on h.o 1/e 11" Reserve Remain 20. AD wls 0/82. oR 52 E 7/2. OR 74 R 10 (Buttle Canaller 285 g HC ammum)	He L.

1875 Wt. W393/826 1,000,000 4/15 J.B.C. & A. A.D.S.S./Forms/C.2118.

Army Form C. 2118 & M.C.
134th FIELD AMBULANCE.
3

Instructions regarding War Diaries and Intelligence
Summaries are contained in F.S. Regs., Part II.
and the Staff Manual respectively. Title Pages
will be prepared in manuscript.

WAR DIARY
or
INTELLIGENCE SUMMARY

(Erase heading not required.)

134 Fd Amb.

Place	Date	Hour	Summary of Events and Information	Remarks and references to Appendices
ACHEUX	9.9.16	6pm	Remain 10 Admitted OR 41 E OR 39 Remaining 12 Lieut BOYERS reported with Capt SMYTHE Proceeded to MESNIL took to Camp. (Battle Casualties 3)	See inside
"	10.9.16	7am	Remaining OR 12 Admitted OR 2 OR 35 E 37 Remaining 2 OR 10 OR. Capt PORTER reports for duty. Went to A Dvn. back to Camp. (Battle Casualties 1)	HCH
"	11.9.16	7am	R 2 OR 10 OR Admitted 1 OR 25 OR E 1 OR 8 OR R 2 OR 27 OR (Battle casualties 7). Capt PORTER + Lieut BOYERS proceed to look over MESNIL Post & A Dvns	14 CH
"	12.9.16	6pm	OR 2. OR 27 (Remain) Admitted OR 10 E 1 OR 5 OR R 1 OR 40 OR. A Dvns. looks Ambulance. Camp Equipment being checked + stores - Ambulance being fitted up.	HCH
"	13.9.16	9am	OR 1 OR 40 Remain Admits 1 OR 27 OR. E 1 OR 19 OR R 1 OR 48 OR Cookhouse at A Dvn S Thes 2.30 pm to Saved inspection + Roll operation	HCH
"	14.9.16	7am	R 1 OR U S OR Ad OR 22 E 1 OR 27 OR Remaining OR 43. Orders received at 11.30am to prepare Camp for possible wedding over of Canadian Division. Rearrangement of Ambulance + preparation for Receiving Police "Raid" - Lieut BOYERS looks 15 4/3 Black head	15CH
"	15.9.16	1pm	OR 43. Remain Admitted OR 2. OR 24 E OR 2. OR 46. Remain OR 21 - orders to trans Queralin. took Camp 9 Lines. ordinary visits - Inspection in St. Peter at A DS MESNIL + Teas	HCH

1875 Wt. W593/826 1,000,000 4/15 J.B.C. & A. A.D.S.S./Forms/C. 2118.

Army Form C. 2118.
134th FIELD AMBULANCE
4

WAR DIARY
or
INTELLIGENCE SUMMARY
(Erase heading not required.)

134 Fd Amb

Place	Date	Hour	Summary of Events and Information	Remarks and references to Appendices
ACHEUX	15/9/16	8 a.m.	39 Div. Casualties. Arms 10 OR v 11 OR. Evacuated to CCS. O.Brown. Canadian 7 OR v 3/3 OR. Walking Cases. 2 OR v 44 OR German wounds. Evac. Pari. through CCS Labor. First 9 Stns. D.A.M.S. v A.D.M.S.	ACH
	16/9/16	10 a.m.	OR 21 Remained. Wounded 10 OR 36 OR. E 10 OR 49 OR. R 60 OR. Lt. Glenn of Canadian wounded through Capt C Station - Thigh case injured twice & our Colonel history account prior to his being a dressing. Journey & is frist thro' this wound to 193 of all ranks first up to the night v Evac. at 9:30 am the following morning	HCH
	17/9/16	7 a.m.	R. OR 6 ad mls 3 OR OR 22. E 10 OR 10 OR D1 Ramsey of 2 OR. Pt. Holt of R.C. wounded sharply wounded & the shoulder. Both v wls. O.C. A.W. & also wounded.	HCH
	18/9/16	10 a.m.	Rem. and 2 OR OR 17. admls. 19 OR 23. E 17 OR 27 OR. R 2 OR 13 OR. 69 other Evacn. from through CCS Labor + has 16 hr. wards for the night health etc.	HCH
	19/9/16	8 a.m.	Remained. OR 2. OR 13. Admls 17 OR 21 OR. E 10 OR 12 OR. R OR 2 OR 22. 29 other Evacn. through CC Station. Walki. still evy act.	HCL
	20/9/16	6 a.m.	R 2 OR 1. 22 OR. admls 33 OR E 17 OR 26 OR R 1 OR 29 OR 31 other Own. Evacn. from through CC Station - First act. For inject gar v Evacd & at 9/16	ACH
	21/9/16	9 a.m.	Rem. 10 OR 29 OR. ad mls 2 OR 16 OR. E 18 OR 19 OR. 10 at'd Manic ADHS v wls. Walki gain.	HCH

Army Form C. 2118.
134th FIELD AMBULANCE.
5

WAR DIARY
or
INTELLIGENCE SUMMARY
(Erase heading not required.)

134 F.D. Amb.

134th FIELD AMBULANCE
1 OCT 1916

Place	Date	Hour	Summary of Events and Information	Remarks and references to Appendices
ACHEUX	22/9/16	10p.	Remain 7 Off OR 26, Acheux Off 1 OR 19 EOR 17. Remain 2 Off 28 OR. Rondu: work.	McNoule
"	23/9/16	9h.	Remain 2 Off OR 26 Acheux 2 Off 28 OR. E 23 OR. Died 1. Remain 7 Off 4 OR 30	Nett
"	24/9/16	"	Remain 4 Off. 38 OR Acheux 3 Off 44 OR E 3 Off 46 OR R Off 4 OR 32 Section formed of B.P. 0 & Lushey J holding & from then	HCN
"	25/9/16	10p	R 40f. 36. OR. Acheux 1 Off 20 OR E 2 Off. 20 OR Orders received 13 Inspan Coy. Orderly Sister to Army. On arrival of wounded Lent by Detn. IV & Dem. S. 134 Fd. Amb. Sgt. P. & artist. Lieut RACEY reported sent.	Joe H
"	26/9/16	10p.	Remain 2 Off OR 28 Acheux 1 Off OR 28 R 1 Off OR. 2 Off. E 33. R 1 Off. 2 Off. Rondu: work	HCN
"	27/9/16	10p.	Remain 2 Off 14 OR Acheux 1 Off 4 OR R. 2 Off. 18 OR. Pans Kings C CS 454 2 Off a 10 OR 92° Bn. arrived to Relieve the Ground & Kent J ADS	HCN
"	28/9/16	10p.	Been to Infantry & Cap. Sar. Denny J. Taken Into Strand. Kent 16 ADS to Bn. hut as prepared new pass. R. 2 Off. 18 OR. Acheux 2 Off. 17 OR. R 2 Off 21 - 131 travel through C.C.S. taken	HCN
"	29/9/16		Remain 2 Off OR 21 Acheux 2 Off 4 OR E 3 Off 26 OR R 2 Off 36 OR. Capt. PORTER Reats from ADS MESNIL to Buys at ADS S, Off in Lieut COYLE	HCN

WAR DIARY
INTELLIGENCE SUMMARY

134 Field Ambulance

Army Form C. 2118
134th FIELD AMBULANCE

Place	Date	Hour	Summary of Events and Information	Remarks and references to Appendices
ACHEUX	30.9.16	10b.	Remained O/c 2. OR 35 A.S.R. 165 O/c 2. OR 19. E. O/c 2. OR 20 Died 2 Remaining H.2. OR 24. During the week the Ambulance has been particularly busy. I had to find Stretcher dealers into Courcelles on a large scale. In addition to running the E. Bgs MESNIL & the Cookers, Baths &c about Forceville from the R.A.P. — It is also in charge of the F Park Collecting Station. When it Keeps a Reserve of am. Dressings &c. On 3rd Sept. the total number was Stretcher Cases 1090 of which 2 were handled by the Ambulance. On 17th of August 700 Cases were handled Stretcher Cases in addition to the numbers of Sitting & Walking Cases. In addition to the Capt. A.Slater, arranged for the Ambulance 9/13 FB Regt. during the night has been Received at the Ambulance & in the opening Westmans of the Period of 24hrs in Wickable ½ 25 woundes relating, but their Comfort & skill also kept busy, it was highly made when he greatly needed. LIEUT MITCHELL The A.D.S. was

30.9.16

H.C. Kilmile Lt. Col.
O/C 134 Fd. Amb. |

140/949

134th F.A.

6/4/16

COMMITTEE FOR THE
MEDICAL HISTORY OF THE W...
Date 30 APR. 1917

WAR DIARY or INTELLIGENCE SUMMARY

Army Form C. 2118
134th FIELD AMBULANCE

(Erase heading not required.)

Vol 7

Place	Date	Hour	Summary of Events and Information	Remarks and references to Appendices
ACHEUX	1.10.16	11hr	Ords recd to hand over C.C.S Station & Amb. & 15 remain ratios	100 WAR LI CAP sick
P.132.a.3	2.10.16	3hr	Handed over to D.S. staff & CCS Station.	
"	"	8hr	15 100th Fd. Amb. arrived & handed & tookover	
"	3.10.16	8hr	Ambulance remained trucks. All sick admitted to 100th Fd. Amb. On right bank	FOR
"	4.10.16	5ft	Subhgos still holds Orders recvd. from Ol S.	
"	"	"	Orders recvd to take over Cabstand at Knees Quarles	
CABSTAND	5.10.16	5ft	Ambulance troves to CABSTAND & Dirst's Court.	172/4
No.10 bus	6.10.16	9hr	Splits ADM S.V.46 T. R M.L AD M.D SOM E'S OR R.N.K	HQ47
"	"	"	Took over CABSTAND from 57 Fd Amb. & half of 20 S.R. v 1 bat MACBRAE detail...	
"	"	9hr	9f & C.C.S. CONTAY Advanced 4 Eu.	No K
"	7.10.16	7hr	D.D.M.S. & Capt. visited amb. Inclusion of COOKERY MEUNIL 39 OR attached 15	HQK
"	"	"	132 Fd Amb A2M Days 5 OR 7mr.	
"	8.10.16	9hr	Cap. SMYTHE Evacuated to 1st F 21 OR E 1st F 21 OR	
"	9.10.16	"	Visit J.A.D.M.S. 12 OR sent to 132 Fd Amb A.D. 19/2 16 OR Evaced	HQ K
"	10.10.16	10hr	Visit to a Do MEUNIL & COOKERS. Orderly Exercises 10 R.	HQK
"	11.10.16	9hr	Coy. S. VW S. Co. v Ill. & Evaced 3 W 12 OR.	HQ H
"	12.10.16	10hr	Bonus I Capt. visits. Handed our ADV. POOKERS to 132 Fd Amb v MEUNIL to	HQ K
"	"	"	Hand brown Pool on Collecting Post MAILLY MAILLY	
"	13.10.16	"	Lucid RACEY details for the Purp. & v handed 2 10 R	HQ K
"	14.10.16	9hr	V S to MAILLY MAILLY. Oh 380 cases From Merger CROSSTAD A.M.S. R.A.	HQK

Army Form C. 2118

WAR DIARY
or
INTELLIGENCE SUMMARY
(Erase heading not required.)

134th FIELD AMBULANCE

134th FIELD AMBULANCE
- 2 NOV 1916

Place	Date	Hour	Summary of Events and Information	Remarks and references to Appendices

(handwritten entries illegible)

Army Form C. 2118
R.A.M.C.
134th Field AMBULANCE

WAR DIARY
or
INTELLIGENCE SUMMARY
(Erase heading not required.)

Place	Date	Hour	Summary of Events and Information	Remarks and references to Appendices
ABSTAND W.10.C.4.3	28.10.16	9am	Remained nil A 3 off 9 9 OR E 3 off 10 v OR R nil – Routine work.	1st Exhibit
"	29.10.16	6am	Remained nil A 2 off 90 OR E 2 off 90 OR R nil – Conducted 9 a turning share for troth horses & men	HeH
"	30.10.16	8pm	Remained nil Adm.to 9 OR E 92 OR R nil	HeH
"	31.10.16	10pm	Adm 5 rdr R nil Ad 10 R 76 OR E 76 OR R nil –
During the week the train clearing of sick & wounded took place. The train after having through S.B of 132 Fd Amb. on through Air locals at the C.C.S. and v Dick were loaded at the Main Dressing sta Ember – Two trains running Slitteries to Key, the other running Regenery to Knitrand, Recessed the same – 2 ards cel at 10ft. y sore-to A.C.C.S. 9 Mens subsistence to Brit 132 Amb Siutes for Walkey Canon Brain. Ve also Mulud a Quintroit Peabody thus keeping clear a very Salient. The Division & 13 y 5 y Lan. Div. between us. We hand D v thereby N.C. Hand being ... 1663. During the Selestran he himd Out Travel 5 casualties were killed attached to 132 Fd Amb. Our complements to the 132 Fd Amb. The unit is till under Canvas Kings huts are dany theek.

1/11/16

H.C.H.Sueh Lt.Col RA RO 13 U Ed hum | |

Confidential.

War Diary
of
134th Field Ambulance

from 1st November to 30th November, 1916

WAR DIARY / INTELLIGENCE SUMMARY

Army Form C. 2118

134th FIELD AMBULANCE

Place	Date	Hour	Summary of Events and Information	Remarks and references to Appendices
CRASTRAND N.10.c.4.5. Map 57 D SE	1.11.16	9 a.m.	Remaining Nil. Admissions & Evacuations 6/5. Health Ord'y & Showery	1/C H/Orl
"	2.11.16	10 p.m.	Admissions & Evacuations 10/4 7/5 OR. Health conditions same. Preparation for operations continued.	A.1 & 2
"	3.11.16	7 a.m.	Operations postponed. Health condition same. Vide 1st A D M S reference orders re Aphurie	1/C H
		8 p.m.	2 Admissions & Evacuations 10/4 6/5 OR.	
"	4.11.16	8 p.m.	Conference at CRASTRAND re operations. 2 p.m. A.D.M.S. O.C. 132 & Brown O/Green attached.	1/C H
"	5.11.16	9 a.m.	Admissions & Evacuations 6/6. Routine duties - health still nil	H C H
"	6.11.16	6 a.m.	Admissions & Evacuations 2 Off 33 OR. Capt. CRAVEN to 60 10/174 Bde.	1/C H
"	7.11.16	10 p.m.	Admissions & Evacuations 1 Off. 41 OR. Capt. MILNE Taken on the strength & the same day posted to "Sussex" - nil health	H C H
"	8.11.16	9 a.m.	Admissions & Evacuations 8 Off 54 OR. A.D.M.S. visit - Shelling & close vicinity 10 CRASTAND	H C H
"	9.11.16	10 p.m.	Evacuation 6 Off 47 OR. Health now normal.	H C H
"	10.11.16	1 p.m.	G.O.C. 39 Div accompanied by A.D.M.S & his heads arrived 9.30 a.m. E 37 q 55 OR. February 2	H C H
"	11.11.16	10 p.m.	Evacuated 370 preparation for operation continued	H C H
"	12.11.16	7 p.m.	Evacuation 25H 42 OR. Lieut HARRIS & MATCHELL with a field ambulance took up their HdQuarters at LANCASHIRE DUMP - 16 evacuees other lands down in ambulance 2.	H C H
"	13.11.16	11 a.m.	Heavy guns around about 8.30 a.m. Total 9.697 3 Off 9.39 a.m. Am Shell with "12 h.m. Can 8.19 Own men also duty with but 3 h.m & there are trucks. An there was no Lorry for the Tent sub-division to form an E 37 at ST. PIERRE DIVION the word O/arrived when troops were greatly approved - a number of them walking cases had duty with at the CRASTAND - the Cookers to await ambulances after having dried & fed by Motor bernes to EAST CLAIRFAYE	H C H

1 DEC 1916

WAR DIARY or INTELLIGENCE SUMMARY

Army Form C. 2118

134th FIELD AMBULANCE

Place	Date	Hour	Summary of Events and Information	Remarks and references to Appendices
CRASTAND W 10 C43	14.11.16	10h.	Orders received to hand over CRASTAND to a Ambulance of 19th Div. On 16/6/27 - Relinquished	16 hours Allocation 3
WARLOY	16.11.16	11h.	Bearer subdivision reformed, and from 1322 and Headquarters were at Y CRASTAND. Evacuation of sick v 20 min into defined ground to Camp in field billets. The Unit marches out at 2 hr. Billets the night at WARLOY. Evacuation 2 off. 9.00a.m. Party from Hrs Q CONTAY beyond Head Quarters	HCH
WARLOY	16.11.16	8h.	Unit marches out of WARLOY 10.45am and 11.50 Bn. billets at AMPLIER the	IKN
AMPLIER	17.11.16	9h.	2hr. 30 m.c. - Marches on CRASTAND to 59th Fd Amb. Start the day at AMPLIER. Motor Ambulance Convoy loaded for WATON	HCH
DOULLENS	18.11.16	10h.	Regt Billet, v marches to DOULLENS arrived at 0.30am billed by the Canadian Stationary Hospital - Arrived at 10.30am	HCH
WORMHOUDT	19.11.16	"	Arrived at HOPOUTRE 7.30am Red of Dr Maj. S orders 15 kilom to WORMHOUDT arrived in billets 5.30am orders received to take over of in Corps Rd Mornival R.A.P. + 16 Rest table & section at BOLLEZELE. Took over CRS y ORS Lieut Hamm unit A Sulin.	No 4
"	20.11.16	10h.	A.D.M.S. A.Q.M.G. visited the unit + inspected billets	HEH
"	21.11.16	8pm	A.D.M.S. A.Q.M.G. visited the unit + inspected billets	HEH
"	22.11.16	9h	Unit engaged in taking our Posts billets + general fatigues	HEH
"	23.11.16	18/p	General fatigues covering Count + improvement ADMS DDMS Visit Capt TAYLOR Joined Capt HARRIS	HEH
"	26.11.16	10h	Routine work of general fatigues - improvement + DDS S	HCH

WAR DIARY or INTELLIGENCE SUMMARY

Army Form C. 2118
134th FIELD AMBULANCE

1 DEC 1916

Place	Date	Hour	Summary of Events and Information	Remarks and references to Appendices
WORMHOUDT	25.11.16	10p	Routine order & instruction for Q and S	App'x
"	26.11.16	do	Routine work - Billets	App H
"	27.11.16	10a	Evt. to Offrs 15 C.R.S. & DRS -	App H
"	28.11.16	10a	Lieut HARRIS proceeds to Temporary Charge of 1st HERTS - Routine Order	App H
"	29.11.16	11p	A/S Black Wd? Sgt-1st Lieut Routine Order Extr within set in	App H
"	30.11.16	9a	Routine work - in Camp. Rub'n 15 instr'ct'n to h and ? 78/1n'ts mot/lees	App H

During the first half of the month the unit Chief duties were confined to the evacuation of sick & wounded: from the front area - & within 15 mls a dismounted a drew ambulance attending on hand/and for the Division. 9/15th Centre 15 9 CCS CORBIE - a Tent Subdiv.? ... on 14-15.11.16 2 pl Amb. further to THIEPVAL - 2nd Pr the Sdiv Cav div & din a Aspidran. 2 P.u, the 2nd Amb. enrol to the R/A, 1 Amb. ? Corps at tu. lu 2.7yds. During the Division Rech to later opened Coll. Post. Reg & a Cotton? Post at BOUZINCOURT chiefly attending evac. the sick of the Guards front & the Division and hf bring in Moment 15 the 2nd & Bry 3 & half. Sure 16/11/16 the Division on the Dh/PS Engaged not all ch Ap the west & whose strong an adv. beg. completed Total Ad'nm'n dy unrb - 1552. Ft 1st the 2nd Amb not having about 600 Miles for other Division - 201 Cars was hr dwlt with-n the DhPS

1.12.16 O.C. 134 Fd Amb?

OC 134 Fd Amb? Ht 10 Unk-le Cert

Appendix 1.

SECRET

IInd CORPS MEDICAL INSTRUCTIONS. No. 5.

1. **Alternative routes.**

   In the event of one of his evacuation lines being put out of action each Field Ambulance Commander must have alternative routes definitely decided upon before the action commences.

   Equally important is the ability of the Field Ambulance Commander to switch his evacuation line from one route to another with as little delay as possible.

2. **Collateral routes.**

   Each Field Ambulance Commander must know accurately and exactly the evacuation lines on his immediate right and left. It may become necessary for him to utilise them in an emergency.

3. **Roads.**

   (a). There is little doubt that the GRANDCOURT - ST. PIERRE DIVION road is passable for G.S. wagons. This increases the probability of our using the ST. PIERRE DIVION - MILL ROAD - HAMEL evacuation line referred to in Medical Instructions No. 2.

   (b). It is also possible that the HAMEL - BEAUCOURT SUR ANCRE road may be useful.

   (c). The BEAUCOURT SUR ANCRE - MIRAUMONT Road is good and is at present being used by enemy motor ambulances.

   (d). Intelligence consider that none of the roads running South from GRANDCOURT will be of any use to us.

4. (a). A.D.M.S. 39th Division will be responsible for having these roads reconnoitred and reporting, as soon as the situation permits, on their passability for motor ambulances or wheeled stretchers.

   (b). 39th Division will have as many wheeled stretchers as possible collected at one or more places suitable for getting them up to ST. PIERRE DIVION.

   (c). 19th Division will also collect wheeled stretchers in the forward area with the same object in view.

   (d). 39th Division will keep at least one Tent Sub-division in readiness with equipment that can be carried on pack animals or by hand. This personnel will be prepared to open an advanced collecting post in ST. PIERRE DIVION as soon as the situation permits.

P.T.O.

SECRET

AMENDMENT TO IInd CORPS MEDICAL INSTRUCTIONS No. 5.

(1). Cancel Section 9 and substitute

"Traffic over BLACKHORSE BRIDGE will be from East to West only.
POPLAR BRIDGE, West to East.
BROOKERS PASS is now impassable.
AVELUY CAUSEWAY - passable in both directions."

(2). Section 12, para. a.

For "9" read "10".

- - - - - - - -

H.Q. IInd Corps.
2nd Nov., 1916.

Colonel, A.M.S.
D.D.M.S. IInd Corps.

Distribution.

Same as Medical Instructions No. 5.

5. Marking of Medical Posts.

Every post opened by Field Ambulances must be conspicuously and clearly marked. Directing flags should be available. In default of these a cross can be stained with Iodine on a white triangular bandage.

6. Colaboration with collateral posts.

Medical Officers in charge of Posts established after the advance must endeavour to establish lateral touch with neighbouring Medical Officers. Much energy is misdirected through neglect of this measure.

7. Red Cross Flag.

At present wounded are being cleared pretty extensively on this front by Bearers working under the Red Cross flag. In a difficult situation it would be comparatively safe to use this flag as a safeguard.

8. Water.

Arrangements must be made for pushing up water testing gear, chlorine and metallic, as early as possible. Tested wells must be clearly marked.

9. Bridges.

Traffic over BLACK HORSE BRIDGE will be from East to West only.
KELLY BRIDGE and BROOKERS PASS will be available for motor ambulance in both directions.

cancelled - see attached slip. 2/11/16

10. 1st Cavalry Division (u/c Fifth Army).

(a). The Tent Divisions (heavy echelons) of Cavalry Field Ambulances will not open collecting posts South of our present front line.

(b). The motor ambulances of 1st Cavalry Division will, at Zero hour, be parked at 20 M.A.C. carstand, BOUZINCOURT, and will, at that hour, pass under orders of D.D.M.S.

(c). The horse transport of 1st Cavalry Division should be parked near AVELUY POST (W.11.d.5.9.). The Officer i/c Transport will be in touch with and be prepared to render assistance at AVELUY POST.

(d). Medical Officers of Cavalry Field Ambulances must be sufficiently "au fait" with the collecting posts and evacuation lines of 18th and 4th Canadian Divisions to know how to adapt to them any temporary line they may themselves establish.

(e). Suitable liaison must be arranged between Cavalry and other Field Ambulances particularly those of 32nd Division. This should prevent the indiscriminate opening up and consequent overlapping of Aid and Collecting posts.

P.T.O.

Page 3.

(f). Particular attention is to be paid to para. 5 by Medical Officers of Cavalry Field Ambulances.

(g). When in "S" area and in front of it, the Rest Station sick of 1st Cavalry Division will be admitted to the Divisional Rest Station at VADENCOURT.

11. 18th Division.

18th Division will open up their Section of the Schoolhouse, ALBERT, by Noon November 1st.
All arrangements regarding the division of duties of their respective personnel will be made direct between the A.Ds.M.S. concerned.

12. 32nd Division.

(a) Paras. (b) (d) (e) (f) of Section 10 referring to 1st Cavalry Division, will refer equally to 32nd Division.

(b). In the event of complete success by IInd and Vth Corps casualties in the IRLES - PYS area should be evacuated via GRANDCOURT and ST. PIERRE DIVION.
Partial success will probably render evacuation through GRANDCOURT impossible and will involve a very heavy carry through COURCELETTE.
The opening up of an evacuation line through LE SARS need hardly be discussed.

H.Q. IInd Corps.
31st Oct., 1916.

Colonel, A.M.S.
D.D.M.S. IInd Corps.

Distribution.

A.D.M.S. 18th Division.)
A.D.M.S. 19th Division.)
A.D.M.S. 32nd Division.)
A.D.M.S. 39th Division.) 4 copies each.
A.D.M.S. 4th Can. Divn.)
A.D.M.S. 1st Cav. Divn.)
O.C. 20th M.A.Convoy.
O.C. No. 26 M.A.Convoy.
D.M.S. Fifth Army.
IInd Corps "A".
IInd Corps "G".
IInd Corps A.P.M.
M.O. i/c IInd Corps Mounted Troops.
War Diary (2 copies).
Office. (6 copies).

Appendix 2.

Secret and Pressing

O.C. 134 Fd. Amb.   Appendix 2.

In accordance with II Corps Medical Instructions No. 5 dated 31/10/16 para 4 (d) you will detail one Tent Sub-division to be in readiness with its equipment packed to move at zero hour on Z day to open an advanced collecting post in St. PIERRE DIVION.

Submit names of officers and personnel selected, and all details for the completion of this order to be submitted to this office as soon as possible

1.11.16

B. Horbury
Capt.
for A.D.M.S.
39th Div.

appendix 3.

SECRET. Copy No. 3

R.A.M.C. Operation Order No.15

by

Colonel G.W. Brazier-Creagh, C.M.G., A.D.M.S. 39th.Div.

Ref.Map
1/40,000 57D.
1/20,000 57D SE.   No.6/627.   14-11-16.

The 19th.Division will take over the 39th.Divisional front by 6am. 15th.November, 1916.
On relief, the 39th.Division will be withdrawn to X.area.
In connection with the above, the following reliefs will take place.

1. No. 132 Field Ambulance will hand over the A.D.S. at LANCASHIRE DUMP and the medical evacuation lines through PAISLEY AVENUE, and all subsidiary posts, including the Head-quarters site at Q.33.b.9.5., to a Field Ambulance of the 19th. Division.

2. No.134 Field Ambulance will hand over the CABSTAND to a Field Ambulance of the 19th. Division.

3. No.133 Field Ambulance will hand over the EAST CLAIRFAYE to a Field Ambulance of the 11th. Division.

4. Relief to be completed by 12 noon on Nov.15.
On relief, No.133 Fld.Amb. will move to BEAUVAL and will be temporarily attached to and will march under the orders of the G.O.C. 116th. Infantry Brigade Group.
No.132 and 134 Fld.Ambs. will move on relief to WARLOY and will be temporarily attached to and march under the orders of the G.O.C. 118th. Infantry Brigade Group.
Duplicate lists of non expendable stores and equipment handed and taken over, will be signed by units concerned and forwarded to this office.

5. After noon on the 16th.inst. Rest Station sick of the 39th. Division will be sent to VADENCOURT. In moving from the forward area, 39th.Divisional Rest Station sick and evacuations will be carried out by Field Ambulance cars.

6. Report completion of moves.

7. Acknowledge.

Capt.
for A.D.M.S. 39th.Div.

B H Odlum

Copies to:- 1. No.132 F.Amb.
2. " 133 "   "
3. " 134 "   "
4. " 82 San.Sect.
5. G.
6. A.Q.
7. Div.R.A.
8.   R.E.
9. 116 Inf.Bde.
10. 117 "   "
11. 118 "   "

12. 13 Gloster Regt.
13. ADMS. 19th.Div.
14. ADMS. 11th.Div.
15. ADMS. 63rd(RN)Div.
16. DDMS. IInd.Corps.
17-19. Office records.

Nos.5-16 For information.

WAR DIARY.

134th FIELD AMBULANCE
1 JAN 1917

COMMITTEE FOR THE
MEDICAL HISTORY OF THE WAR
Date 31 JAN 1917

Army Form C. 2118
R.A.M.C.
134th FIELD AMBULANCE

WAR DIARY
or
INTELLIGENCE SUMMARY
(Erase heading not required.)

134 Fd Amb

Place	Date	Hour	Summary of Events and Information	Remarks and references to Appendices
WORMHOUDT.	1.12.16	8 hr	Remaining 209 570 R. Admitted 1 of 17 OR E 300 R Remain, 47. Routine work. Brought Bart Student Remaining 94	1st Field Amb 2 Corp
"	2.12.16	6 hr	Admitted 30 E 20 Remain, 55. Routine work	1st "
"	3.12.16	10 h	Admitted 18 Evacuated 16. Remain, 63. DRS. 112	1st CH
"	4.12.16	10 h	Admitted 11. E 18 Remain, 56. DRS 113. Routine work- ADMS visits Ambulance	1st CH
"	5.12.16	6 h	Admitted 14 E 11 Remain, 79. DRS 92. Routine work	1st CH RCH
"	6.12.16	10 h	Admitted 33 E 5 R 98 DRS. 100 Routine work	1st CH
17	7.12.16	10 h	Admitted 16 E 27 Remain, 76. DRS 116. Routine work	1st CH
"	8.12.16	10 h	Admitted 20 E 21 Remain 75. DRS 113 Routine work	1st CH
"	9.12.16	6 h	Admitted 6 OR E 21 Remain 60 R.P.8. 95 —	1st CH
"	10.12.16	10 h	Admitted 16 E 28 Remain, 47. DRS 102	1st CH
"	11.12.16	6 h	Admitted 39 Evacuated 26 Remain, 50. DRS 104	1st CH
"	12.12.16	11 h	Admitted 8 E 30 Remain, 60. DRS 124. Orders received to hand out of WORMHOUDT. Loading was 16/131 Fd Amb. & taken over from 12/9 Fd Amb. L.O.S v ADS. Advance Rwd. Process & stores over ADS ESSEX FARM C.19.C.4.1 SUSSEX FARM Ambulance C. 19. C. 2. 6. R.A.S.C. Post P. 28. b. 6. 5. 11.	1st CH
A23.C29 Pop Shop Map 28/NW20	13/12/16		R an Advance of 7 Ambulance left at 9 a.m. & marched to new position at A23 C 2.9 arrived at 1pm. Other 3 hr all cars & ambulances arrived at position of about 3 hr. arrived at position & all cars hands & ambulances with advance of lot to ADS under command of Capt. GATCHELL. R.A.M.C	1st CH

WAR DIARY or INTELLIGENCE SUMMARY

Army Form C. 2118

134th FIELD AMBULANCE

Place	Date	Hour	Summary of Events and Information	Remarks and references to Appendices
A.23 C.29	14/12/16		Admits 3 Off. 34 O.R. E 1 Off. 30 O.R. Remnay S 2. Personnel employed in unloading our billets & Establishing kitchens	1/E/returns
"	15/12/16		Admits 2 D. 5 T.R. E 6. Remnay 5 B. Personnel engaged & fatigues around camp	18 CH
"	16/12/16		Admits 47 O.R. and S 7. Unit is ADS & workshop of whole camd back & advanced posts	18 CH
"	17/12/16		Admits 33. E 26. Remain. Duties & fatigues	NCH
"	18/12/16		Admits 25. E 29. Dis S. 5 admits 2. Duty & Dig	1/E/H
"	19/12/16		Lieut. A.C. MURRAY R.A.M.C. appointed acting M.O. to 13th Royal Sussex Reg. CO's & Ends. 2 cases of Cerebro spinal Meningitis (fulminating type) admitted & Evac to CCS 117 T M B. Remaining 4 Off. 154 O.R. Admitted 30 O.R. 2 O.R. battle casualties Evac. 10H 35 O.R. Rems 129 O.R.	1/2 Sussex 39 Dn Ophthalmican
"	20/12/16		Seven cases Trench feet - 1st Camps. all precautions taken in each case - no his care are showing swelling & discolouration	
"	21.12.16			
"	22.12.16	noon	Lt.Col. M.C. HILDRETH R.A.M.C. commanding 134 Fd Ambulance proceeded on 10 days leave to Great Britain. Authority HQ. A.A. & Q.M.G. 39 Dn 5/9/1176/A7 d/19.12.16 Under instruction from A.D.M.S. 39 Div Capt. G.D. ROBERTSON R.A.M.C. 133 Fd Ambulance is detailed to take on temporary Command of 134 Fd Ambulance I took on Command of 134 Fd Amb at 12 noon 22.12.16 Photostatureine sent. There were 6 officers and 129 O.R. Admitted 47 O.R. and 2 O.R. were battle casualties. Evacuated 36 A. 32 O.R. Remaining 3 Off. & 144 O.R. } Trench foot 1 case all precaution taken up rigid reserve.	CDR

WAR DIARY / INTELLIGENCE SUMMARY

134 Fd Ambulance Army Form C. 2118

Place	Date	Hour	Summary of Events and Information	Remarks and references to Appendices
A.23.c.29 Sheet 28 1/40000	22-12-16		Lieut. N. PATEY. R.A.M.C. proceeded to 179 Bde. R.F.A. for duty. Capt. J.P. CHARLES. R.A.M.C. reported for duty with this unit on relief by Lieut. Paley, R.A.M.C. Any was taken in the strength accordingly. Two wards of Cuebos of small coutacto under "friendly" pain -	Authority A.D.M.S. A.P. Nº 39/105
		3 p.m.	I inspected O.C. Nº1 Mobile Lab and reported several nights to taken. The conditions of outacts were therefore sent with the Ward Orderly for examination - The ward orderly 72273 Pte H.T. MACKNESS RAMC was reported as a "career" and was evacuated. The remainder of ward & orderly men were liberated.	
	23.12.16	9 a.m.	Made a thorough inspection of the unit. From the A.S.C. personnel from the Sergeant Billets hutted hive been to a dressroom behind the QM stores. The A.S.C. are now in the hut & I took room. Started to erect a drying room next to the washroom. This is urgently needed for the drying of Pain boots and clothing. The lean to shed at the entrance was pulled down and rebuilt with proper timber & covered. Mess Pauline obtained from the Salvage dump. I have continued for a further 20 yards. This will serve for the storing of blankets and stretchers for exchange with M.A.C. cars. A stove has been placed in the meat store for thawing the meat when received in bulk. Attempted to obtain some extra water to catch any juices from the meat. A few new chairs being dug - the ground being very sodden. Admitted 2 F.O.R. 1 battle casualty. Evac. 1 off. 51 OR. Reinf. 2 off. 12 OR. Accommodated Normally 97.	8-12-16 HERZEELE French Lieut I wounded slung & lying up etc. Capt. Neville Cp. Saunders apparently intoxicated. Little pain - injections after being wounded.

War Diary / Intelligence Summary

Army Form C. 2118

134 Fd Ambulance

Place	Date	Hour	Summary of Events and Information	Remarks and references to Appendices
Q.23.c.29 Hut 38 1/40000	24.12.16		Continued work in camp. Drying room nearly finished. Two horse tents for personnel again during - evacuated NAR and obtained two linings below class - Are making them locally from tent linen. Stoves arrived from RE for heating wards. Do not appear to give much heat. One ward lined with canvas rooms down half. Erected two latrines at west end. I was ATB for one of patients. They were working the ordinary stoves in one part of the wards which was leading to unnecessary smoke. Much high. Some falling down away but this is being repaired. Recalled the truck party from Ypres to man convoys tomorrow. Erected a stage in the main patients dining hall for the concert.	
			ADMS 39 Div has kindly agreed to the general. M.O. 1132/42 Pte R. M'Jvn Gaskint to ND 17 Cr'S and evacuated to Bane - Defective brain. (? wounded 28.10.16.) Pte. [?] [?] ND [?] [?] of the Aug'd [?] 39 Div. Trench foot. Capt Liebeault Ry'd referred by Capt Aquenette (8th from Brighton). Aust in divit adunn inn.	Written statement will follow.
			75 RAMC personnel were balloted & obtained change of clothing at D camp. Party 4/3 [?] service at 9pm. Three Divisional Chaplains of Division. ADMS 39 Div invited to repelled being unable to attend the dinner. Dinner to all ranks x officers at 10pm. Read out greetings from Capt [?] & spoke in behalf ADMS. Know the Change of diet. A very large fig augmented by Mount Lieut 38 Div. A special field [?] was erected for the purpose with excellent result. Written patients in ward. Excellent Talent displays at a concert. organised by the men in the afternoon.	L. WALKER
	25.12.16	9pm	Admitted 2 FA 49 OR 9 births. Evac 6 OR Nomading S-ff 136 OR Care of [?] handed over to Malaria sent from ADS can transferred	

WAR DIARY / INTELLIGENCE SUMMARY

Army Form C. 2118

134 Fld Amb.

Place	Date	Hour	Summary of Events and Information	Remarks and references to Appendices
Q.23.c.2.9. Sheet 28 1/40,000		6pm	Captain J.P. Charles RAMC transferred to 132 Fld Amb. and Lieut. CA WEST R.E. and Chick of Strength accordingly – could not be sent till his work was handed over – ADMS 39 Div notified of this.	Auth: ADMS 39 Div
	26.11.16		Work resumed. Telling round huts nailed down and patched, drying room completed. LT C.A.WEST R.E. reported & evacuated to CCS (46 Prov). Table erected between the wards for the brushing of clothes of patients. The work though the Camp is receiving my urgent attention, but a great many loads of bricks required to complete this work, there being no proper base to work on. NGOL WAYBREW & Pte ARIGNO RAMC reported to ADMS for duty at baths. Admitted 39 DR Evac 19 DR died 1 OR Remaining 50 ft. Trench foot 1 swollen disc severed 2/am/ There was a conference of OC's Fld Ambulances at the ADMS 39 Div office at 2.30 pm 24-12-16. The importance of providing out-patient work & heavy jobs / medical officers was pointed out. Also the necessity for strict discipline in the way of escorts out by NCOs, Ventilation & clean supervision by OC's was called for. A protest was put forward to others fields of accommodation for patients in which therefore 2 huts have been had worries be necessary. It was also pointed out that large care must be taken over War Diaries. Care of Mumps & evacuated at once. Car disinfected. Rly ordinary work being carried on –	
	27.11.16	1.30pm	101189 Pte V.R.CLAY taken off the strength of the Unit and proceeded to the Base on leave aft. measles contacts (8) admitted for observation proceeded to A.2.1.c.2.8. Sheet 28 for huts – was informed home in area – surfirlaint and myself required for visiting great dangers (expected) in front area.	Auth ADMS 39 Div 7/428.

WAR DIARY
WAR or DIARY INTELLIGENCE SUMMARY

Army Form C. 2118

134 Fd Amb

6

Place	Date	Hour	Summary of Events and Information	Remarks and references to Appendices
A23c2.9. Sheet 28 Ypres		3pm	informed ADMS in writing that permission to go to OMER to obtain it and ch from lime kiln - Feb 11.	
	28.12.16		Admitted 1 Off. 27 OR. 10R Battle casualty. Evac. 32 OR. Penn Boff. 136 OR. Obtained some spare wood. ADMS invited Capt GATCHELL RAMC SMO Canal guard. Continued drainage & started making a road I hopes through the Camp. He has marion huts being lined by unit carpenters. Lt Huggins RAMC detailed to join his return 4th & 5th prob. in CHIROPODY. Admitted. 10ff. 33 ott. Evac. 16ff. 22 or Remg. 6 off. 14) 172.	
	29.12.16		J62 + 3 Pte ATHERTON 27. NMWe returned to Unit from Hospital Brought two TU men before AD.m.S for inspection - both passes to 82 San Cast. No order to ensure fuel supply, indicates no fuel in billet till 2pm daily. Paraffin supply very short. Obtained the 2 load in urgent on loan. Admitted. 5 off. 27 OR. Evac. 36 OR. Remaing 6 off.138 OR. Harnes to prepare for visit of Majr General CHICHESTER 2nd Army - he did not visit - Camp clean & tidy.	
	30.12.16		Road progressing rapidly. Host of the officers he wood & metal required for same - he promised to rebuild the bridge at the Entrance. Tried to obtain some taved felt but was from Kerosene canvas - will serve when faced over in roofing material 73/.06.0107 Col BAXTER ASC (charge) with Irregular conduct - allowing a fire to lighted in a hut continuing tor - ADm awaited 30/12/16. G.D.Miller	

Army Form C. 2118

WAR DIARY
or
INTELLIGENCE SUMMARY
(Erase heading not required.)

134 Fd Amb

Place	Date	Hour	Summary of Events and Information	Remarks and references to Appendices
A 23 c 2.9 Sheet 28 4/40.000	30.12.16		Abbeville 30.OR. Evac 15 OR. Reing. 6A. 161 OR. Built ADS and found all correct.	
	31.12.16		Continued work in camp. Proceeded to HAZEBROUCK and obtained B.K's linen – Abbeville. 19A. 41 OR. Evac 44 OR. Reing. 7A. 156 OR. Report called for on best method of dealing with rats in tent area – wound dressed more used (Expanded metal to flooring & sides) QM. Stores the envelope & corrugative alcove full rauts avoided by joints or wood dog, the whole overrun by cleanliness in all departments. Lieut HILDRETH DAMC leaves expires 31.12.16.	

Signed
Lt Colonel
for the Quota Ambulance
for 134 [Field Ambulance]

39
Original

140/19+3
Vol XI

WAR DIARY.

COMMITTEE FOR THE
MEDICAL HISTORY OF THE WAR
Date 13 MAR. 1917

39 F.Amb

Jan. 1917

WAR DIARY or INTELLIGENCE SUMMARY

Army Form C. 2118

134th FIELD AMBULANCE R.A.M.C.

Place	Date	Hour	Summary of Events and Information	Remarks and references to Appendices
A.23.c.2.9 Sh.28	1.1.17	9hr	Received 7 O.R. 15'8 O.R. Admitted 10 O.R. 36 O.R. E 174. 35 O.R. Remaining 7 O.R. 159 O.R. Trench day. 2 Battle casualties	14th A.D.S. & C.R.
	2.1.17	6hr	Admission 66 O.R. E 46. 180 to Ambulance. Battle Casualties 12 O.R. Routine work & improvement.	14 CH
	3.1.17	10p.	Admission 32. E 36. 176 to Ambulance. No battle casualties. Visit to ELVERDINGHE 1st Prest site for Divisional Collecting Station. Chateau 2.2.23.	N CH
	4.1.17	6hr	Admission 38. E 30. 184 to Ambulance. Attended 5th meeting of II Army Medical Society. Routine duties.	N CH
	5.1.17	10p.	Admission 43. E 30. 197 to Ambulance. 4 Battle Casualties. Routine work.	H CH
	6.1.17	11h.	Admission 34. E 42. 190. Remaining. Visit 15 A.D.S. & Scheme of evacuation in 14th Bde. of a Raid – hot weather.	N CH
	7.1.17	10p.	Admission 33 O.R. E 27. 196 Remaining. Visit to 2/1st W.L. Field Ambulance which relieve us to take over.	N CH
	8.1.17	10p.	Admission 19 O.R. 28 O.R. E 47. 178 Remaining. Routine duties. Personal Interviews & enlightenment.	14 CH
	9.1.17	10p.	Admission 43. E 32. 189 Remaining. Routine work.	14 CH
	10.1.17	9h.	Admission 57. E 34. Remaining 205. Routine duties.	N CH
	11.1.17	10p.	Admission 28. E 63. 171 Remaining. Duties – Conference at A.D.S. Office – Discussion. From & ambulance.	14 CH
	12.1.17	7h.	Admission 52 O.R. E 31. 191 Remaining – Routine duties & preparation for move to Right Sub & hand.	N CH

WAR DIARY
or
INTELLIGENCE SUMMARY

Army Form C. 2118
R.A.M.C.
134th FIELD AMBULANCE.

134 Fd Amb.

Place	Date	Hour	Summary of Events and Information	Remarks and references to Appendices
"	13.1.17	11h.	Admission 43 E 37 Remains 198. Lieut MURRAY joined 16 17th Warks. Handed over A Dy Guesin v Essex Farm v took over B Dy Reim YPRES	He Whands L.Cot
RED FARM G.5.D.93 Sheet 28	16.1.17	10h.	Handed our ambulance sub-site over RED FARM from 2/1 W. Lancs Fd Amb. owing to lack of accommodation of 52 hd. a gain of 95 b. this Fd Amb - a number of details had to be inserted. Admin 41 E 72. R.154	HCH
"	16.1.17	8pm	Admission 32. E 16. R.120. A.D.M.S finds camp - embarkin of A. Dy v reconnaissance of outpost showsite.	15 CH
"	18.1.17	10h.	40 Admin. 30 E 130 Remains Inspection of LODGE FARM which is in Falcon over by Bosch. Capt. PORTER i command. Accommodation of 30 Sick + lame	HCH
"	17.1.17	10h.	Admin 25 E 41. R.114 Routine and - very heavy snow.	HCH
"	18.1.17	10h.	Admission 49. E 34 R.129. Snow v frost.	HCH
"	19.1.17	10h.	43 Admin E 48 124 R. Routine ord- holy orders Lieut PATEY attached to Julys	HCH
"	20.1.17	8h.	Admission 33. E 36. 121 R. Routine ord - recruit this v kings	HCH
"	21.1.17	10h.	43 Admin 53 E 111 R. Routine ord- medical inspection same.	HCH
"	22.1.17	9h.	28 Admin 29 E 111 R. Capt. TAYLOR relieves Capt. GERATY - temporarily as Sn. o. H. H. Hooge	HCH
"	23.1.17	10h.	31 Admin E 25 R.117. Routine ord- medical condition same	HCH
"	24.1.17	9h.	25 Admin E 28 R.115. Routine ord- medical condition same.	HCH
"	25.1.17	10h.	Admin 48 E 33 R.129 Routine ord.	HCH

Army Form C. 2118

R.A.M.C.

3. 134th FIELD AMBULANCE.

WAR DIARY
or
INTELLIGENCE SUMMARY

(Erase heading not required.)

Instructions regarding War Diaries and Intelligence Summaries are contained in F. S. Regs., Part II. and the Staff Manual respectively. Title Pages will be prepared in manuscript.

134 Fd Amb

Place	Date	Hour	Summary of Events and Information	Remarks and references to Appendices
Red Farm B5 D 9 b Central	26.1.17	10h	39 Admission. 37 E 131 R main; BDzS VIII Corps moved to H.Q Ambulance - zondui math Weather continues same.	HC Wesulu
"	27.1.17	9h	Admission 24. E 30. 125 R. ADHS ends Ambulance - Visit to ADs v LEEDS FARM zondui Weather - weather still continues fine v frosty	HCH
"	28.1.17	10h	Admission 40. E 29. 136 R. zondui duties	HCH
"	29.1.17	10h	Admission 36. E 35 R. 137. Advice received of a hostile bombardment of our - Kortendun at ADs v h Bos Cambells - v me any walking wounded duties	HCH
"	30.1.17	10h	Admission 57. E 47. 143 R. zondui duties. no Shound Casualties received bombardment attack on Rothem. owing to heavy fall of snow.	HCH
"	31.1.17	10h	Admission 47 E 31 R. 140 Rombie duties - weather bright v sunny.	He returned to Corp

During the month the Ambulance dealt with 1194 Cases - mostly sick v owing to have of the Division moved di Rear quarters v A.D.s to the Right side - The weather was the 15th Jan. army, has been technically good - Frosty Snow.

H C Wesuler
Lt Col.
O C 134 Fd Amb.
1.2.17

WAR DIARY.

134th FIELD AMBULANCE
−1 MAR 1917

COMMITTEE FOR THE
MEDICAL HISTORY OF THE WAR
Date 4 − APR. 1917

Army Form C. 2118

WAR DIARY
or
INTELLIGENCE SUMMARY
(Erase heading not required.)

134 Fd Amb.

R.A.M.C.
134th FIELD AMBULANCE.

Place	Date	Hour	Summary of Events and Information	Remarks and references to Appendices
R.E.D. Front (9.5.d.9.1. Sheet 28)	1st Feb	5 pm	Remaining 138. Admitted 47 OR. E 10H. 39 OR. Remain 7 145. Routine orders. Walked > sits sick & prob.	1st & 141st N.M. & C.D.T
"	2.2.17	10 am	Remaining 145. Admitted 5 OR. E 2. Ordinary 52. R 149. Battle Casualties.	1st H.
"	3.2.17	9 am	Remaining 149. Admission 54. E 1. Ordinary 28. R 175. 1 battle casualty - Routine	1st CH
"	4.2.17	10 am	R 173. Admission 66. E & D 70. 169 Remaining. 4 battle casualties. Walked sick same	1st CH
"	5.2.17	8 pm	169 R. Admission 38. D & E. 23. 182 Remaining. 3 battle casualties. Bn S II Army. Stores. 4 ADMS buds Camp. Inches CDMS.	1st CH
"	6.2.17	10 am	162 R. 46 Admitted. 32 E & D. 146 Remaining. Routine ord.	1st CH
"	7.2.17	9 am	146 R. 37 or Admitted 52 E. 179. + hidden Ca brain	1st CH
"	8.2.17	10 am	179 R. 52 or Admitted 46 E. 185. Remain. Routine ord.	1st CH
"	9.2.17	10 am	185 R. 44 or Admitted 40 E. 181. Remain. walked Cabris 14 Jan.	1st CH
"	10.2.17	10 am	181 R. 60 Admitted 56 E. 185. Remain. walked and. 15 battle casualties	1st CH
"	11.2.17	10 am	185 R. 76 OR Admitted 99 E. 162 Remaining 26 batt casualties. CDMS Met a Confine & The Ambulance	1st CH
"	12.2.17	"	162 R Admitted 85 D & D 104 E 84 Died OR 2. R 163	1st CH

WAR DIARY or INTELLIGENCE SUMMARY

Army Form C. 2118

134th FIELD AMBULANCE
134 Fd Amb

Place	Date	Hour	Summary of Events and Information	Remarks and references to Appendices
RED FARM (G.5.d.9.1)	13.2.17	10a	R.163. Admission 77. E.80. R.160. Battle casualties 10. Rankin wnd - shelling of Ypres	Heywood at Cr
"	14.2.17	"	R.160. Admsn 105 E.102. 163 R.	ACH
"	15.2.17	"	R.163. Admsns 48 E.63. R.148. Battle casualties 7. Rankin wnd. hesitates for the time in hand	NCH
"	16.2.17	"	R.148. Admsns 39 E.R. Brigade 51. R.133. Battle casualties 11. Rankin wnd	NCH
"	17.2.17	"	Hands on A.D.S. YPRES PRISON & POL: RED FARM & LIDDLE FARM to 2/1st WESSEX Amb. & took over Ambulance site at HERZEELE. Rankin and B. Admsns 49 E.102	NCH
HERZEELE (D.10.C.1.7. Sheet 27F)	18.2.17		R.83. Admsns 10 R. E.16. R.68. Band rejoins & ---- --- over grounds	NCH
"	19.2.17	"	R.88. A.9. E.10. 67 Remg. Rankin wnd	BCH
"	20.2.17	"	A.D.M.S. inspected unit R.67. admsn 10 R. E.10. 67 R. rankin and	BCH
"	21.2.17	"	67.R. admsn 6. E.4. R.69. rankin and & fatigues	ACH
"	22.2.17	"	69.R. admsns 7 E.10 R.66.	NCH
"	23.2.17 8p	R.66. admsns 12 E.9 69 R. rankin ---- 10th ar ---- preparing for same in Furegem	BCH

WAR DIARY or INTELLIGENCE SUMMARY

Army Form C. 2118
R.A.M.O.
134th FIELD AMBULANCE.

134 Fd Amb.

Place	Date	Hour	Summary of Events and Information	Remarks and references to Appendices
HERZEELE (D.10.c.17.)	24/2/17	10th	69 R. 16 ORs. 10 OR E 75 R. walker into q/m	HC/McDowell Lt Col
"	25/2/17	"	75 R. 16 ORs. 14 E 77 R. 2nd packing up	"
"	26/2/17	"	77 R. 22 ORs. 14 E R 80. C. Section under Capt FIELD proceeded to take over sites + DRS (G.15.a.3.0.)	"
"	"	"	as an advance party	"
"	27/2/17	"	Ambulance wached out & arrived at new site 12.30 p.m. Took on from BC 69 Fd Amb. DRS etc. CDHS under Ambulance	"
WARATAH CAMP. (G.15.a.3.0.) (sheet 28).	28/2/17	"	DDmS visits Ambulance & inspects & chooses up the sites & settling in 64 ORs. Camp for 132 Fd Amb. & are handed to this until all over from 14 69. 20 Fd Amb. has remained.	HC/McDowell Lt Col
			During the week the total number of admissions was 1140. This high rate of admission is apparently due to the severe weather from recently & the fact that there is an immense front of the Sambulance (70 ± Flanders). During the week we had a spell the Bath Fell Accidentally when carrying out a change of the water VPRES, several men slightly & the asst.7 Fd 15/14 = 20. Casualties have occurred amongst Fd Amb	
				HC/McDowell Lt Col
			O/C 134 Fd Amb	

CONFIDENTIAL.

War Diary
of
134th Field Ambulance,
from March 1st. to March 31st., 1917.

(Volume 1.)

Army Form C. 2118

R.A.M.C.
134th FIELD AMBULANCE

WAR DIARY

Intelligence Summary (Erase heading not required)

Instructions regarding War Diaries and Intelligence Summaries are contained in F.S. Regs., Part II and the Staff Manual respectively. Title Pages will be prepared in manuscript.

Place	Date	Hour	Summary of Events and Information	Remarks and references to Appendices
WARATAH CAMP G.15.a.3.0. Sheet 28	1.3.17	10 h.	Demand Rak: Vehicles R.140 OR. Wounded 45. Evacuated 10. Remaining 184. Ambulance Remaining 8 OR. DO OR Wounded 2 R. 2 OR. Evacuated 25 OR. R. 8 OR 840 R. Unit supplied on Gun L. + Jatigue duties	ACH Louth A.C.S.
"	2.3.17	8 h.	D.R.S. Remaining 180 OR. Admitted 24. Evacuated 13. R.191. J Ambulance 8 OR 840 R. Remaining Admitted 2 OR. 11 OR. Evacuated 20. R. 10 OR. 75 OR.	HCH
"	3.3.17	9 h.m.	D.R.S. Remaining 195 OR. Admitted 12. Evacuated R.185 OR. J Aul. R. 76. Admitted 26. Evacuated 4. Remaining 107. Gen'l rout duties	HCH
"	4.3.17	10 h.	D.R.S. Remaining 185. Admitted 35. E.V.D 22. R.198. Fd Aul. Remaining 107. Admitted 40 E.V.D 21. R. 127. Unit Engaged in Construct road	HCH
"	5.3.17	9 h.	ADkS X. Cook Visits unit + hospitals DRS v Fd Aul. Remained in DRS 198 A 70. E.V.D 20. Remaining 198. Fd Aul. 127. Admitted 14. E.V.D 35. R. 106. ADkS visits camp	HCH
"	6.3.17		DRS. Remaining 198. Admitted 37 E.V.D. 40. R.195. Fd Aul. R.106. Admitted 19. E.22. Remaining 103. Routine duties. ADkS visits unit	HCH
"	7.3.17	10 h.	D.N.S. 195 Remained Ad 49. E.24. R.220 OR. Fd Aul R.103 Admitted 37 E.V.D 22. Remaining 114. Capt J.M.Taylor reported unit	HCH
"	8.3.17	-	DRS. 114 remained Admitted 15 OR. Fd Aul. 114. Ad 15 E.V.D 26. R.103. Unit Employed on hospital + fatigue duties	HCH
"	9.3.17	12 h.	Remaining in DRS. 214.	HCH
"	10.3.17	6 h.	ADkS visits unit. Remaining in DRS. 209 Remaining Fd Aul 115	HCH
"	11.3.17	9 h.	R. DRS 219. R. Fd Aul. 118. Routine work + Construct road	HCH
"	12.3.17	10 h.	Remaining in DRS 213. R. Fd Aul. 122.	HCH

Army Form C. 2118

WAR DIARY or INTELLIGENCE SUMMARY

(Erase heading not required.)

134th FIELD AMBULANCE

Place	Date	Hour	Summary of Events and Information	Remarks and references to Appendices
WARATAH CAMP (9.15.a.3.d. Sheet 28)	13.3.17	6h.	Reman'g "c" D.R.S. 198 & Fd. Amb. 122. Routine work.	WCH/Walsalt [?] Fd Camp
"	14.3.17	10h.	R. D.R.S. 190 & R. Pulso Amb. 114. Genrl. Routi. orders.	HCH
"	15.2.17	6h.	D.R.S. 181 of Fd Amb. 123. A.D.M.S. proceed on leave & J Amend orders of A.D.M.S.	HCH
"	16.3.17	"	Sunday g patients. D.R.S. 170. & Fd Amb. 143. Visit to A.D.M.S. OPP. re F Amb.	HCH
"	17.3.17	"	D.R.S. 167 & whilst of Fd Amb. 133. Routine Hospital orders	HCH
"	18.3.17	9h.	Remain'g "c" D.R.S. 172. Fd Amb. 132. Personal employee in General order	HCH
"	19.3.17	10h.	D.R.S. 160 whilst. Fd Amb. 124. D.D.M.S. to whilst Camp	HCH
"	20.2.17	6h.	146 patient "c" D.R.S. 119 "c" Fd Amb Buttery removed - routi. work in Count.	HCH
"	21.3.17	10h.	D.R.S. 145 Patients. Fd Amb. 130.	HCH
"	22.3.17	6h.	Patient "c" D.R.S. 143. Fd Amb. 139. nothing to record.	HCH
"	23.3.17	"	D.R.S. 132. Fd Amb. 153. Routine orders	HCH
"	24.3.17	9h.	Patient "c" D.R.S. 148 "c" Fd Amb 143. Routine work.	HCH
25	25.3.17	"	R. D.R.S. 153 Patient "c" Fd Amb. 153. Routine work in Count.	HCH
"	26.3.17	-	D.R.S. 147 Patient. Fd Amb. 152. Routine work	HCH
"	27.3.17	"	D.R.S. 106 Fd Amb 179. A. & G. & G visits Ambulance & whilst Count.	HCH

WAR DIARY

Army Form C. 2118
134th FIELD AMBULANCE

WAR DIARY OR INTELLIGENCE SUMMARY
(Erase heading not required.)

Place	Date	Hour	Summary of Events and Information	Remarks and references to Appendices
WARATAH CAMP (9.15 a.3.0. Sheet 28)	28.3.17	6h	Remaining in camp were 9 c Fd Amb. 166. Remainder went	H.C. Howorth Lt Col
	29.3.17	10h	DMS 151 Fd Amb 145	A.C.H.
	30.3.17	2h	f.o.c. 39. Brown inspected the Camb, Itinerary of letters – DMS 162. Fd Amb 147	15 C.H.
	31.3.17	10h	L. DMS 158. Fd Amb 157. The day the bn. has been somewhat [...] to the line at 4 a.m. it's been drills, they had the Divisional R.S.P [Staff?] [...] a good deal of [...] had — There is [...] been employed as Field Ambulance to receive the [...] from 133 Fd Amb. which has moved to [...] their site away to [...] accommodate. The next convoy consisted of the bad & [...] to hospital & [...] cases & 166. Evac. 9 Fd. a. 169. 145. [...] has attended to 133 Fd. The total number of cases dealt under during the week is 1574 dressed. 6 732 . 2 Fd Amb. The weather throughout has been [...] at 145 up to the [...] which have changed. Has a pronounced snowstorm. The health of 145 Personnel as Good. Capt. HARRIS-En, admitted to duty [...] Capt Candy = 31.3.17. H.C.Howorth Lt Col. O.C. 134 Fd Amb	13.C.H.est Lt Col

1.4.17.

ORIGINAL.

CONFIDENTIAL

WAR DIARY
OF
134th FIELD AMBULANCE
FROM APRIL 1st. TO APRIL 30th,
1917.
(VOLUME 14).

COMMITTEE FOR THE
MEDICAL HISTORY OF THE WAR
Date 6 JUN. 1917

WAR DIARY
or INTELLIGENCE SUMMARY

Army Form C. 2118
R.A.M.C.
154th FIELD AMBULANCE

(Erase heading not required.)

Instructions regarding War Diaries and Intelligence Summaries are contained in F. S. Regs., Part II. and the Staff Manual respectively. Title Pages will be prepared in manuscript.

13 4 Fd Amb
39 Divsn

Place	Date	Hour	Summary of Events and Information	Remarks and references to Appendices
WAR FARM CAMP (G.15.Q.3.0 Sheet 26)	1/4/17	10b	The Unit 7120 combined 16 run a Combined D.R.S. & Fd Ambulance - & 5 agaza a Combination of Unk. for the 2 Corps. A Dressing Station to supply wounded Patients - DRS 160 Fd And 3 off 137 OR	HC Uh Uls & Cap
"	2.4.17	"	D.R.S. 179. Fd Amb. 2 off 128 O.R. routine medn med. shery	HCH
"	3.4.17	"	D.R.S. 181. Fd Amb. 1 off 110 OR	HCH
"	4.4.17	"	D.R.S. 177. Fd Amb. 2 off 133 OR D&S II Army - Accompanied by D.A.D.M.S II Corp Inspected the Unit	HCH
"	5.4.17	"	D.R.S. 168 Fd Amb. 1 off 125 OR Capt HARRIS- Shield of the Shiqth- Capt TAYLOR took a party B motor lorries to HERTZELE & obtend with a collecting hosp for the 110 MB.	HCH
"	6.4.17	"	D.R.S. 169. Fd Amb. 1 off 120 OR Capt WARWICK- 133 Fd Amb. returd Capt TAYLOR who was transferred to the 47. Division v Struck off the Strength	HCH
"	7.4.17	"	DRS 176. Fd Amb. 2 off. 113 OR Amb at C.R.D.S. to Sigtly wounded uls a hand	HCH
"	8.4.17	"	DRS 162. Fd Amb. 2 off. 119 OR routine work. Capt. FIELD rejoined unit	HCH
"	9.4.17	"	D.R.S. 153 Fd Amb. 3 off. 183 OR Capt FIELD took over duties at HERTZELE	HCH
"	10.4.17	"	DRS 144 Fd Amb 4 off. 130 OR	HCH
"	11.4.17	b	DRS 147 Fd Amb 3 off. 151 OR routine work. v constructed work. 2 Lieut and Corpmed	HCH
"	12.4.17	"	DRS 124 Fd Amb 4 off 117 OR. Lieut Bullock A.D.S to unit	HCH
"	13.4.17	"	DRS 124 Fd Amb 5 off 113 OR A D.h.S visits unit Stn	HCH

WAR DIARY
or
INTELLIGENCE SUMMARY

Army Form C. 2118
R.A.M.C.
134th FIELD AMBULANCE

134 Fd Amb
39' Division

—1 MAY 1917—

Place	Date	Hour	Summary of Events and Information	Remarks and references to Appendices
WARATAH CAMP (G.15.a.3.0. Sheet 28.)	14/4/17	10h	DRS S.123 Fd Amb 2 off 95 OR - orders to hand over DRS to 23rd Bde second.	HCH wh Lt Col HCH
	15.4.17	"	DRS: 109 Fd Amb 2 off 55 OR. Unit engaged in packing & transport cleaning at further day to hand-by over	HCH
	16.4.17	"	Hands over DRS & C.R.D. S.th highly wounded to 70° Fd Amb. - Unit left WARATAH Camp at 8am for BOLLEZEELE. 3 pm 2 nd night at HERTZEELE. 13 miles from HERTZEELE. Took over WATOU from 70° Fd Amb. hand-by over HERTZEELE to the 55 Div. All cases of 39 Div sick now transferred to DRS PROVEN other Divisions new hand-by with to hand-by unit. Jam Fd Amb cases now hand-by to 133 Fd Amb	HCH
BOLLEZEELE	17.4.17	-	R & C Sections left HERTZEELE at 8am arriving at BOLLEZEELE at Noon & hand-by opened up to 2 occur patients. No 117 Fy Bde. B Section opens	HCH
"A.24.C Sheet 27).			at 7 oct at 7 oct from the HERTZEELE - WATOU area. Mess being ch'fd. from the R.F.A & Ind Cav, 10 K & 33 OR remaining	
	18.4.17	"	Fd Amb 6 off 77 OR. Admits the blkg of 17 K.R.R's & 17. 2 K. V. D	HCH
	19.4.17	"	Fd Amb. 6 off 92 OR. admits of Reinforcement Camp, Divisional School & Company of Black Regt & takes at RUBROUCK. Fords 2 CO RANCH Div. & amony	HCH
			for Colclen quick	
	20.4.17	"	Fd Amb. 6 off 101 OR. Admits 5 m 16 all shelters beaving the Bde Relieves and gave whole letters of a res. & feed.	HCH
	21.4.17	"	Fd Amb. 6 off 87 OR. admits of 16 K.V.D. & Reinforcements of 18 R.B at MILLAM. Procurations of relief of Fiends & Lar B billing	HCH

Army Form C. 2118

WAR DIARY or INTELLIGENCE SUMMARY

(Erase heading not required.)

134 Fd Amb
39 Division

134th FIELD AMBULANCE
R.A.M.C.

Instructions regarding War Diaries and Intelligence Summaries are contained in F.S. Regs., Part II and the Staff Manual respectively. Title Pages will be prepared in manuscript.

Place	Date	Hour	Summary of Events and Information	Remarks and references to Appendices
BOLLEZEELE (A.24.C.) (Sheet 27).	22/4/17	10 h	Fd Amb Off. 4 Offrs 86 Ranks + Cook chin't. Ord. Continued unpacking. The whole history + Cook chin. of chaf's line Completed.	HC Wesselt Lt Col
"	23/4/17	"	B.A.S. & Corps. + O.B.'s inspected. 117 Bde - a Fancy Ground afterwards inspected. HC Ambulance R. 4 Off. 81 OR.	HCH
"	24/4/17	"	Fd Amb. 4 Off. 90 OR. General Duties.	HCH
"	25/4/17	"	Fd Amb. 6 Offs. 95 OR - Reconnamen HOUTKERKE - WATAU. amn. for Fd Ambulance site. Parties & tons in accordance with Schemes	HCH
"	26/4/17	"	Remaining 40 ff. 102 OR. Routine Duties.	HCH
"	27/4/17	"	Fd Amb. 4 Off. 72 OR. Lord hockey up. moved A 2 echn. lorries to WATOU. A D.M.S. visited WATOU orders. C section 15 men of 116 Bde received. G D M S visited WATOU orders. C section remained on awaiting further orders. The Padre's van transferred to WATOU A. recomments the amn. available. A section arrived WATOU. 2 pm.	HCH
"	28/4/17	"	Fd Amb. B off. 85 OR. A section moves to WATOU. Orders to move a sickers 15 men of unit 116 Bde received	HCH
WATOU (K.4.b.) (Sheet 27).	29/4/17	"	Fd Amb. 4 Off. 81 OR. Cox. FIELD proceeds on 2 am - orders to GOC 116 Bde received. 15 ARQUES on the morning & report to GOC 116 Bde received.	HCH
"	30/4/17	"	Fd Amb. 5 off. 76 OR. Reshuffle of amn to be carried by 116 Bde - hardships to the recommits of who recommits that BAYENGHEM CHATEAU be allotted to O.C. C Section r & enormous and - arrangement now made for Coy ams 116 Bde.	HC Wesselt Lt Col OC 134 Fd Amb.

1.5.17

HC Wesselt
Lt Col
OC 134 Fd Amb.

ORIGINAL.

CONFIDENTIAL

WAR DIARY
OF
134th FIELD AMBULANCE
from May 1st to May 31st, 1917.
(VOLUME 15).

COMMITTEE FOR THE MEDICAL HISTORY OF THE WAR
Date 10 JUL. 1917

Army Form C. 2118

R.A.M.C.

WAR DIARY
INTELLIGENCE SUMMARY
(Erase heading not required.)

134th FIELD AMBULANCE

39th Division

Place	Date	Hour	Summary of Events and Information	Remarks and references to Appendices
WATOU (K.4.b.9.15) (Sheet 27)	1.5.17	10 a	Remaining in Ambulance 4 Officers & 85 O.R. healths this routine duties	H/Q/Details Lt Col. H.C.H
"	2.5.17	"	Admitted 6 O.R. discharged & transferred 1 S.O.R. Remaining 4 Off. 76 O.R. - P. Section	
"	3.5.17	"	A company 116 Bde. & an Tables established a Collecting Post at BAYENGHEM LEZ-SENINGHEM whilst Bde. was in Camp - Section under command of Capt HUGGINS	
"	"	"	Remaining 4 Off. 71 O.R. A & B Sections Engaged in routine duties healths fine	H.C.H
"	4.5.17	8 p	Remaining 4 Off. 78 O.R. - routine work - Fine - Fair	H.C.H
"	5.5.17	"	Remaining 3 Off. 85 O.R. healths fine	H.C.H
"	6.5.17	"	Capt. HARRIS reported 63 15 hr - 4 Off. 78 O.R. to Ambulance routine work & fatigues	N.C.H
"	7.5.17	8 p	Remaining 3 Off. 78 O.R. Fair weather nothing particular to note	H.C.H
"	8.5.17	"	Remaining 3 Off. 75 O.R. weather overcast Clearing towards noon - routine duties	H.C.H
"	9.5.17	9 p.	Remaining 10 Off. 83 O.R. The units 2 1/3 tons hr the 132 2nd And. completion above - Bath to hang for Horse Ambulance & 2 CO's change 5 Reinforcements in t/r chief in Front line into 133 3rd And. weather particularly fine.	H.C.H
"	10.5.17	10 h	Remaining 10 Off. 83 O.R. routine duties	H.C.H
"	11.5.17	"	Remaining 10 Off. 86 O.R. nothing particular	H.C.H
"	12.5.17	"	Remaining 10 Off. 79 O.R. routine duties	H.C.H

WAR DIARY / INTELLIGENCE SUMMARY

Army Form C. 2118
R.A.M.C.
134th FIELD AMBULANCE

134 Fd Ambulance   39 Division

Place	Date	Hour	Summary of Events and Information	Remarks and references to Appendices
WATOU (Sheet 28 G.1.5)	13.5.17	9 h.m.	Remaining 10ff 79 OR. Weather fine, brilliant sunshine. Zonnebeke shelled.	He/Fd/Amb & Cap H.C.H.
	14.5.17	"	Remaining 10ff 69 OR. Bright shower — nothing special to report.	H.C.H.
	15.5.17	"	Conference at A.D.M.S office. Discussion of various subjects remaining 2 off 44 OR. Divnl Light M.T.O.U. + moved to 16 Red Chateau, Poperinghe + 5 Tablns in Ambulance. Remaining all ranks 15 now sick.	H.C.H.
POPERINGHE (J.2.Q.2.4. Sheet 28)	16.5.17	10 h.m	A.D.M.S. Accompanied A.D.M.S. & worked near A.D.S. (Dutallow) also side to Divnl Cavalry stables. D.W.S. visited Ambulance. Remaining 2 off 44 OR.	H.C.H.
"	17.5.17	"	Visited C. section at Wormhoudt. Capt Harris sick — has 92 OR knees + lost our A Dy (Dutallow) from 133 Fd Ambulance which is under Australia. Also advance post outskirts Farm. Admr 3 OR	H.C.H.
"	18.5.17	9 p.m.	Remaining 2 off and 32 O.R. Weather fine. Routine duties. Lt Col Mitchell proceeded on leave to England — Capt H.B.Field acting during his absence.	H.B.Field Capt.
"	19.6.17	10.25 p.m	ADMS visited Fd Ambce in morning. Capt Ambeet on proceeded on leave to Eastbourne. Remaining 2 off & 34 O.R. Admr 2 10 off & 13 ORs Sick & Evac. 1 off 49 ORs. Visited A.D.S. Weather fine but dull intervals	H.B.
"	20.5.17	6 p.m.	Remaining 2 off + 44 OR. Adm 2 10 off & 11 OR. Sick & Evac 1 off 3 5 OR. Weather fine but brilliant sunshine. A.D.M.S. visited in evening Routine duties	H.B.
"	21.5.17	10 p.m	Remaining 2 off 44 + 5 OR. Adm 1 4 16 OR. Sick & Evac. 12 OR. Weather fine with dull intervals. Capt Meech returned to 133 Fd Amb from C section Wormhoudt Capt Hufford evacuated to 46 Cct from C section in his place. Capt Irwin M.C. 132 Fd Amb becoming O.C. C section in emergency. Lieut Bullock returned to H.Q. 134 Fd Amb from the 133 Fd Amb. A.D.S.	H.B.

WAR DIARY or INTELLIGENCE SUMMARY

Army Form C. 2118
R.A.M.C.

134th FIELD AMBULANCE
3rd DIVISION

Place	Date	Hour	Summary of Events and Information	Remarks and references to Appendices
POPERINGHE G.2.a.2.4. Sheet 28	22.5.17	10. p.m	Remaining 18ff & 41 OR. Admitted 10ff & 12 OR. Sick & Evac'd 20ff & 19 OR. Weather Showery in morning, fine in the afternoon. Routine duties & fatigues. Visited Dunallow A.D.S. in afternoon, thence to visit A.D.M.S. with whom the A.D.S. and other arrangement were discussed.	A/S Field Capt.
"	23.5.17	6.30 pm	Remaining 20ff & 46 OR. Adm'd 10ff & MOR. Sick & Evac'd 9 OR. Routine duties. Weather fine and clear. Instructional conference of R.M.O.s at Hd Ambs. Various subjects discussed.	A/S
"	24.5.17	9. p.m	Remaining 32 OR. Adm'd 10ff & MOR. Sick & Evac'd 3 off & 20 OR. Routine duties and fatigues. Weather fine and sunny throughout day – very warm	A/S
"	25.5.17	10. pm	Remaining 29 OR. Adm'd 10 OR. Sick & Evac'd 13 OR. Weather fine and brilliant sunshine and very excellent visibility. An enemy high velocity gun shelled Poperinghe in the afternoon – 4 to 6 shells. Prepared scheme of evacuation in case of shelling A.D.M.S. visited Hd Ambs at 5 P.M.	A/S
"	26.5.17	10.30pm	Remaining 34 OR. Adm'd 10ff & 13 ORs. Sick and Evac'd 10ff & 6 OR. Duicke and Poperinghe again shelled between 7.45 pm and 9 pm – some 15 to 20 shells apparently light calibre, the nearest to the Ambce site being some 400 yards away. Two sergeants and two privates hit & injured.	A/S
"	27.5.17	10 p.m.	Remaining 31 off Adm'd 1 off & 12 OR. Sick and Evac'd 15 OR and 1 off. Weather continues as yet today. The shelling was repeated at 6.15 AM and 4.15 PM. four or five shells on each occasion. Visited 132 Hd Ambce unit Yor. 133 Hd Ambce for conference.	A/S
"	28.5.17	10 p.m	Remaining 36 OR. Adm'd 8 OR. Sick & Evac'd 8 OR. Weather unchanged 1 H.D. Hoss taken on strength. 1 A.C.C. driver taken on strength. Capt. Huggins returns from C.C.S.	A/S
"	29.5.17	8.3pm	Remaining 45 ORs. Adm'd 23 ORs. Sick & Evac'd 13 OR. One of the sergeants taken to Staff Sergt (Roumin) transferred to strength 16.5.17 transferred to 133 Hd Amb o. the private increased to Intelligence dept D.D.M.S. VIII Corps on this unit in evening one taken off strength accordingly England as candidate for Infantry commission & was taken off but fine. Drifting towards evening Weather over cast Capt Huggins visited Capt Morris & O.C. C section	A/S

Army Form C. 2118
R.A.M.C.
134th FIELD AMBULANCE.

WAR DIARY
or
INTELLIGENCE SUMMARY

(Erase heading not required.)

134 - Fld. Ambulance   Sg. Division

Place	Date	Hour	Summary of Events and Information	Remarks and references to Appendices
POPERINGHE (9.2.a.2.4. Sheet 28)	30.5.17	9 p.m.	Remaining 34 O.R.s. Admitted 1 Off and 8 O.R.s. Routine duties and fatigues. Weather fine and clear. Hussein and Capt. Potts of this unit "mentioned in despatches" — Gazette 28.5.17.	H.Stuin Capt.
"	31.5.17	12 noon	Remaining 34 O.R.s. Admitted 9 O.R.s. Dick & Evans 1 Off. & 19 O.R.s. to A.D.M.S.; 2nd Cor. Anderson, Capt. Anderson returned from leave. Nickle and Evans 9 O.R.s. Poperinghe again shelled. Weather fine and clear.	H.St.

Summary for May 1917.

1st May (Remaining from 30/4/17) 81
Admitted during May/17.   364
                                 ―――
                                 445

In HP during the month

DISPOSALS
To CCS . . 150
"   DRS . . 171
"   Duty . .   90
              ―――
              411 = 411
                    ―――
                    445

No remaining in HP 31.5.17 = 34

H.Stuin Capt.

ORIGINAL COPY.

CONFIDENTIAL

WAR DIARY
OF
134th/T FIELD AMBULANCE
from 1st. June to 30th June, 1917.

(VOLUME 16).

WAR DIARY
or
INTELLIGENCE SUMMARY
(Erase heading not required.)

Army Form C. 2118
R.A.M.C.
134th FIELD AMBULANCE.

Instructions regarding War Diaries and Intelligence Summaries are contained in F. S. Regs., Part II. and the Staff Manual respectively. Title Pages will be prepared in manuscript.

134th Field Ambulance
39th Division

Place	Date	Hour	Summary of Events and Information	Remarks and references to Appendices
Chateau Rouge Poperinghe (G.2.a.2.H. Sheet 28)	1/6/17	10 P.M.	Weather fine with Brilliant sunshine. Remaining 84 ORs Admitted 2 Off + 13 ORs Discharged & Evacuated 1 Off + 11 ORs. Remaining 1 Off + 36 ORs	Appx Field State 134 Hd Am
	2/6/17	10 P.M.	Weather fine overcast at intervals. Lieut I.P. CARMODY R.A.M.C., 132nd Fd Ambulance proceeded to DUHALLOW A.D.S. for attached duty. Remain up 1 Off + 36 OR. Adm² 1 Off + 11 OR. Sick & Evac² 2 Off + 8 ORs. Died 1 OR. Rem⁴ 38 OR	≠BP
	3/6/17	9 P.M.	Brilliant weather - very hot. ADMS visited in evening. Rem⁴ 36 OR. Adm² 1 Off + 9 OR Sick & Evac² 1 Off + 8 ORs Remaining 39 OR	≠BP
	4/6/17	9.30 PM	Weather continue very hot and fine. Capt J.H. PORTER RADC reported for duty. Capt J. ANDERSON proceeded to WORMHOUDT for duty with "C" Section. Remaining 39 ORs Adm² 1 Off + 5 ORs RAMC Sick & Evac² 1 Off + 14 ORs Rem⁵ 1 Off + 33 ORs. Routine work	≠BP
	5/6/17	10.0 PM	Lieut-Col H.C. HILDRETH R.A.M.C. O.C. 134 Fd Amb. awarded D.S.O. in Birthday Honours Gazette Weather continue brilliant fine. Remaining 1 Off, 3 OR. Admitted 1 Off 22 OR. Discharged and Evacuated 1 Off + 8 ORs Remaining 1 Off + 47 OR.	≠BP
	6/6/17	10 P.M.	Weather fine with thunder & rain in evening. Routine duties during day. Rem 1 Off + 47 ORs Adm² 24 OR. Evac² 1 Sick, 1 Off + 5 ORs. Surroundings of Chateau wired in afternoon.	≠BP
	7/6/17	10 PM	Hot weather continues. Capt PORTER visited A3rd in afternoon. Patient and personal of ROUSE shelly during afternoon, was evacuated in order. After remaining for minutes & a shell near the SUTFOL Ra heavily included in evening. Lieut WALNER there for an hour, the CHATEAU was reoccupied shortly after 3 P.M. of coming to a rest & Bulloch, RAMC were lent to O.C. 133 Fd Ambce to assist him owing to Battle Casualty having been pown. Included enemy prisoner. 2 mtr ambulances and Officers and transport returned at 9.45 P.M. I Have ambulance were also sent. Evac² Sick 2 1 Off + 30 ORs Adm² 1 Off + 28 ORs Remaining (latest) 1 Off 50 ORs Remaining 1 Off + 48 ORs	≠BP

WAR DIARY / INTELLIGENCE SUMMARY

Army Form C. 2118

134th Field Ambulance
39th Division

Place	Date	Hour	Summary of Events and Information	Remarks and references to Appendices
Red (Chateau) Poperinghe G.2.a.4. Suisse	8/6/17	10 pm	Weather continues brilliant. Sun - Patient remaining 1 Off + 48 ORs. Admitted 1 Off + 34 ORs. Evact & Sick 1 Off + 926 ORs. Remain 1 Off + 63 ORs. Routine duties. Died 1 OR.	HQ Files 7 Oct 134 Fd Amb
	9/6/17	11 pm	Weather continues the same. Lt Col ANDRETH D.S.O. R.A.M.C. returned from leave. Inter-ambulance sports were held at PROVEN during the afternoon and were well attended. A challenge shield was presented by ADMS who attended, as did the General Off commanding 39th Divn. Patients admitted 2 Off + 47 ORs. Evact & Sick 2 Off + 30 ORs.	He Returned L/Cpl RAMC at 134 Fd Amb
	10/6/17	10 pm	Remaining 1 Off + 40 ORs. Capt MORRIS RAMC 137 Fd Amb attached to this unit. Weather cloudy, with rain at night. Capt HUSSINE proceeding on leave. Sent details for duty as O/c "C" Section VII Corps from IInd Army to Vth Army from Capt PORTER returned to ADMS Office. Admit 2 OPs + 14 ORs. Evact + Sick 210 R. Remainent 1 Off + 70 ORs.	HCH
	11/6/17	9 pm	Remaining 1 Off + 63 ORs. Visited A.D.S. DUHALLOW and outposts. Two servicemen wounded. Weather cloudy with rain at intervals shell fire by enemy shells for 4-day on ear early slightly wounded. Ambulance were slightly damaged. Routine duties. Admit ASPE. Evact & Sick 59 ORs. Remaining 1 Off + 9 ORs	HCH
	12/6/17	11 pm	Weather fine during day, overcast in evening, thunderstorm at night. 1 Reinforcement (Private) 5 day Visited A.D.S. DUHALLOW, heavily shelled - no casualties in the unit. Routine duties. Admits 1 Off + 42 ORs Remainen 33 ORs. Adm'd 260 Rs Evact & Sick 26 ORs	HCH
	13/6/17	10 pm	Weather fine with dull intervals. Adm 1 Off + 32 ORs. Attended Horspa unfinals came. Col GERRARD D DMS VIII Corps visited Fd Amb to-day. Evact & Sick 2 1 Off + 22 ORs Remain 1 3 ORs	HCH
	14/6/17	10 PM	Fine weather throughout day. Lieut CARMODY RAMC relieved by Lieut WALKER R. RANC at DUHALLOW ADS. K-day visited fwd ambce site at WATOU and reported its occupation by RFC. & ADMS. Adm 1 22 ORs Evact & Sick 15 ORs Remain up 50 ORs	HCH

WAR DIARY or INTELLIGENCE SUMMARY

Army Form C. 2118
134th FIELD AMBULANCE
39th DIVISION

Place	Date	Hour	Summary of Events and Information	Remarks and references to Appendices
CHATEAU ROUGE POPERINGHE (G.2.9.a.4.4 Sheet 28)	15/6/17	10 P.M.	Weather fine & clear. Routine duties. Army Billet changed from 35 to 53 Rue de Forbes. R.C. Club Sh. H. Rev. K.B. Denany attached to the unit for duty. Admn 1 Off + 17 ORs. Evacd 4 Offs + 11 ORs. Remaining 57 ORs.	HCH
"	16/6/17	9.30 PM	Weather continues fine and hot. Visited DDMS XVIII Corps. Admn 21 ORs. Evacd 4 + Evacd 15 ORs Remaining 62 ORs	HCH
"	17/6/17	11 PM	Weather exceedingly hot. ADMS visited. Ambce fete and inspected T.U. men. Admn 16ff + 32 ORs. Sick & Evacd 1 Off + 25 ORs Remaining 69 ORs. 2 NO Removed	HCH
"	18/6/17	10 PM	Weather fine during morning, rain and heavy thunderstorm after mid-day. Admn 2 Off + 23 ORs Remaining 71 ORs. Sick & Evacd 2 Off + sundry. During all the exceedingly hot weather which there has been, no cases of sunstroke have been admitted. Enemy shelled POPERINGHE	HCH Admn 2 Off
"	19/6/17	8 PM	Weather cloudy with intermittent heavy showers and fine intervals. Arrangements have and the district — patients and most of personnel removed to Cellars been made for 133rd Fld Ambce to receive all patients on this unit to admit & remain started in anticipation of move. Visited ADMS this morning. Admn 15 ORs Evacd & Sick 12 ORs Remaining 70 ORs	HCH
"	20/6/17	9 PM	Showery weather. Lieut RN. WALTER RAMC taken ill. Strength on hand up to 28th taken group Visited ADMS Office. POPERINGHE again shelled by enemy. A working party of 25 NCOs and men have been lent to the M.O.K. 17 NOTTS & DERBYS to reinstated R.A.P. at LA BELLE ALLIANCE. Lieut WM BULLOCK proceeded to ADS. for duty in relief of Lieut WALTER. Admitted 9 ORs. Sick & Evacd & Transferred 52 ORs. Remaining 31 ORs. Sunken car slightly damaged by enemy shrapnel.	HCH
"	21/6/17	10 PM	Weather fine. This unit remains posted with the exception that a dressing station for local casualties has been opened. Admn 13 ORs Sick & Evacd & Transferred 18 ORs Remaining the shelling of the last few nights which is still in the track area. Leaving moved to 26 ORs. The figures refer to "C" section. AMBCE: from whom "C" section SALPERWICK, NR ST OMER to-day. The 1/3rd HIGHLAND FD. took over CHATEAU ROUGE to-day, at which site the 134th Fld Ambce still remains	HCH

WAR DIARY
or
INTELLIGENCE SUMMARY

Army Form C. 2118

134th FIELD AMBULANCE

Instructions regarding War Diaries and Intelligence Summaries are contained in F.S. Regs., Part II. and the Staff Manual respectively. Title Pages will be prepared in manuscript.

134th "F" Field Ambulance
39th Division

(Erase heading not required.)

Place	Date	Hour	Summary of Events and Information	Remarks and references to Appendices
CHATEAU ROUGE, POPERINGHE. (G.2.a.2.4s)	22/6/17	10 P.M.	Weather finer. "Ford" car damaged by shellfire at A.D.S. DUHALLOW & can for this afternoon be handed over to the 133rd Field Ambulance, and Capt. HARRIS, M.C., R.A.M.C. has returned from the ADS to the MDS with his personnel. Admitted 6 ORs, Sick, 1 OR Died 1 O.R. Remaining 30 ORs. (Your figure up to & inc sick section with the exception of the "Died")	HCH
"	23/6/17	8 P.M.	Weather showery. Sick 2 & 6 ORs Remaining 25 ORs	KCH
"	24/6/17	10 PM	Weather fine. Visited "C" section at Mil. 51st Division visited Fd. Ambce. Capt PORTER R.A.M.C. detailed to "C" section on relief of Capt. HARRIS, M.C., R.A.M.C. Admitt 26 O.R. Sick & Evac'd 19 ORs Remaining 4 & 2 ORs (C section). Three men of this unit have been hit & the 133 Fd Ambce 2 ORs wounded at DUHALLOW A.D.S. last night.	KCH
CHATEAU ROUGE POPERINGHE TO GWALIA FARM N. ELVERDINGHE (A. 23. C. 2. 9) Sheet 28	25/6/17	9 PM	Weather overcast with heavy rain at night. The unit proceeded from CHATEAU ROUGE to GWALIA FARM where the 130th Fd. Ambce 38th Division are in occupation this morning. The unit has parked at this site in anticipation of the 130th Fd. Ambce moving out. "C" section attached 14 ORs. The funeral of the 2 ORs killed in action took place this afternoon. Sick & evac'd 10 ORs. 4 & 6 ORs Remaining	KCH
"	26/6/17	10PM	Weather fair & clear. Unit engaged in pitching marquees and generally cleaning up. Sick & Trans 2 OFF & 14 ORs. "C" section admitted 2 OFF & 14 ORs. Sick & Trans 2 OFF & 5 ORs Remaining 55 ORs. Capt HUGGINS returned from leave.	KCH
"	27/6/17	9.30PM	Weather fine with occasional showers. Noisier shelter Kind STEEL attacked by 134th from 132 Fd Ambce to-day. R.A.M.C. 53 ORs Remaining "C" section admitted 17 ORs. sick"? ex inc.? 19 ORs Fd Ambce took from the evening violent thunderstorm at night.	KCH
"	28/6/17	8 PM	Weather fine. Routine duties. Commence running patient throughout the day. Sick & Evac'd 3 OR Remaining 64 ORs. Admits 14 ORs	KCH
"	29/6/17	10PM	Weather fine. 130th Fd Ambce handed over GWALIA FARM site and personnel. The unit spent the day in generally cleaning up and preparing. Admitted 35 ORs Evac'd 14 ORs Remaining 86 ORs.	KQX

… 5.

Army Form C. 2118
R.A.M.C.
134th FIELD AMBULANCE.

WAR DIARY
or
INTELLIGENCE SUMMARY
(Erase heading not required.)

134th Field Ambulance Intelligence Summary, Part II
30th Division

Place	Date	Hour	Summary of Events and Information	Remarks and references to Appendices
GWALIA FARM NR ELVERDINGHE. A.23.c.2.9 Sheet 28.	30/6/17	10.P.M.	Weather wet. Unit engaged in routine duties, also in loading stores for Corps M.D.S. at PROVEN and unloading at this site, where the Corps M.D.S. is to be. Admitted 2 off + 41 ORs – Died 2 ORs and Evac'd 2 off + 34 ORs. Remaining 59 ORs.	ACA
			Summary for Month.	
			1st June Remaining ——— 34	
			Admissions during June ——— 664	
			Total 698 cases	
			Details	
			To C.C.S. ——— 329	
			" D.R.S. ——— 89	
			" Other Ambulance ——— 100	
			" Duty ——— 89	
			Died ——— 2	
			Remaining 30/6/17 — 89	
			Total = 698 cases	
			During the month, the unit has been performing Routine Field Ambulance Work, has constructed an A.D.S. at DUHALLOW, YSER CANAL BANK, and has been preparing the GWALIA FARM site for a Corps M.D.S.	
	1.7.16		A.C.Midwich Col. R.A.M.C. O.C. 134th FIELD AMBULANCE.	

B.E.F.

SUMMARY OF MEDICAL WAR DIARIES OF 134th F.A. 39th Div.
18th Corps. 5th ARMY. (from 10/6/17).

Western Front Operations - June 1917.

Officer Commanding - Lt.Col. Hildreth D.S.O.

SUMMARISED UNDER THE FOLLOWING HEADING:,
Phase "D" - Battle of Messines, June 1917.

B.E.F.

1.

134th F.A.   39th Div.   18th Corps.   5th ARMY.   Western Front.
Officer Commanding - Lt.Col. Hildreth, D.S.O.   June 1917.

PHASE "D".   Battle of Messines.   June 1917.

Headquarters at Chateau Rouge, Poperinghe.
G.2.a.2.4. (28).

June 10th.	Transfer. To 5th ARMY.
12th.	Ops. Enemy. Duhallow A.D.S. heavily shelled.
19th-20th.	Poperinghe shelled.
21st.	Ops. R.A.M.C. 1st aid rendered to numerous casualties from shelling. Unit packed in readiness to move.
24th.	Casualties R.A.M.C.

        O & 2 killed.)
) attached to 133rd F.A.
        O & 2 wounded.)

25th. Moves. To Gwalia Farm. A.23.C.2.9. (28).

30th. Ops. R.A.M.C. Summary for month:-

1st June.	Remaining 34.	To C.C.S.	329.
		D.R.S.	89.
Admissions for month	664.	Other F.As	100.
		Duty	89.
	698.	Died	2.
		Remaining 30/6	89.
			698.

B.E.F.

SUMMARY OF MEDICAL WAR DIARIES OF 134th F.A. 39th Div. 18th Corps. 5th ARMY. (from 10/6/17.)

Western Front Operations - June 1917.

Officer Commanding - Lt.Col. Hildreth D.S.O.

SUMMARISED UNDER THE FOLLOWING HEADING:,

Phase "D" - Battle of Messines, June 1917.

B.E.F.

134th F.A. 39th Div. 18th Corps. 5th ARMY. Western Front.
Officer Commanding - Lt.Col. Hildreth, D.S.O. June 1917.

PHASE "D". Battle of Messines. June 1917.

Headquarters at Chateau Rouge, Poperinghe.
G.2.a.2.4. (28).

June 10th.	Transfer. To 5th ARMY.	
12th.	Ops. Enemy. Duhallow A.D.S. heavily shelled.	
19th-20th.	Poperinghe shelled.	
21st.	Ops. R.A.M.C. 1st aid rendered to numerous casualties from shelling. Unit packed in readiness to move.	
24th.	Casualties R.A.M.C.	

                0 & 2 killed.)
) attached to 133rd F.A.
                0 & 2 wounded.)

25th.   Moves. To Gwalia Farm. A.23.C.2.9. (28).
30th.   Ops. R.A.M.C. Summary for month:-

1st June.	Remaining 34.	To C.C.S.	329.
		D.R.S.	89.
	Admissions for month 664.	Other F.As	100.
		Duty	89.
	698.	Died	2.
		Remaining 30/6	89.
			698.

Original / Vol 17

CONFIDENTIAL.

WAR DIARY
OF
134 FIELD AMBULANCE.

FROM JULY 1st 1917 TO JULY 31st 1917.

(VOLUME 17.)

COMMITTEE FOR THE MEDICAL HISTORY OF THE WAR
Date 10 SEP. 1917

WAR DIARY / INTELLIGENCE SUMMARY

Army Form C. 2118
R.A.M.C.
134th FIELD AMBULANCE

134th FIELD AMBULANCE, 39th DIVISION

Place	Date	Hour	Summary of Events and Information	Remarks and references to Appendices
WALIA FARM, Nr ELVERDINGHE (Map Reference A.23.B.2.9 Sheet 28)	July 1st 1917	10 P.M.	Remaining 89 ORs. Admitted 64 ORs. Sick & Evac = 74 ORs. Died 1 OR. Remaining 83 ORs. Routine duties. Weather, overcast and cool.	
"	2/7/17	9.30 PM	Admitted 2 Off. 31 OR. Died 1 OR. Sick & Evac = 2 Off, 120 R. Remaining 71 ORs. Weather fine. 134: Fd Ambce sustained my unit in hospital eye accident and was Capt Huggins RAMC 134: Fd Ambce evacuated to No. 10 Stationary Hospital, St Omer. Routine duties.	
"	3/7/17	9.30 PM	Admitted 34 ORs. Sick & Evac of 32 ORs. Remaining 72 ORs. Lieut Burrock, O.H. RAMC, this unit. H.D. now evacuated killed. 50 ORs of 1/2 Highland proceeded to No 6 Reserve Park for duty to assist with construction work in connection the Field Ambulance reported at Casualty Clearing Station (XVIII(S) Corp) to be erected in this site at C Section of this. Capt Ham Dressing Station (SALPERWICK, N. St OMER). Weather fine & cool Ambulance is still in the Back Area	
"	4/7/17	10 PM	Admitted 49 ORs. Sick & Evac = 39 ORs. Remaining 84 ORs Routine duties. C.M.D.S. constructional work in progress. Weather fine & cool.	
"	5/7/17	10 PM	Admitted 5 Off, 147 ORs. Died 1 OR. Sick & Evac = 84 Off, 37 OR. Remaining 1 Off & 93 OR. Visited D.D.M.S. afternoon. Ordinary duties — routine and constitutional. Weather continues fine and cool.	
"	6/7/17	8.30 PM	Admitted 2 Off & 40 OR. Sick & Evac = 2 Off & 24 OR. Remaining 1 Off, 9 106 ORs. Weather fine and warmer. 3 MAC (104) Cart attacked for duty & 133 Fd Ambce for duty Capt AL Shearwood RAMC (SR) & 1 Sanitary Section and Lieut J.D. Clay, RAMC (TC) 135 Fd Ambce attached 5 the Unit for duty to-day 34 Fd Ambce.	
"	7/7/17	10 PM	Admitted 3 Off, 5 ORs. Sick & Evac = 4, 1 ORs. Remaining 1 Off & 102 OR. Weather fine — brilliant sunshine 15 hrs. XIII Corps visited the morning — Visited him in the afternoon Lieut J. Steele on temporary duty with this unit, attached to 133 Fd Ambce for duty at A.D.S. the evening.	
"	8/7/17	11 PM	Admitted 5 Off, 95 OR. Sick & Evac 5 Off, 69 OR. Remaining 1 Off & 105 OR. Weather wet. He SS was evacuated by Rail. Personnel & Horse Transport at 9.145 owing to enemy shelling. Some 18 or 20 very HE shells being thrown into adjoining field. No casualties. Its greater number its men returned at 1.45. Capt T.H. Porter RAMC this unit. proceeded 5 days to Canadian Mobile DIEPPE	

Army Form C. 2118

R.A.M.C.
134th FIELD AMBULANCE

WAR DIARY
INTELLIGENCE SUMMARY
(Erase heading not required.)

134th Field Ambulance. 30th Division

Place	Date	Hour	Summary of Events and Information	Remarks and references to Appendices
GWALIA FARM NEVERDINGHE (Map Ref A23.C.7.9 Sheet 28)	9 July 1917	9.30 PM	Admitted 2 Off & 38 OR. Sick & Wound. 1 Off & 49 OR Remaining. 2 Off & 99 OR. Weather fine but colder. Capt G.W. Huggins, RAMC, this unit, in hospital as the result of a motor cycle accident. Struck off strength today.	
"	10/7/17	10 P.M.	Admitted 4 Off & 40 OR. Sick & Wound. 5 Off & 36 OR. Remaining 1 Off & 103 OR. Weather continues fine and C.M.D.S. constructional work are being proceeded with. No horse died.	
"	11/7/17	10 P.M.	Admitted 1 Off & 65 OR. Sick & Wound. 1 Off & 45 OR. Remaining 1 Off & 450 R. Weather fine & summer. Lieut J.R. CLAY RAMC on temporary duty with this unit, attached today to 133 Fld Ambce. Visit D.D.M.S.	
"	12/7/17	8 P.M.	Admitted 2 Off & 61 OR. Sick & Wound. 1 Off – 62 OR. Remaining 2 Off & 109 OR. Weather fine. D.M.S. 5th Army visited Field Ambulance midday today.	
"	13/7/17	9.30 PM	Admitted 5 Off & 93 OR. Died 3 OR. Sick & Wound 2 Off & 100 OR Remaining 10 Off & 99 OR. Weather fine & clear. Lieut D.H.BURTON, this unit, struck off strength to-day on posting to No 8 Armour Park.	
"	14/7/17	10 PM	Admitted 3 Off & 77 OR. Sick & Wound 3 Off & 89 OR. Remaining 10 Off & 89 OR. C.M.D.S. constructional works are weather fine, though there was heavy rain during night. Ronton & CMDS continued work during night.	
"	15/7/17	10 PM	Admitted 52 ORs. Died 1 OR. Evac & Sick & 34 ORs. Remaining 10 Off & 101 ORs. Weather brilliant & fine.	
"	16/7/17	8.30 PM	Admitted 1 Off & 62 OR. Sick & Evac & 1 Off & 6.32 ORs. Remaining 10 Off & 102 ORs. Weather fine. Visited BDHQ. 2 Officers, 5 NCOs & 17 men of 1/2 Highland Fld Ambce reported here for duty. Conference with CMDS work.	
"	17/7/17	9 PM	Admitted 10 Off & 72 OR. Evac & Sick & 10 Off & 62 OR. Remaining 10 Off & 112 OR. To 24 MAC returned to 4 MAC on duty with the Fld Ambce. Weather brilliant.	
"	18/7/17	10 PM	Admitted 2 Off & 62 ORs. Evacuated & Sick 10 Off & 43 OR. Died 1 OR. Remaining 20 Off & 130 OR. A.D.M.S. 39th Div & D.D.M.S. XVIII Corps visited Fld Ambce to-day. Weather fine & very hot.	
"	19/7/17	10 PM	Admitted 65 ORs. Evacuated Sick & 1 Off & 77 ORs. Remaining 10 Off & 118 ORs. Visited BARLETTE spin stretcher fetching fittings for CMDT. Barletti chutes and Weather brilliant and very hot. CMDT continued work proceeding.	
"	20/7/17	10.30 PM	Admitted 65 ORs. Evac & Sick & 10 Off & 49 OR. Remaining 1 Off & 116 ORs. Weather sunny and extremely hot.	

Army Form C. 2118

R.A.M.C.

134th FIELD AMBULANCE

WAR DIARY
INTELLIGENCE SUMMARY
(Erase heading not required.)

Title Pages will be prepared in manuscript 134th Field Ambulance. 39 Division

Place	Date	Hour	Summary of Events and Information	Remarks and references to Appendices
GWALIA FARM Nr ELVERDINGHE Map Ref A.23.c.9. (Sheet 28)	21st July 1917.	9 P.M.	Admitted 3 OFF & 46 OR. Evacuated 3 OFF & 67 OR. Remaining 95 OR. Weather fine and very hot. Baths under construction.	
"	22/7/17	10 P.M.	Admitted 92 OR. Evac'd & Disch'd 2 97 OR. Remaining 90 OR. Weather continues very hot.	
"	23/7/17	10 P.M.	Admitted 10 OFF & 81 OR. Evac'd Disch'd & 10 OFF & 85 OR. Remaining 86 OR. Weather brilliantly fine.	
"	24/7/17	9.30 AM	Admitted 3 OFF & 90 OR. Disch'd & Evac'd 3 OFF & 62 OR. DIED 1 OR. Remaining 9.5 OR. "C" Section returned from Bach area. One ASC (M.T) Sergeant died of Acute Cardiac Dilation en route. 50 Cars, 6 Motor Cycles, & 99 Personnel of 24th MAC reported for duty at CMDS. ADMS visited Fd Amb site & area. Weather extremely hot.	
"	25/7/17	8 P.M.	Admitted 3 OFF & 84 OR. Disch'd & Evac'd 3 OFF & 86 OR. DIED 2 OR. Remaining 89 OR. ADMS visited CMDS in evening. Capt M.W. ROBERTSON RAMC attached to CMDS for duty. Weather very wet in morning, fine in afternoon. 1/2 Highland Fd Amb, 5 OW arrived 7ed & daytime duty but CMDS.	
"	26/7/17	10 P.M.	Admitted 4 OFF & 106 OR. Discharged Evac'd 4 OFF & 112 OR. DIED 2 OR. Remaining F3 OR. ADMS 39th DIV and G.O.C 39th DIV visited C.M.D.S at 2.30 P.M. CMDS constructional work is now practically completed. 11th Corps visited CMDS at noon. Weather extremely hot – brilliant sunshine.	
"	27/7/17	9 P.M.	Admitted 3 OFF & 54 OR. Disch'd Evac'd 3 OFF & 51 OR. DIED No OR. Remaining 89 OR. ADMS 46th DIV visited CMDS to-day. 3 N.C.O.s and 44 OR reported for duty as bearers at CMDS Line men an "temporary" duty.	
"	28/7/17	10.30 AM	Admitted 1 OFF & 58 OR. Disch'd and Evac'd 1 OFF & 59 OR. Remaining 66 OR. 18th C.M.P.S opened 12 noon 6 day – personnel consist of 1/2 Highland Fd Amb, 57th Division D 134 Fd Ambulance and 1 Tent division of 1/2 Highland Fd Amb. RAMC Corps, and AAPM'S, 18 Corps visited CMDS to day. Weather fine and clear.	

1875 Wt. W593/826 1,000,000 4/15 T.B.C. & A. A.D.S.S./Forms/C. 2118.

WAR DIARY or INTELLIGENCE SUMMARY

Army Form C. 2118

134th FIELD AMBULANCE

134 Field Ambulance 39 Division

Place	Date	Hour	Summary of Events and Information	Remarks and references to Appendices
GWALIA FARM ELVERDINGHE Map Ref: A.25 C.1.9. Sh.28	29th July 1917	10 P.M.	Admitted 9 Off. 489 OR. Discharged and evacuated 8 Off. 108 OR. Died 2 OR. Remaining 1 Off. 67 OR. G.O.C. XVIII Corps and DDMS visited. Capt RA KERR RAMC reported for temporary duty. 60 men "temporarily unfit" men, reported for duty at C.A.D.S. Weather showery.	
"	30/7/17	10.30 pm	Admitted 7 Off. 234 OR (8 whilst 7 Off and 226 OR were Batt.d Casualties) Evacuated 8 Off. and 227 OR. Remaining 6 Off. Died 7 OR. Discharged. Intense bombardment by our artillery every hour. Weather fine. Captain J ANDERSON RAMC and Lieut A.C. MURRAY RAMC RAMC attached the night. Captain ARR MURRAY ADS Bearer sub division & DUHALLOW A.D.S. proceeded with his Bearer sub division & Lieut DUHALLOW to reconnoitre arrangements having been received by Capt A.P.R MURRAY. A.D.M.S. 39th Division visited.	
"	31/7/17	10 PM	Admitted 14 Off. 329 OR (Of which 10 Off and 294 OR were Batt.d Casualties) Evacuated 14 Off. 352 OR. Remaining 4 Off. Died 2 OR. Discharged 4 Off. 57 " Intense operations commenced at 3.31 a.m. this morning. Try casualties commenced coming through CMDS at about 7 a.m. Capt Johns. and Col Maynard SMITH, Consulting Surgeon to Army, visited in morning. 2 Officers Bearer sub division in reserve sent to warn & DUHALLOW this evening. Lieut BORD, BROWN and VISGER, RAMC attached for temporary duty. Weather dull and cool. Occasional showers.	

SUMMARY for JULY.

Admitted 2424
171/TR Remaining 89
Remaining 2516

Transferred to C.C.S.	389
Evacuated to C.R.S.	1812
Died in Hospital	20
Died in C.R.S. & C.R.S.	25.3
TOTAL	2474 (+ Remaining 42 = 2516 for month)

Heatwole
Lt Col
O.C. 134th FIELD AMBULANCE
R.A.M.C.

B.E.F.

SUMMARY OF MEDICAL WAR DIARIES OF 134th F.A. 39th Div.

18th Corps. 5th ARMY.
To 2nd Army Area from August 7th.

Western Front Operations - July - ~~August~~ 1917.

Officer Commanding - Lt. Col. Hildreth, D.S.O.

SUMMARISED UNDER THE FOLLOWING HEADINGS:-
Phase "D" 1. Passchendaele Operations, "July - Nov.1917."
    (a) - Operations commencing July - Nov.

B.E.F.

1.

134th F.A.   39th Div.   18th Corps.   5th ARMY.   Western Fro
                                                   July-Aug.19
Officer Commanding - Lt.Col. Hildreth, D.S.O.

To 2nd Army Area from August 7th.

PHASE "D" 1.   Passchendaele Operations, "July-Nov. 1917."

    (a) - Operations commencing 1/7/17.

Headquarters at Gwalia Farm A23.c.2.9. (28).

July 1st-30th.   Ops. R.A.M.C.   C.M.D.S. Routine.
    31st.   Operations. 39th and 51st Division commenced attack at 3.31 a.m.

Casualties. 1st arrived at C.M.D.S. at 7.0 a.m.

Moves. Detachment. B.S.D. sent forward to Duhallow in evening.

Ops. R.A.M.C. Summary for month:-

Admitted.	2427.	Transferred	389.
Remaining		To C.C.S.	1812.
1/7	89.	Died.	20.
		Disch. to duty	253.
	2516.		2474.
		Remaining	42.
			2516.

B.E.F.

1.

134th F.A.   39th Div.   18th Corps.   5th ARMY.   Western Front
                                                    July-   .1917.

Officer Commanding - Lt.Col. Hildreth, D.S.O.

To 2nd Army Area from August 7th.

PHASE "D" 1.   Passchendaele Operations, "July-Nov. 1917."

   (a) - Operations commencing 1/7/17.

Headquarters at Gwalia Farm A23.c.2.9. (28).

July 1st-30th.   Ops. R.A.M.C.   C.M.D.S. Routine.

31st.   Operations. 39th and 51st Division commenced attack at

3.31 a.m.

Casualties. 1st arrived at C.M.D.S. at 7.0 a.m.

Moves. Detachment. B.S.D. sent forward to Duhallow in

evening.

Ops. R.A.M.C. Summary for month:-

Admitted.	2427.	Transferred	389.
Remaining		To C.C.S.	1812.
1/7	89.	Died.	20.
		Disch. to duty	253.
	2516.		2474.
		Remaining	42.
			2516.

ORIGINAL.

CONFIDENTIAL.

WAR DIARY
OF
134th FIELD AMBULANCE
from 1st to 31st August, 1917.

(VOLUME 18).

COMMITTEE FOR THE
MEDICAL HISTORY OF THE WAR.
Date -1 OCT.1917

1. Original.

WAR DIARY
INTELLIGENCE SUMMARY
(Erase heading not required.)

Army Form C. 2118
R.A.M.C.
134th FIELD AMBULANCE

39 Division
134 Fd. Ambulance

Place	Date	Hour	Summary of Events and Information	Remarks and references to Appendices
GWALIA FARM A.20.c.2.9. Sheet 20	1.9.17	10pm	The Fwd Divisions of this Unit were employed at the XVIII Corps Mn Dressing Station. Admissions 75 Offrs + 1111 OR. Died 1 Offr + 14 OR. D.D.M.S. & Consulting Surgeon to V Army visited. Heavy rain fell. Lieut VIESGER taken on the strength.	H Chalwin Lt Col
"	2.8.17	8h	Admissions 20 OR. + 572 OR. Wounded 19 Offrs + 509 OR. Died 2 Offrs. Remain 1 Offr + 3 OR. Weather wet	HCH
"	3.8.17	10h	Admitted Pat Officer + 365 OR. E 230 Offrs + 269 OR. Died 1 Offr + 15 OR. Remaining 1 Offr + 4 OR. Weather overcast + showery. Lieut MACNEILL taken on the strength.	HeK
"	4.8.17	"	Admitted 13 Offr + 226 OR. E 130 Offrs + 224 OR. Died 2 OR. Remaining 1 Offr + 4 OR. Weather fine. The Bn l/0th knives of Ambulance returned to Bridon. A O/h3 visits	HCH
"	5.8.17	8h	Admitted 9 Offr + 172 OR. E 10 Offr + 172 OR. Died 2 OR. Remaining 2 OR. Capt J. ANDERSON wounded + evacuated to CCS. Aerodrome hit. Ground impossibly routine order	HCH
"	6.8.17	10h	Admissions 8 Offr + 186 OR. E 6 Offr + 165 OR. Died 3 OR. A.D.M.S. visits Ch.D.S	HCH
"	7.8.17	"	The Team Cdy of the Unit Lyte Ch.O.S. + proceeded by Car to EECKE Marching Line. The B.C. + O.R.E. Fwd 2nd made Island to hand over Ch.D.S. Admitted 12 Offr 197 OR. E 12 Offr 197 OR. Weather fine.	HCH
W.S.C.8.9. Sheet 27	8.8.17		The Rr Div. Ambulance for this Unit Admits 2 Offr. Capt. R.B. JOHN + Capt J W STONE Posted to Unit. Remain 2.	HCH

1875 Wt. W593/826 1,000,000 4/15 I.B.C. & A. A.D.S.S./Forms/C. 2118.

2. Original. 2.

Army Form C. 2118
R.A.M.C.
134th FIELD AMBULANCE.

WAR DIARY or INTELLIGENCE SUMMARY

(Erase heading not required.)

134 Fd Ambulance 39th Division

Instructions regarding War Diaries and Intelligence Summaries are contained in F.S. Regs., Part II. and the Staff Manual respectively. Title Pages will be prepared in manuscript.

Place	Date	Hour	Summary of Events and Information	Remarks and references to Appendices
W.S.@5.9 Shut 27	9.8.17	6 pm	The Unit was engaged in truck-making. The Ambulance Equipment & personal kit a Tent Band was opened to the ADMS of Corps Armlets SOTR.	HC/Bind
"	10.8.17	10 a	Routine. Unit orders received. 16 9s O. 1 Orck inter O.C. 138 Fd Amb with a view to taking over the Unit. Admitted 30TR medical line.	BCH
"	11.8.17	5 h	Unit's O.C. 138 Fd Amb a ADS VOORMEZEELE. The Ambulance was ordered to packing up again - orders received for Bearer Relations to proceed to relief of Bearers of 138 Fd Amb under Capt HARRIS Admits & Evans to 3 OTR	HCH
"	12.8.17	10 a	The Bearer Division proceeded at 5.30 am. 9 reports at VOORMEZEELE	HCH
"	13.8.17	8 pm	The unit moved out & proceeded to 16" Fd Amb area - Reinforced arriving about 3 am	HCH
1-31.C.47 VOORMEZEELE	14.8.17	10 a	Relieved 138 Fd Amb at 6 pm. Taking over the A.D.S. BRASSERIE & other lines. The A.D.S. exists of Cellars in a Ruined brewery. The BRASSERIE is Cellaring. Post in Cellars at (NB 6 22) Horses kire in open fields at (W105.9) The Evacuation from Fd Amb has carried out by the Bearers to a Collecting post NORFOLK. Under the orders of ADS, & from him (132 d 33) by motor Ambulance to the A.D.S. fur Corps on the river Rent thence 132 Fd Amb at M.6.d.8.8 BRIDGE	HCH
"	15.8.17	10 am	Admits 3 OR. 120 OR. To Duty, 46 OR. E.73. Routine duties - weather fine	HCH
"	16.8.17	"	Admits 1 OR. 15 BR. To duty 36 OR. E.127. weather fine	HCH
"	17.8.17	"	Cases dealt with 140. To duty 26. E.114. Capt HARRIS wounded & evacuated. 1 OR. killed y 19 wounded. Capt JOHN South relief of Capt HARRIS	HCH

1875 Wt. W593/826 1,000,000 4/15 J.B.C. & A. A.D.S.S./Forms/C. 2118.

Original.

3.

Army Form C. 2118
R.A.M.C.
134th FIELD AMBULANCE.

WAR DIARY
or
INTELLIGENCE SUMMARY
(Erase heading not required.)

39th Division
134 Fd Ambulance

Instructions regarding War Diaries and Intelligence Summaries are contained in F. S. Regs., Part II. and the Staff Manual respectively. Title Pages will be prepared in manuscript.

Place	Date	Hour	Summary of Events and Information	Remarks and references to Appendices
VOORMEZEELE I 31 C 47 Sheet 28	18/8/17	10h	A D M S visits 1st line & inspects W.C Lats. Cases dealt with – 148. To duty 32. E 116. Routine & fatigue duties. Weather fine	HCH/ads
"	19/8/17	"	Total numbers of Cases dealt with – 113. To duty 35. E 75. Died 3. Relief Room from 133 Amnc. Guns epileptique + routine duties. Weather fine.	HCH
"	20/6/17	9h	Cases dealt with 114. To duty 46. E 68. Reinforcements at ADS undertaken : undertaken by 9 MC men & ambulance 9 bath to Offrs on weather fine	HCH
"	21/8/17	10h	Admission 149. E 95 To duty 54. Routine duties. weather fine	HCH
"	22/8/17	10h	Cases dealt with – 129. E 62. To duty 66. Weather showery. Lieut HARRIS R.O.R.C. M.S.A posted to the unit. Weather showery. 20 Reinforcements arrived.	HCH
"	23/8/17	"	Cases dealt with 92. E 58. To duty 36. Capture at A D M S Offcr on recent operations	HCH
"	24/8/17	9h	D D M S visits ADS Cases dealt with 87. E 60. To duty 27. weather showery	HCH
"	25/8/17	10h	A D.M.S. & G.O.C 118 Bde. visits ADS 82 Cases now dealt with 29 returns to duty. 53 reach 65	HCH
"	26/8/17	"	Capt JOHN detained by Capt FIELD as Bearer Offcr. Vice former detained to 133 Fd Amb. 92 Cases dealt with – 58 E + 36 returns to duty. Heavy rain at night.	HCH
"	27/8/17	"	Cases dealt with – 75. Reach 61. To duty 14. Showery weather – routine duties & fatigues.	HCH

1875 Wt. W593/826 1,000,000 4/15 J.B.C. & A. A.D.S.S./Forms/C. 2118.

134th FIELD AMBULANCE 1 SEP 1917

4. Original

WAR DIARY
INTELLIGENCE SUMMARY
(Erase heading not required.)

Army Form C. 2118
R.A.M.C.
134th FIELD AMBULANCE
39th Division

Place	Date	Hour	Summary of Events and Information	Remarks and references to Appendices
ROORNEZEELE 13.10.47	28.8.17	10p	Cases admitted – 54. To Duty 27. F=27 Headline fire – Rendin order	HC Woods Lt Col
	29.8.17	"	55 Cases admitted. 37 Evacuated. 17 retained. 10 duty. Headline fire.	154
"	30.8.17	11h	At 10pm Sunday – Sunbeam 2nd 10 members of a lion column – BLANEY & Pwk ADDINGTON injured 44 Cases admitted 15 sent to Duty 29 Evacuated	HCW
"	31.8.17	7h	Cases admitted 40 Duty 15 Evacuated 22 Headline fire	HCW

Summary. During the month the unit has been habitually busy. At first Divn has mainly attended to the XVIII Corps under the Rearrangement employed in the Line – for hour of the first week. After a few day's of the unit was again employed in the Line. The 132d members of Casualties sustained viz. 10H. 250R. Deaths. 3. Ribbons 10 Duty. 4 in recognition of service in bringing in and wounded men snow. The total number of cases dealt with by the unit was 4666 during the month.

1.9.17

H C Woods
Lt Col
OC 134 Fd Amb

Aug. 1st.	Operations R.A.M.C. T.D's of unit employed at 18th C.M.D.S.					
1st-6th.	Admissions etc.		Admitted.	Died.	Evacuated.	
		1st.	75 & 1111.	1 & 14.		
		2nd.	20 & 512.	2 & 0.	19 & 509.	
		3rd.	24 & 305.	1 & 15.	23 & 289.	
		4th.	13 & 226.	0 & 2.	13 & 224.	
		5th.	9 & 172.	0 & 2.	10 & 172.	
		6th.	8 & 186.	0 & 3.	8 & 185.	
7th.	Moves and Transfer. 150 &512					
	To W.5.c.3.9. (27). 2nd ARMY AREA.					

Aug. 1st.	Operations R.A.M.C. T.D's of unit employed at 18th C.M.D.			
1st-6th.	Admissions etc.	Admitted.	Died.	Evacuated.
	1st.	75 & 1111.	1 & 14.	10 & 500.
	2nd.	20 & 512.	2 & 0.	19 & 509.
	3rd.	24 & 305.	1 & 15.	23 & 289.
	4th.	13 & 226.	0 & 2.	13 & 224.
	5th.	9 & 172.	0 & 2.	10 & 172.
	6th.	8 & 186.	0 & 3.	8 & 185.
7th.	Moves and Transfer.			
	To W.5.c.3.9. (27). 2nd ARMY AREA.			

B.E.F.

SUMMARY OF MEDICAL WAR DIARIES OF 134th F.A. 39th Div.

18th Corps.   5th ARMY.

To 2nd Army Area from August 7th.

Western Front Operations - ~~~~ - August 1917.

Officer Commanding - Lt. Col. Hildreth, D.S.O.

SUMMARISED UNDER THE FOLLOWING HEADINGS:-

Phase "D" 1. Passchendaele Operations, "July - Nov.1917."

(a) - Operations commencing July - Nov.

ORIGINAL

Vol 19

CONFIDENTIAL.

WAR DIARY
OF
134th Field Ambulance,
from 1st Sept. to 30th Sept., 1917.
(Volume 19).

COMMITTEE FOR THE
MEDICAL HISTORY OF THE WAR
Date −5 NOV. 1917

WAR DIARY

Army Form C. 2118

INTELLIGENCE SUMMARY

134 Fd Amb 39 Div

Place	Date	Hour	Summary of Events and Information	Remarks and references to Appendices
VOORMEZEELE (I.31.C.4.7. Sheet 28).	1.9.17	6pm	Dealt with S.B Crew men reinf to 112th amb. for 5 km 72 Fd Amb.	He rel'd by Col.
"	2.9.17	10pm	Ordering of armed party of 72 Fd Amb. Constr Tower Canada Street Larch wood 2L. Ridwis. 72 Fd Amb. L. arrived pm lost one Billowed VOORMEZEELE - oenthin jour. 53 OR stretcher bearers to A.D.M.S	He N
"	3.9.17	"	52 OR cleared into Bathing minimal routine work. The temporary Commander rode to the 4 QMS Tent mess all posts from 72 Fd Amb. Report to Dressing Station	He N
"	4.9.17	9am	5 off 126 OR. Suppl. SDBR health cleaning. Routine work.	12 N
"	5.9.17	8pm	2 off 103 OR To Ruf Surf 41 health fine E.D.M.S ruled & unrest Colonel Tullen wsr SCR.	He N
"	6.9.17	6pm	2 off 122 OR To Suf 54 health fine thro' rainy day. Storm at night. Routine work -	He N 4 CH He N
"	7.9.17	10am	3 off 112 OR 7 OR Suf 49. Routine work.	
"	8.9.17	"	1 off 110 OR To Ruf 62.	
"	9.9.17	"	10 off 136 OR To Ruf 50. Chapman at A.D.M.S (rear) Cap FIELD totch lamp of LARCH WOOD	He N He H
"	10.9.17	"	2 off 113 OR To Ruf 42. Routine orders.	
"	11.9.17	"	5 off 215 OR To Ruf 40. Canadian Infantry trenches local knowing Lieut BOGART 2.O RCHSA attaches for duty.	
"	12.9.17	"	6 off 195 OR To Ruf 69. 10 OR 1.5 3 Fd armed to ass in building SCP BARTELEM etc. Cerft BROWN MC to Bornards 141 Grouts	H 2 N

Original 2

WAR DIARY
~~INTELLIGENCE SUMMARY~~
(Erase heading not required.)

Army Form C. 2118

134th Bde. R.F.A.
Bde. D. And. 39" How

Place	Date	Hour	Summary of Events and Information	Remarks and references to Appendices
VOORMEZEELE (I.31.C.4.7. Sheet 28)	13.9.17	6h	577 & 149 OR Troops 2 pr & 7 pr. A.Drs & under VOORMEZEELE. Weather fine	H/Heads ref. C.S.T.
	14.9.17	10p	147. 113 OR to Drf. 47. Preparation for following operation in hand.	He.11
	15.9.17	"	3 OR 174 OR to Drf. 52. BDR S x Corps orders another fine. Reconnt. work.	He.11
	16.9.17	"	8 pr. 82 OR Drf. 57 Preparation for handing over horses & taking over new scale in hand.	He.11
	17.9.17	"	577. 117 OR Drf. 25" Handed over VOORMEZEELE & advanced post to 140" Field Amb. & moved to hr/a reg of ZWARTELEEN & SPOILBANK, where had been established the former on Dormont Colliery Post, the Potter in a Building known as the BRASSERIE (N.6.a.2.2). Becoming the Advanced Dressing Station.	He.N
BRASSERIE N.6.a.2.2 Sheet 28	18.9.17	Nh	194. 62 OR. 5-16 Drys. The land very heavy, setting into new A.D.S. also filling up new posts.	He.11
	19.9.17	10h.	holes & gunfire & 6 hrs. raid. Preparation for offensive Northern walks in hand. 2 OR & 134 OR. Reported Beam and Battn Green. Cart. FIELD a 6c Beam. Capt. LIMBERY as Capt. PORTER as 2/c. OR of R.I.	
	20.9.17	11h	Offensive commenced 5.40 a.m. Casualties arrived by train. Lineable Salvador for the first two days. The former at A Baker. Coll. FIELD. G Con. S. x Others. Later Con. clay & lort. EnEg SPOILBANK. Cavilli 82 OR 52> OR Lowers Mounting	He.L
	21.9.17	"		

Original 3

WAR DIARY
INTELLIGENCE SUMMARY
(Erase heading not required.)

134th Field Ambulance
3rd Bn Brigade

Army Form C. 2118

Place	Date	Hour	Summary of Events and Information	Remarks and references to Appendices
BIRR-asse (R.17.c.2.8) Sheet 28	22/9/17	6pm	13 OR 13 OR horse trans - preparation to return to VOORMEZEELE & the taking over of front a trench. Weather fine	He has all to cap
"	23/9/17	8am	2 OR. 1 2nd OR. Awaiting tramways to another attack & awaiting arrival Capt Brown McG Capt STONE with 100 stretcher bearers to work a rear post the night 23/24	He H
VOORMEZEELE (I.31.c.6.4.7) Sheet 28	24/9/17	"	Landed at ZWARTELEEN & SPOILBANK 18 OR and 7.19 Br & 16th on beds from 140 OR 9 A.C.C Q. Bgh - S. bight VOORMEZEELE hang wire & form 4 th lin - 4/4. 2.78 O.R Advance post 9 A.M. S. 240 O.R. Adv spent Q am under shellfire with Lt 2/Lt 3 First horses advanced Repeated Brown Ken & Lloyd as Runs become more hard - Capt FIELD & Capt STONE in back wards at the front & Capt KIMBERY takes on. Causality was heavy 19 v 10 OR killed 3 OR 4/2 OR wounded. The known hum this amb'c King a Sgarant Crean/drain - ADMS lights heard LOC C B.V	Kin A
(R.25.ell 6.91)	"	"		
VOORMEZEELE (R.17.c.6.52)	27/9/17	8pm	VOORMEZEELE Br's S. bite - 11 OR. 287 OR. + 52 92 O.R. Relief of Front line 27/28 night C. 2b - back men landed out 16 9/4 Pak's Ecarle. by 12 5m Sft & the bn of Ratchers? to hand KOKEREELE. 64 & 12 mom. A/T 3pm. 2b Br 4/5 80. 9th. when & took over. am (R.17.6.5.2. Sheet 27)	He H
MONT KOKEREELE	28/9/17	"	Kept allowed the trimed of CAPFIELD & Corporal TALLON & CAPKIMBERY all found 9 bn at GODSWARSWELDE D-5 + 6-3-8. Borr's 9 Dists - 1 off. 28 O.R. Q-18. 6-3-8.	He H
FARM 27	28/9/17	"		
R-17. 6.5.2	29/9/17	"		
	30/9/17	"	Unit resting, reequipping & refreshing the Sty - 1 off. 18 O.R. The month, on the whole has been the harshest the battn has experienced since its arrival in France, previous to this last battle it	Ken

Army Form C. 2118

WAR DIARY
INTELLIGENCE SUMMARY
(Erase heading not required.)

134 F¹ Bn.

Place	Date	Hour	Summary of Events and Information	Remarks and references to Appendices
134 F¹ Bn.	1.10.17		It has been two had been a week with 4th Bear Division working forward. 91st and during operation angles of the 9th and 2nd Ardennes suffered great casualties of all ranks were in groups, but reformed also has lost ret. the results that the Ennemie has a serious & dealt with during the period 20/25 November 62 R 1717 O.R. — D.R.H.B.	H.Q. Mobile A Coy. H.Q. Moluik A Coy O.C. 134 F Bn. O.C. 134 F Bn.

ORIGINAL.

CONFIDENTIAL.

WAR DIARY

of

134th FIELD AMBULANCE.

from Oct. 1st, 1917. to Oct. 31st, 1917.

(VOLUME 20).

COMMITTEE FOR THE
MEDICAL HISTORY OF THE WAR
Date — 8 DEC. 1917

Vol 20

Original 1.

WAR DIARY
INTELLIGENCE SUMMARY

Army Form C. 2118

R.A.M.C.
134th FIELD AMBULANCE

(Erase heading not required.)

Instructions regarding War Diaries and Intelligence Summaries are contained in F.S. Regs., Part II. and the Staff Manual respectively. Title Pages will be prepared in manuscript.

134 Fd Amb.
3 G Division

Place	Date	Hour	Summary of Events and Information	Remarks and references to Appendices
MOUNT KOKEREELE (R.17.b.5.2.) Sheet 27	1/10/17	6h.	Admitted 43 OR. 1 Died 1 to Duty. Evacuated 25 OR. Remaining 25 included fine worker mob.	Methersole to CCS
	2/10/17	9h.	Admitted 33 OR Duty 7. F 7. R 47. Included Capt HARMANS proceed in relief of Capt DELGADO.	OR's & Halls 140 H
"	3/10/17	10h.	Admitted 42 OR To Duty 2. E 34. R.S.R. included fine workers mob.	14 H NOH
"	4/10/17	9h.	Admitted 31 OR. E 22. Remaining 63. included Cols & neh.	N°H
"	5/10/17	10h.	Admitted approx 23 OR E 10. 130 OR Duty 110R. Q Bn & OR's 3 inches headed out.	15 H
"	6/10/17	10h.	Admitted 45 Ev Duchamp 26 OR. Remaining 9 OR. included fine	16 H
"	7/10/17	6h.	Admitted 39. 150R E 30R 32 OR Remaining 64 OR included fine Q Bn S & OR'S	18 H
"	8/10/17	10h.	Admitted 18 H 210 R Ev Duchamp 34 included mi Capt ... Duties	18 H
"	9/10/17	1h.	Admitted 29. 43 OR Ev Duchamp 31. Remaining 10 & 7 STR Sheny included workers mob	16 H
"	10/10/17	6h.	Admitted 31 OR Ev Duchamp 36 Remaining 71. included workers mob Q Bn S hills	17 H
"	11/10/17	8h.	Admitted 31 OR Ev Duchamp 28. 74 OR remaining included nel	16 H
6	12/10/17	9h.	Admitted 21 OR. Ev Duchamp 26. Remaining 69 OR. included	16 H
"	13/10/17	8h.	Admitted 36 OR. Ev Duchamp 50 OR. Remaining 32 OR. included sheney	14 H
"	14/10/17	9h.	Admitted 18 OR. Ev Duchamp 32 OR. Remaining 41 included sheney Q Bn S hills	14 H

WAR DIARY

INTELLIGENCE SUMMARY
(Erase heading not required.)

Army Form C. 2118
134th FIELD AMBULANCE

Place	Date	Hour	Summary of Events and Information	Remarks and references to Appendices
At rest KOKEREEL	15/10/17	6 p.m.	Advanced party 3 Offrs and KEERSEBROM (S.10.d.5.7) Sheet 28 admitted 3 O.R. 32 O.R. Ev.D. Work Remarks 53.	134 Mobile Lab Ew
(R.17.b.5.2 Sheet 27) KEERSEBROM	16/10/17	10 a.m.	Sent [?] to KEERSEBROM. Took over D.R.S. from 132 F.A. and V Ladies ours. 4 F.A. Ambl. Rout KOKEREEL	HEW HEW
(S.10.d.5.7 Sheet 28)	17/10/17	8 h.	M.S. L. chut. Later on 145 admitted 62. D.S. 51. Remain ? 156. Orders received to take over D.R.S. METEREN	BCH HEW
METEREN (L.15.d.3.7 Sheet 27)	18/10/17	10 h.	Handed over KEERSEBROM. Leaving 3 offr, Brown patients, with 48 F.A. Ambl.	HEW
"	19/10/17	6 h.	Transporting 3 F. Bri Cars to METEREN	HEW
"	20/10/17	10 h.	Unit establishing daily + new quarters. D.R.S. - 171 Patients E. 45. Remain ? 175 Routine work.	HEW
"	21/10/17	8 h.	D.R.S. 175 admitted 27 F. 8 O.R. E.39. Remain ? 226. O.R. routine work.	HEW
"	22/10/17	6 h.	Remain ? 307 223 O.R. E.81.O.R. P.189 routine work.	HEW
"	23/10/17	8 h.	Remain ? 40 F. 165 adm.M.S. 10 F. 520 R. E.38. Remain ? w O F. 200 O.R.	HEW
"	24/10/17	8 h.	R.26 F. 200 O.R. a. 10 F. 220 O.R. E.64. R.50 Off. 158 O.R. Routine work.	HEW
"	25/10/17	8 h.	R.50 Off. 158 O.R. a. 280 O.R. Ev.D. 380 O.R. M. 5 O.R. 146 O.R. Routine work.	HEW
"	26/10/17	8 h.	R.50 Off. 146 O.R. Do 2 O.R. 43 O.R. Ad 2. W O.R.R. 78 F. 150 O.R. "	HEW
"	27/10/17	9 p.m.	R.50 Off. 193 O.R. a.52 O.R. E.73 R.54 H. 212 O.R. routine work. ADnS Visit	HEW
"	28/10/17	7 h.	R.50 Off. 212 O.R. Do 10 R. w O.R. F.52.O.R. R.63 N. 180 O.R. routine work. BDMS visit. No 65	HEW
"	29/10/17	6 p.	R.50 Off. 180 O.R. a V. A 3.2.O.R. R.6 N. 157 O.R.	HEW
BAD	30/10/17	6 h.	126 Off. 156 O.R. Do V. A.3.2.O.R. R.6 N. 157 O.R. Opens Field Ambulance a. 31. E.17. R.19. routine work	HEW

Original 3.

Army Form C. 2118
R.A.M.C.
134th FIELD AMBULANCE

WAR DIARY
INTELLIGENCE SUMMARY
(Erase heading not required.)

134 Fd Amb.   39' Brown

Instructions regarding War Diaries and Intelligence Summaries are contained in F.S. Regs., Part II. and the Staff Manual respectively. Title Pages will be prepared in manuscript.

[Stamp: 134th FIELD AMBULANCE 1 NOV 1917]

Place	Date	Hour	Summary of Events and Information	Remarks and references to Appendices
METEREN (X.15.d.3.7. Sheet 27)	Oct 31 - Nov 1	12 Noon	Field Ambulance: Admitted 49 O.R. Discharged & evacuated 12 O.R. Remaining 56 O.R. D.R.S. Running 60 Officers 1310 O.R. Admitted 7 O.R. Discharged & evacuated 7 O.R. Rem. 6 Officers 1311 O.R. Summary D.R.S. Admitted 975 Evacuated 9 Transferred 384 Discharged Dead 456 Running 87 ____ 56 984	
			Summary Field Ambulance Admitted 132 Figures Evacuated Transferred 141 Discharged 698 Running 332 122 226 157n 839	A C Webster Lt. Col. O.C. 134 Fd Amb.
			1.11.17.	

CONFIDENTIAL.

WAR DIARY.
OF
134TH. FIELD AMBULANCE

FROM Nov. 1ST. 1917. TO Nov. 30TH. 1917.

(VOLUME 21.)

Vol 21

ORIGINAL

COMMITTEE FOR THE
MEDICAL HISTORY OF THE WAR
Date   17 JAN. 1918

WAR DIARY
or
INTELLIGENCE SUMMARY
(Erase heading not required.)

Army Form C. 2118

R.A.M.C.
134th FIELD AMBULANCE.

Place	Date	Hour	Summary of Events and Information	Remarks and references to Appendices
METEREN Sheet 27 X.15.d.37.	1.11.17	2 P.M	Censorship orders read to guards. Lt. Colonel HILDRETH, D.S.O. granted leave to ENGLAND from 1.11.17 to 3.11.17.	
		6. A.M	Capt L. WAY. R.A.M.C assumed temporary command of the Field Ambulance. Admitted to Field Ambulance 400.O.R. discharged & evacuated 260.O.R. Remaining 700.O.R. Remained in the D.R.S. 6 officers 151 O.R. admitted 30.O.R. Discharged & evacuated 17.O.R. Remaining 6 officers 137.O.R.	1 brar Capt R.A.M.C
	2.11.17		Admitted to Field Amb. 1 officer 49 O.R. Discharged & evacuated 10 officers & 14 O.R. Remaining 1050 O.R. In D.R.S. Remaining 6 officers 137 O.R. evacuated 2 officers & 15 O.R. Remaining 5 officers 134 O.R. Weather rainy.	L.W.
	3.11.17	10-15.	The A.D.M.S. 39th Division visited this unit. Capt WHARMAN S.R.Q.M.C posted to 6th Cheshire Regt. vice Capt H. JEFFREYS. The O.C. 132 Field Ambulance informed me that 6 men from the Rangoon subdivision assisting him were evacuated. Lieut Colonel HILDRETH, R.A.M.C having returned for embarkation to MESOPOTAMIA was struck off the strength of this unit. Admitted to the Field Ambulance 130.O.R. Discharged & evacuated 150.O.R Remaining 1030.O.R Admitted to D.R.S. 15 O.R. Discharged & evacuated 10 officers 2 5. O.R. Remaining 4 officers 124 O.R. Weather fine.	L.W.

Army Form C. 2118

WAR DIARY
INTELLIGENCE SUMMARY
(Erase heading not required.)

134th FIELD AMBULANCE

Place	Date	Hour	Summary of Events and Information	Remarks and references to Appendices
ETEREN Sh.27 X.15.c.3.7.	4.11.17		Admitted into F.d Amb. 6.O.R. Discharged & evacuated 33 O.R. Remaining 76 O.R. Admitted into D.R.S. Discharged & evacuated 1 officer + 18 O.R. Remaining 3 Officers + 133 O.R.	1. Weather R.G. Inc.
		7 A.m.	Col. Taylor a.y. + 6 O.R. proceeded to 132 F.d Ambulance at VOORMEZEELE (I.31.C.4.7.) as reinforcements. Sheet 2	L.W.
		6 P.m.	Lieut. P.E. CARROLL, R.A.M.C. reported for duty at this Field Ambulance. Admitted to F.d Amb 8 O.R. Discharged & evacuated 33 O.R. Remaining 78 O.R. Admitted to D.R.S. 27 O.R. Discharged & Evacuated 1 officer + 18 O.R. Remaining 3 Officers + 133 O.R. Weather overcast.	
	5.11.17		Lt Colonel HILDRETH D.S.O. having departed from this unit is struck off the strength. Admitted to the F.d Amb. 2. Transferred. Discharged & evacuated 10 O.R. Remaining 70 O.R. Admitted to the D.R.S. 3 officers. 133 O.R. Discharged & Evacuated 32 O.R. Admitted 1 officer. Remaining 1 officer, 151 O.R. Weather stormy.	
	6.11.17	7 A.m.	6 hen proceeded as reinforcements to 132 F.d Amb. + the men above returned. Admitted to F.d Amb 6. 2. O.R. Transferred. Discharged & evacuated 2 s O.R. Remaining 4 17 O.R. In the D.R.S. 1 Officer 151 O.R Remaining. Admitted 1 officer 39 O.R. Discharged & Evacuated 12 O.R. Remaining 2 Officers + 178 O.R. 1 N.C.O. + 5 hen proceeded to 132 F.d Amb. as Pushups, 1 N.C.O. + 5 air returned the name day.	L.W.

Original

Army Form C. 2118

Instructions regarding War Diaries and Intelligence Summaries are contained in F.S. Regs., Part II. and the Staff Manual respectively. Title Pages will be prepared in manuscript.

WAR DIARY
INTELLIGENCE SUMMARY
(Erase heading not required.)

134th FIELD AMBULANCE. R.A.M.C.

Place	Date	Hour	Summary of Events and Information	Remarks and references to Appendices
METEREN ts. d 3.7. Sheet 27.	7.11.17	3.15 P.M.	Proceeded to Berthen (R.22.C.4.4) to remain troops at the 39th Divisional Rhine reinforcement Camp. Having received orders from the A.D.M.S. to do this inspection.	L.W.
			Remaining in D.R.S. 2 officers, 178 O.R. Admitted 2 officers 32 O.R. discharged + evacuated 4 officers 193 O.R.	
			Admitted to Fd Amb. 2 O.R. Discharged, Transferred + evacuated 18 O.R. Remaining 31 O.R. Weather cold + wet.	
	8.11.17		Capt H.C. GOMPERTZ posted to this unit from today + attached to 132 Fd Amb for duty.	
			Admitted to Fd Amb nil. Transferred + evacuated 17 O.R. Remaining 14. O.R. In the D.R.S. Admitted 193 O.R. Admitted 29 O.R. Discharged + evacuated 38 O.R. Remaining 4 Officers 184 O.R.	
			Weather showery + cold.	
	9.11.17	9-30 A.M.	Capt L. WAY, visited I Corps reinforcement camp to medically examine reinforcements of the 39 division.	
			Two Nissen huts taken into use which have been erected today.	
			Remaining in the D.R.S. 4 Off, 195 O.R. Admitted 550 O.R. Evac to discharge 4 + 40 O.R. Admitted GOR.	
			Remaining in Fd Ambce 14 O.R.	
	6.P.M.		I handed over Command of this unit to Lieut L. Way, Capt Rawle. Colonel C.M. DREW R.A.M.C.	

Army Form C. 2118

R.A.M.C.
134th FIELD AMBULANCE

WAR DIARY
or
INTELLIGENCE SUMMARY
(Erase heading not required.)

Place	Date	Hour	Summary of Events and Information	Remarks and references to Appendices
METEREN Sheet 27 X 15 d 37	10/11/17		D.R.S. Remained 4 Officers 195 O.R. admitted 6 O.R. Evacuated & discharged 19. Remaining 4 Off. 182 O.R.	
			Fd. Ambce – Remained 16 O.R. admitted 2 O.R. Evac. discharged 3 O.R. Remaining 15 O.R.	
		2.30 p.m	Major-General FEETHAM, Commanding 39th Div. visited & inspected the D.R.S. & Fd. Ambce.	
		4 p.m.	1 N.C.O. & 20 O.R. and 2 Ford Cars proceeded to 132 Fd. Ambce for temporary duty.	
		10 p.m	Captain L.F.K. WAY proceeded to 6th CHESHIRES for temporary duty.	
	11/11/17		D.R.S. Remained 4 Off. 182 O.R. Admitted 27 O.R. Evac. & discharged 45 O.R. Remaining 4 Off. 164 O.R.	
			Fd.Ambce Remained 15 O.R. Admitted 1 Off. 2 O.R. Evacuated & discharged 8 O.R. Remaining 1 Off. 9 O.R.	
		10 a.m.	Lieut P.E. CARROLL left the unit & joined the 4th Division for duty.	
		9 p.m.	Lieut R.M. VANCE M.O, R.C. U.S.A., posted to unit & taken on strength.	
	12/11/17		D.R.S. Remained 4 Off. 164 O.R. admitted 53 O.R. Evac. & discharged 11 O.R. Remaining 4 Off. 210 O.R.	
			Fd. Ambce Remained 1 Off. 9 O.R. admitted nil. Transferred 1 O.R. Base 1 O.R. Remaining 1 Off. 7 O.R.	
		5 p.m.	Lieut C. VISGER returned to unit from temporary duty at X Corps Central Runners.	
		8.30 p.m	George Clovis, French civilian, treated in D.R.S. evacuated to 53 CCS. He had been seriously injured.	

1875 Wt. W593/826 1,000,000 4/15 J.B.C.&A. A.D.S.S./Forms/C. 2118.

Army Form C. 2118

R.A.M.C.
134th FIELD AMBULANCE

WAR DIARY or INTELLIGENCE SUMMARY
(Erase heading not required.)

Place	Date	Hour	Summary of Events and Information	Remarks and references to Appendices
METEREN Sheet 27 X 15 d 39	13/11/17		Fd Amba Admitted NIL Evac &discharged NIL. Remaining 16ff 7 OR. DRS Admitted 1 off 23 OR. Evac &discharged 16 OR. Remaining 5 off + 21 OR	
	14/11/17		Fd Ambce Admitted 1 OR. Evac 1 OR. To DRS 1 off. Remaining 7 OR. DRS Admitted 4 off 13 OR. Evac &discharged 4 off + 1 officer 20 OR. Remaining 5 off 210 OR. Seemed good covered horse lines a little outside town on BERTHEN ROAD.	
	15/11/17	9 a.m. 10 a.m. 3 p.m.	Fd Ambce Admitted 1 off Evac transferred 2 OR Remaining 16ff + 5 OR DRS Admitted 10 OR. Evac &discharged 4 off 68 OR. Remaining 1 off 152 OR. Capt C.W. McCLANAHAN, M.O., R.C., USA posted temporary to 132 Fd Amba. Proceeded to BAILLEUL & arranged re taking over site at 6 Rue BENOIT CORTYL as a D.R.S. METEREN is outside the IX Corps Area. Lt Col Cpl CM DREW, Comm't 134 F.A. assumed duties D.A./A.D.M.S. 2 D.H.Q.	
	16/11/17		Capt R.A. MacNEIL assumed duties a/o Surg. TA Rev J FURLONG CF (R.C.) attached to Field Ambce. Fd Ambce Admitted 4 OR Evac &discharged 3 OR. Remaining 1 off 4 OR DRS. Admitted 12 OR 9 1 off. Evac &discharged 7 1 OR. Remaining 2 off 93 OR.	
	19/11/17		Fd Ambce. Admitted 11 OR. Remaining 1 off 15 OR. DRS. Handed over to 50th Fd. Ambce. 91 OR. Admitted 36 OR. To dut 1 off. Remaining 1 Officer 222 OR.	

original

1 DEC 1917
134th FIELD AMBULANCE

WAR DIARY or INTELLIGENCE SUMMARY

Army Form C. 2118

134th FIELD AMBULANCE R.A.M.C.

Place	Date	Hour	Summary of Events and Information	Remarks and references to Appendices
BAILLEUL No 6 Rue BENOIT CORTYL	17/11/17	2 p.m.	Took over site at No 6 Rue BENOIT CORTYL, BAILLEUL as D.R.S. from 50th Fd. Ambce. Left holding party at METEREN	6
	18/11/17		No. 4 (Mobile) Dental Unit attached for return to billets. — 1 Off. & 7 O.R. Retaining Officers D.R.S. at METEREN. Remaining 1 Off. 15 O.R. Fd. Ambce. Admitted 2 O.R., Evac. 2 O.R. Remaining 1 Off. 15 O.R.	
	19/11/17		Retained D.R.S. Admitted 39 O.R. Evac. & discharged 31 O.R. Remaining 1 Off. 230 O.R. Fd. Ambce. Admitted 8 O.R. Evac. & discharged 2. Remaining 1 Off. 21 O.R. D.R.S. Admitted 22 O.R. Evac. & discharged 43 O.R. Remaining 1 Off. 209 O.R.	
		10 p.m.	Lt Col C. M. DREW returns to duty with unit & resumes command.	
	20/11/17		Fd. Ambce. Admitted 14 O.R. Evac. & discharged 3 O.R. Remaining 1 Off. 32 O.R. D.R.S. Admitted 22 O.R. Evac. & discharged 26. Remaining 1 Off. 205 O.R. A.D.M.S. inspected the patients & site at No. 8 Rue BENOIT CORTYL, BAILLEUL	
	21/11/17	3 p.m.	Fd. Ambce. Admitted 10 O.R. Evac. 2 O.R. Remaining 1 Off. 40 O.R. D.R.S. Admitted 30 O.R. Evac. & discharged 1 Off. 14 O.R. Remaining 218 O.R.	
		11 a.m.	D.D.M.S. IX Corps visited to-day & went round the wards. Parties of 70-80 men are attending the Cinematograph every afternoon at 2.45 p.m.	
	22/11/17		Fd. Ambce. Admitted 12 O.R. Evac. & discharged 7 O.R. Remaining 1 Off. 45 O.R. D.R.S. Admitted 36 O.R. Evac. & discharged 43 O.R. Remaining 211 O.R.	

Army Form C. 2118

WAR DIARY
or
INTELLIGENCE SUMMARY
(Erase heading not required.)

134th FIELD AMBULANCE R.A.M.C.

Place	Date	Hour	Summary of Events and Information	Remarks and references to Appendices
No 8 Rue 23/11/17 BENOIT CORTYL, BAILLEUL	23/11/17		Fd. Ambce. Admitted 7 OR. Evac. to/discharged 8 OR. Remaining 10ff/44 OR D.R.S. Admitted 22 OR. Evac to/sick 30 OR. Remaining 208 OR	
	24/11/17		Fd. Ambce. Admitted 16 OR. Evac. to/discharged 21 OR. Remaining 10ff/39 OR D.R.S. Admitted 15 OR. Evac to/discharged 48 OR. Remaining 170 OR	
		5 a.m.	Captain R.A. MacNEILL and 3 Horsed Ambulances proceeded to ABEELE to meet 117th Inf. Bde. Thereafter the Ambulances proceeded with the Brigade to its destination. 21 O.R. reinforcements from Base taken on strength to-day	
		9 a.m.	O.C. MQ's MO inspected new rest for D.R.S. at L.20.b.8.8. (HILHOEK)	
	25/11/17		Fd. Ambce. Admitted 164 9 OR. Evac/disch. 209 7 OR. Remaining 41 OR D.R.S. Admitted 104 19 OR. Evac/discharges 42 OR. Remaining 144/145 OR	
		9:30 a.m.	"C" section transport & equipment proceeded by route march to new site at HILHOEK	
		11:30 a.m.	Lieut C. VISGER & 12 OR proceeded to HILHOEK as advance party.	
HILHOEK Map 27 L.20.b.88	26/11/17		Fd. Ambce. Admitted 26 OR. Handed over to 96 FA 26 OR Remaining 41 OR D.R.S. Admitted 144 OR. Handed over to 96 FA 20 OR. Discharged 8 Remaining 1, left 261 OR	
		12 noon	Handed over site at No. 8 Rue BENOIT CORTYL, BAILLEUL to 96th Fd Ambce	
		11:45 a.m.	The Fd. Ambce less C section details required for special duties proceeded by route march for HILHOEK, Arrived there at 3 h.m. St. Jean Cappel Church was passed at 12.30 p.m. as ordered	

Army Form C. 2118

WAR DIARY or INTELLIGENCE SUMMARY

(Erase heading not required.)

Original

134th FIELD AMBULANCE

1 DEC 1917

Instructions regarding War Diaries and Intelligence Summaries are contained in F.S. Regs., Part II. and the Staff Manual respectively. Title Pages will be prepared in manuscript.

Place	Date	Hour	Summary of Events and Information	Remarks and references to Appendices
HILHOEK L20 6.88 Sheet 27	26/11/17		The patients were transferred by Ambulance car, 12 M.A.C. Cars being put at my disposal for this purpose. Altogether 140 patients were moved. The transfer began at 8.40 a.m. & was completed by noon. 101 British & 38 Colonial patients were taken over from 98 & 7th Ambce before they vacated the site.	
DRY	27/11/17		7th Ambce Admitted 38 OR & vac. recharges 7 OR Remaining 72 OR. D.R.S. Admitted 101 OR & vac. recharges 144 115 OR Remaining 14ff & 37 OR Cond	
		10 a.m.	Revd R.M. VANCE, M.O., R.C., USA proceeded to take over medical charge of 19 K.R.R.C. during absence on leave of Lieut. McELROY, M.O., R.C., USA.	
		9 p.m.	3 Ambulance Cars reported to O.C. 133 7d Ambce for temporary duty	
		2 p.m.	Capt. McCLANAHAN, M.O., R.C., USA & 46 OR returned from temporary duty with 132 7th Ambce	
WET	28/11/17		7th Ambce. Admitted 19 OR Most Evac & Transd 3 OR Regm. 85 OR	
DRY			D.R.S. 28 OR discharged to duty on recovery, 61 OR Remg. to Casualty	
		12 noon	Captain P. F.R. WAY returned to duty from on medical charge of 19 K.R.R.C.	
			All ranks employed in getting camp cleaned up, made ship-shape. Patients' comfort.	
		8.20 p.m.	Captain McCLANAHAN, M.O., R.C., USA proceeded to take over temporary medical charge of 13 Gloucesters vice Capt. A.C. MURRAY sick	

Original

Army Form C. 2118

Instructions regarding War Diaries and Intelligence Summaries are contained in F.S. Regs., Part II. and the Staff Manual respectively. Title Pages will be prepared in manuscript.

WAR DIARY or INTELLIGENCE SUMMARY
(Erase heading not required.)

R.A.M.C.
134th FIELD AMBULANCE

Place	Date	Hour	Summary of Events and Information	Remarks and references to Appendices
Hilhoek L20 c 88 Sheet 27	29/11/17		7th Ambce. Admitted 11 OR. Anvold Evac'd 4 sick and 8 OR. Remain 91 OR. D.R.S. Admitted 1 OFF 4 32 OR. Sick'd, Evac'd 4 trans of 32 OR. Remain 2 Off 104 OR.	
		9.45 a.m.	Contractors parts began repair work on road leading to Rest Station.	
DRS		3 p.m.	D.D.M.S. VIII Corps inspected the D.R.S. Began trenching low walls round huts for protection against bombs.	
			7th Ambce Admitted 1 Off /16 OR Anvold Evac'd Evac'd Sine & transf 9 OR Remain 164 OR 99 OR	
DRS	30/11/17		D.R.S. Admitted 40 OR Anvold Evac'd Sick'd & transf'd 31 OR Remain 2 Off 91 80 OR	
DRS		9.30 a.m.	Visited the A.D.M.S. at STEENVOORDE re evacuation from BEGGARS BUSH and the Prison, YPRES. Thereafter proceeded to YPRES & interviewed O.C. 7th Ambce at BEGGARS BUSH & YPRES. I arranged to send 2 A.M.C. clerks to each 7th Ambce and all sick returned attended by them are to be shown as admitted to 134 7th Ambce. Sidecars 1 N.C.O. to load as conducting N.C.O. of party of 39 Div, proceeding by ambulance tram from BEGGAR'S BUSH to POPERINGE where cars from 134 F.A. are to await arrival during the presence. In the DRS at L 20 C 68 sheet	
		4 p.m.	27 Captain R.H.C. GOMPERTZ returned to duty with the 7th Ambce.	
		4 p.m.	6 Patients evacd.	

Army Form C. 2118

WAR DIARY
or
INTELLIGENCE SUMMARY
(Erase heading not required.)

Place	Date	Hour	Summary of Events and Information	Remarks and references to Appendices

Nielles les Bleeds (Sheet 27)	30/11/17		Summary of Admissions & Discharges etc of 39th Divisional Rest Station for November 1917.
			
			Remaining on 1/11/17 159
			Admitted during Nov. 1040
			                                                    1197
			Transferred 61
			Evacuated 359
			Discharges 595
			                   1197
			Remaining 30/11/17 182
			                           1197
			
			Summary of Admissions & Discharges etc of 134th Fd Ambce during Nov. 1917.
			
			Remaining 1/11/17 56
			Admitted during Nov. 335
			                              391
			Transferred 136
			Evacuated 105
			Discharges 50
			Remaining 30/11/17 100
			                              391
			
			Andrew L Tost
			Commanding 134 Fd Ambce
			B.E.F.
				10

CONFIDENTIAL.

WAR DIARY

OF

134TH FIELD AMBULANCE,

FROM DEC 1ST 1917. TO DEC 31ST 1917.

(VOLUME 22.)

COMMITTEE FOR THE
MEDICAL HISTORY OF THE WAR

Date —1 FEB. 1918

Army Form C. 2118

134th FIELD AMBULANCE

WAR DIARY
or
INTELLIGENCE SUMMARY
(Erase heading not required.)

Place	Date	Hour	Summary of Events and Information	Remarks and references to Appendices
H.L.HOEK L.20.b.88 sheet 27	1/12/17		Fd. Amb. 10 OR Surcharges, Evac'd & transferred 21 OR Rein's 1 OM R 8 OR D.R.S. Admitted 16 OR. Evac'd Evac'd & transf'd 26 OR Remain 26/OM/YOR. Capt C.W.M^cCLANAHAN, M.O., R.C., U.S.A. returned to duty to-day from temporary duty with 13th Gloucesters. All patients, whose physical condition allowed, proceed daily for a route march under trained N.C.O.'s, to keep them as fit to proceed in Condition for return to duty. Scabies patients from the 39 Div. are now being treated at D.R.S. allotment of leave from 1/12/17 is 3 per day.	
		1 p.m.		
do.	2/12/17		Fd Amb. Admits 2 Off, 5'0. OR. Sick "Base, France". 1 OM 14 OR Rein's 20M/104 D.R.S. Admits 21 OR Evac'd Transf'd Base 24 OR Rein'g 2 OM + 164 OR Rec'd C.V.I.S.G.E.R. proceeds on leave from 3/12/17 to 17-12-17.	
		10 a.m.		
		2.30 pm	A.D.M.S. 39th Div. visited the D.R.S. The Fd Ambce in collecting such 1/6 CHESHIRES 9/4 KRRC and 12th SUSSEX at POPERINGHE & 1/5- BLACK WATCH at BRANDHOEK.	

1875 Wt. W593/826 1,000,000 4/15 J.B.C. & A. A.D.S.S./Forms/C. 2118.

WAR DIARY or INTELLIGENCE SUMMARY

Army Form C. 2118

(Erase heading not required.)

Instructions regarding War Diaries and Intelligence Summaries are contained in F.S. Regs., Part II. and the Staff Manual respectively. Title Pages will be prepared in manuscript.

134th FIELD AMBULANCE

Place	Date	Hour	Summary of Events and Information	Remarks and references to Appendices
HILHOEK 20 b 88	3/12/17		Fd. Amber admitted 1 O/R 22 O.R. Anchorages wares etc 16 O/R 23 O.R. Remain 2 O/R 123 O.R.	
			D.R.S. admitted 4 3 O.R. Drad'd Evac etc 23 O.R. Remain 2 O/R 187 O.R.	
do	4/12/17		Fd. Amber admitted 16 O/R 41 O.R. Drac'd etc 37 O.R. Remain 3 O/R 127 O.R.	
			D.R.S. admitted 14 O.R. Transit Arrels Verac 50 O.R. Remain 2 O/R 157 O.R.	
do	5/12/17		Fd. Amber admitted 1 O/R 49 O.R. Drad'd etc 2 O/R 44 O.R. Remain 2 O/R 132 O.R.	
			D.R.S. admitted 18 O.R. Drad'd etc 35 O.R. Remain 2 O/R 134 O.R.	
			Captain L.F.K. WAY began course of instruction in first-aid to men J.M.G.C.	
do	6/12/17		Fd. Amber admitted 3 O/R 94 O.R. Drad'd etc 2 O/R 94 O.R. Remain 3 O/R 132 O.R.	
			D.R.S. admitted 18 O.R. Drad'd etc 1 O/R 52 O.R. Remain 1 O/R 100 O.R.	
			The Sergeant Major & 1 N.C.O. Details to proceed as billeting party	
	8.30 p.m.		For the Fd. Amber on 7/12/17. Captain A.E. DELGADO, R.A.M.C. admitted suffering from effects of being buried by shell burst. Captain H.C. GOMPIERTZ left by car for temporary duty with 132 Fd. Amber — and. ADMS 5/40's of 6-12-17	
do	7/12/17		Fd. Amber admitted 1 O/R 73 O.R. Drad'd etc 2 O/R 59 O.R. Rem'g 2 O/R & 116 O.R	
			D.R.S. admitted 21 O.R. Dried's etc 38 O.R. Rem'g 1 O/R 83 O.R	

Army Form C. 2118

R.A.M.C.
134th FIELD AMBULANCE

WAR DIARY
or
INTELLIGENCE SUMMARY
(Erase heading not required.)

Instructions regarding War Diaries and Intelligence Summaries are contained in F. S. Regs., Part II. and the Staff Manual respectively. Title Pages will be prepared in manuscript.

Place	Date	Hour	Summary of Events and Information	Remarks and references to Appendices
HILLHOEK	7/10/17	11 a.m.	Interviewed Brigade Major 116 Inf Bgde in reference to forthcoming move.	
		4.30 p.m.	D.A.D.M.S. 33rd Div'n went round DR's in ref to taking over by a Fd. Amb. of 33rd Div.	
"	8/10/17		Fd. Ambee admitted 21 O.R. Directed etc 41 O.R. Remg 2 off & 96 O.R.	
			D.R.S. admitted 5 O.R. Directed etc 84 O.R. Remg 10 off & 54 O.R.	
		9.30 a.m.	Captain R.F.K. WAY & 20 O.R. proceeded to LUMBRES area as advance party to	
			take over site of AFFRINGUES as a D.R.S.	
		11.30 a.m.	O.C. 101 Fd. Ambee 33 Div went round D.R.S. with a view to taking	
		4 p.m.	it over.	
"	9/10/17		Orders received from 116 Bgde with ref. to move on 9th & 10th.	
			Fd. Ambee admitted 16 off & 18 O.R. Directed etc 2 off & 59 O.R. Remg 10 off & 53 OR.	
			D.R.S. admitted nil Directed etc 25 O.R. Remg 9 1 off & 29 O.R.	
		8.30 a.m.	Transport with mobilisation equipment under command of Capt.	
			C.W. McCLANAHAN set out by route march for new site at AFFRINGUES	
			They are to arrive there on the 10th.	
		11.30 a.m.	Advance party from 107 Fd. Ambee arrived & proceeded to take	
			over site at HILLHOEK.	
HILLHOEK	10/10/17		Fd. Ambee admitted nil Directed nil Remaining 10 off & 53 O.R.	
Fine			D.R.S. admitted nil Directed nil Remaining 1 off & 29 O.R.	

Army Form C. 2118

134th FIELD AMBULANCE

WAR DIARY
or
INTELLIGENCE SUMMARY
(Erase heading not required.)

Place	Date	Hour	Summary of Events and Information	Remarks and references to Appendices
HILL HOEK L.20 c.8.8. Sheet 27	10/12/17	9 a.m.	The site at HILLHOEK was completely handed over to 107 Fd. Amb. 33rd Division	
		9 a.m.	The personnel under command of Capt. R.A MACNEILL proceeded to GODEWAERSVELDE to entrain for new site at AFFRINGUES.	
		9.15 a.m.	All the patients for transfer to new site (27 all told) proceeded by cars from 20th M.A.C. to new site.	
		10 a.m.	Commanding Officer satisfied himself that all patients, personnel, stores etc. of 134 Fd Ambce were now en route for AFFRINGUES & adjud thereto.	
AFFRINGUES Sheet 5 A HAZEBROUK	10/12/17	1 p.m.	Patients arrive at LANNOY where an advance party had prepared accommodation 9 days everything possible to make the patients comfortable. The advance of 39th Div.	
		1.45 p.m.	C.O. arrives.	
		4.30 p.m.	Transport arrived all correct.	
		8 p.m.	Personnel arrived — all correct. At the chateau at LANNOY there is accommodation for about 90 patients. The personnel are billeted in AFFRINGUES — about 50 sleep in the barn of the chateau.	
AFFRINGUES	11/12/17		Fd. Amber. Received 11 OR Drafted 2 OR Evacuated — Deaths etc 2 OR Remains 101/527 OR	
			D.R.S. Admitted nil Drafted etc 2 OR	

WAR DIARY or INTELLIGENCE SUMMARY

Army Form C. 2118

134th FIELD AMBULANCE

Place	Date	Hour	Summary of Events and Information	Remarks and references to Appendices
AFFRINGUES	11/12/17	9 a.m.	Captain P.F.K. WAY proceeded to interview Area Commandant with a view to obtaining further accommodation. He returned with report that none is available.	
		10.30 a.m.	A.D.M.S. visited the D.R.S's and inspected the arrangements.	
		12.45 p.m.	D.O.C. visited the D.R.S.	
			The personnel were engaged all day in cleaning up, fixing latrines, etc. A good deal of work is required on the site in the way of repairs to the building, whitewashing the wallgele. The accommodation is limited to about 90 patients. As the D.R.S. is to accommodate 200 patients (up as up is the present if it were possible to ensure anything available application for including scabies cases) I have therefore submitted an application for 5 marquees. I asked that the same may be expedited. Wood & R.E. material generally is required for making of ablution places, bath houses & other annexes of a D.R.S. Tables, chairs etc have been indented for (Red Cross Hive) A.D.M.S. applied to for stores.	
"	12/1/17		7th Amber. arriving from R.of R. Gradt a/c B.R. Bent 8 13/1/17 × D.R.S. Abucus 13R Read 14/12 Read 14/1/17 ×	
		3 p.m.	Captain C.W. McCLANAHAN, M.O., R.C., U.S.A., proceeded on leave to Paris from 13/12/17 to 17/12/17 - Auth. 8th Corps A.L. 1250 of 8/12/17 a/c of H.A.Q.M.S. A 210 of 9/12/17.	
			All the personnel were occupied on fatigues in cleaning up all O.D.R.S. Patients nursed out of T.R.C. & A. A.D.S.S./Forms/C.2118. Branch under their own N.C.O.'s. Bearer & th C Section on route march afternoon. Returned having begun.	

Army Form C. 2118

WAR DIARY or INTELLIGENCE SUMMARY

(Erase heading not required.)

134th FIELD AMBULANCE

Place	Date	Hour	Summary of Events and Information	Remarks and references to Appendices
AFFRINGUES	13/12/17		7t Ambce. 1st Autd B OR Bracklesh 1st ff/15 OR Rem S 41 OR	
			D.R.S. Admitted OR Brecold 1st M Escort Rem 4 11 OR	
		1.15 p.m.	S.O.C. 39th Div inspected D.R.S.	
			Personnel employed on fatigues.	
		2.30 p.m.	Football match between B & C Sections.	
	14/12/17		7t Ambce Admitted 6 OR Discharge 2.3 OR Rem 7 to OR	
			D.R.S. Admitted 30 OR Dischard 8 OR Escort 8 35 OR	
		12 noon	D.D.M.S. X Corps inspected the D.R.S.	
		9.0 a.m.	Capt A.F.K. MAY proceeded to 14th F.A. on temp duty	
	15/12/17		7t Ambce Admitted 11 OR Discharged 9 R Rem 9 0R (Rem 9 31 OR	
			D.R.S. Admitted 9 OR (Disch) 486 Escort 25 OR	
		13 noon	Red Cross Cinema shown states arrived - Men had been much appreciated	
			W.O. R N 7.013/17 J Jaskson will confirmed	
			7th Ambce Admitted 15 OR Disch 9 OR Rem 9 37 OR	
			D.R.S. Admitted 5 OR Evacuated 5 OR Rem 6 4 6 OR	
	16/12/17		7t Ambce Admitted 15 OR Evacuated 16 OR Rem 5 46 OR	
			Admitted 20 OR Rem 3 45 OR	

WAR DIARY
or
INTELLIGENCE SUMMARY

(Erase heading not required.)

Army Form C. 2118

Place	Date	Hour	Summary of Events and Information	Remarks and references to Appendices
WIMEREUX	18/9/17	9 am	Pte. Rubin. Admitted 1 Off. 8 O.R. Bricknapes evacuated, transferred 1 Off. 5 O.R. Remaining 51 O.R.	
do.		6 pm	Lt. C. Visager & Capt. C.M. McClaughlan to Dr. Rickards & Capt. C.M. McClaughlan transferred. 9 O.R. Remaining 41 O.R. Sick. Ambl. admitted 11 O.R. Bricknapes evac. transport 9 O.R. Remaining 53 O.R. 7 O.R. " " " " 9 O.R. " 39 O.R.	
			D.R.S. Lt. Col. C.M. Breen proceeded on leave to U.K. Capt. R.A. Macneile took over temporary command of unit. Attended conference at A.D.M.S. office. Lt. to M/Car. Capt. R.H.C. Gompertz transferred to 132 Fd. Amb. 134 Fd. Amb. evac. 22 8 M.G. C in Football competition 2-1. Fd. Amb. admitted 10 O.R. Bricknapes evac. & transferred 7 O.R. Remaining 52 O.R. D.R.S. Evac. 1 O.R. Bricknapes & D.R.C. - 30 O.R.	
do.	21/9/17	9 am	Fd. Amb. 1 Off. 26 O.R. Hosp. & Evac. Transport - 1 Off. 26 O.R. Rem'g. 8 D.R. 19 O.R. - 41 O.R.	
do.	22/9/17	6.30 pm 12.30 am	Fd. Amb. admitted - 16 O.R. Bricknapes . 16 O.R. Remaining 36 O.R. D.R.S. - 4 O.R. 9 O.R. 36 O.R. L Beng. S. visited 8-5. 11.15 a.m.	
do.	23/9/17		Fd. Amb. admitted 12 O.R. Bricknapes " 16 O.R. Remaining 52 O.R. 7 O.R. 2 O.R. 27 O.R. 12th Fd. Amb. Sent to No.2 Coy. 13 or 9-10 Cdn. 2 - 4 - D.R.S.	
do.	24/9/17	1 pm	Fd. Amb. admitted 12 O.R. Bricknapes ev. 7 O.R. Remaining 55 O.R. D.R.S. 6 O.R. - 6 O.R. 29 O.R.	

Army Form C. 2118

134th FIELD AMBULANCE

WAR DIARY or **INTELLIGENCE SUMMARY**

(Erase heading not required.)

Instructions regarding War Diaries and Intelligence Summaries are contained in F.S. Regs., Part II. and the Staff Manual respectively. Title Pages will be prepared in manuscript.

Place	Date	Hour	Summary of Events and Information	Remarks and references to Appendices
AFFRINGUES	25/12/17	7.30 a.m.	A.D.M.S. orders to hold transport & tent subdivision ready to move at early hour on 26th. Christmas dinner to patients & personnel. Fd. Amb. detailed 2 Off. 9 O.R. Discharges from & Camps 2 Off/ 15 O.R. Remaining 49 O.R.	
"			D.R.S. admitted — nil. Sick: 2 O.R. Transport to move with 139 Fd. Amb. on 26th. Remaining 27 O.R.	
Post at Snow	26/12/17	2 p.m.	Owing to bad roads — snow — the convt. transport 8/133 Fd.Amb. did not arrive till 6 p.m. Motor lorries (2) sent to assist in AFFRINGUES	
			Fd. Amb. admitted 10 O. 20 O.R. Sick: and. 1 Off. 29 O.R. Remaining 40 O.R. D.R.S. " nil 16 O.R. " 11 O.R.	
"	27/12/17	9 a.m.	Transport moved at 9 a.m. Roads bad especially on ST MOMELIN — LAURE 7½ m. Remaining transport has to move via composition 2 S " road. Fd.Amb. admitted 2 Off. — 38 O.R. Sick: Enve: 2 Off. 16 O.R. Remaining 62 O.R. D.R.S. " 1 O.R. " 2 O.R. " 13 O.R.	
			Capt. C.W. McCLANAHAN M.O.R.C. U.S.A. + 17 O.R. proceeded in advance party to GWALIA FARM (Sheet 28 A-23-c-2-9) to take over site from 91st Fd. Amb. Remainder of transport (less Limber G.S.) to move with 117 Bde. transport.	
"	28/12/17	1 p.m.	Lt. E. VISSER R.A.M.C. evacuated to N.Z. S.H. — INFLUENZA Fd. Amb. admitted 2 Off. 32 O.R. Sick: Enve: 2 Off. 32 O.R. Remaining 63 O.R. D.R.S. " 7 O.R. " 3 O.R. " 15 O.R. 133 Fd. Amb. billeted in AFFRINGUES.	

1875 Wt. W593/826 1,000,000 4/15 J.B.C. & A. A.D.S.S./Forms/C.2118.

WAR DIARY or INTELLIGENCE SUMMARY

Army Form C. 2118

(Erase heading not required.)

Instructions regarding War Diaries and Intelligence Summaries are contained in F.S. Regs., Part II. and the Staff Manual respectively. Title Pages will be prepared in manuscript.

Place	Date	Hour	Summary of Events and Information	Remarks and references to Appendices
AFFRINGUES	29/4/15		Personnel of Fd. Amb. moved at 6 a.m. to entrain at WIZERNES. 1 B.S. Soldier with the Patients (72) moved by car to 37 M.A.C. by road to GWALIA FARM in charge of Lt. A. BROWN 13th Fd. Amb. O/C & officers moved tents at 11.15 a.m. No hotering party left behind. Capt. C.D. COPPE R.A.M.C. attached for temporary duty.	
GWALIA FARM Sheet 28. A-23-c-2-9.			Relief of 91st Fd. Amb. complete at 12 noon. A.D.M.S. visited Amb. at 9 a.m.	
		5 pm	Personnel moved 8 p.m. all present moved. Fd. Amb. Strength was on May 21st Fd. Amb. 114 O.R. Divisional Train 1 Off. 37 O.R. Supply Train 1 Off. 23 O.R. Remaining 130 O.R. Fd. Amb. 15 O.R. Remaining sick.	
do.		9.30 am	D.R.S. admitted — nil	
			D.R.S. works closed	
			Advanced transport arrived 9 p.m. Afternoon Huts / small Nissen 1 large farm. Transport Fd Amb ente- 2 Adrian Huts / small Nissen 1 large farm. GWALIA FARM accommodation 164 normal — expected 200. B.A.M.S. II Corps gave sanctioning to O/C 91st Fd. Amb. to transfer large Nissen Hut from 32 CCS to GWALIA FARM. Southern's rendered over to 13th Fd. Amb.	
	30/4/15		Visited C.M.P.S. 11.30 a.m. 1 Off. (Lt. FARRELL 133 Fd Amb) + 30 O.R. sent to C.M.P.S. for duty 3.30 p.m. visited 133 Fd Amb. at DUNALLOW.	
From. Art. Bde		7.30 pm	Patients transport arrived 6 a.m. to duty off + tempe times massive Fd Amb admitted 28 O.R. Free & discharged to 80 O.R. Remaining 98 O.R.	

Army Form C. 2118

134th FIELD AMBULANCE

WAR DIARY
or
INTELLIGENCE SUMMARY
(Erase heading not required.)

Instructions regarding War Diaries and Intelligence Summaries are contained in F.S. Regs., Part II. and the Staff Manual respectively. Title Pages will be prepared in manuscript.

Place	Date	Hour	Summary of Events and Information	Remarks and references to Appendices
GWALIA FARM Sht.28. A 23.c.2.9. Ypt.	31/12/17	8 p.m.	B.D.R. proceeded to 132 Fd. Amb. with 6 O.R. Pts — to inform Rev.d G. Annow Minister to the attached there Rev.d Yates (Honorary) in neighbourhood.	
		9.15 p.m. to 1.30 p.m.	No damage or casualties in camp. One Stratcher wounded O.R. admitted.	
		9 p.m.	Lieut. C.P. COYLE R.A.M.C. proceeded to 132 Fd. Amb. for temporary duty. 5 O.R. transferred to it. Pt. Amb. attached. 5 2 O.R. Hosptl Evac. vc. v.30R. Remaining 107.	

During the month the Fd. Ambulance has been running as 39th D.R.S. until Dec. 29 when it was sent. All cases/cases were sent on to C.C.Ss. Numbers of patients treated during the month:—

British Sick & Trench feet.
Reward admissions.
Fd. Amb. 100 – 264   260 – 251 – 345 : 1 Permissions Total
D.R.S. 182 – 260   247 – 86 – 109 it. 107 – 964 vit. – 442

Weather fine cold.

P.B.Warwick Capt R.A.M.C.
a/O.C. 134 Fd Amb.

ORIGINAL

CONFIDENTIAL

WAR DIARY

OF

134 FIELD AMBULANCE

from Jan. 1st to Jan. 31st, 1918.

(VOLUME 23).

Original

WAR DIARY or **INTELLIGENCE SUMMARY**
(Erase heading not required.)

Army Form C. 2118

134th FIELD AMBULANCE R.A.M.C.

Instructions regarding War Diaries and Intelligence Summaries are contained in F.S. Regs., Part II. and the Staff Manual respectively. Title Pages will be prepared in manuscript.

Place	Date	Hour	Summary of Events and Information	Remarks and references to Appendices
WALIA FARM. Sh.4.28. V.23.c.2.9. Ref.	1/1/18.	7 p.m.	67 Cases Evacuated 6 133 Fd. Amb. To Antwp. 12.30 p.m. (Remaining 31/12/17 - 107 O.R.) Fd. Amb. admitted 1 Off. 37 O.R. Disch'd re. 1 Off. 63 O.R. 79 O.R. Remaining 92 O.R.	
do.	2/1/18.	6 p.m.	Fd. Amb. admitted - 43 O.R. Discharged re. 32 O.R. Remaining 92 O.R. Weather fine - extr. frosty. 6 O.R. evacuated to 133 Fd. Amb. for entry in Hosneux - 81 O.R. in all	
do.	3/1/18.	6 p.m.	now with 133 Fd. Amb. Fd. Amb. admitted. 3 Off. 32 O.R. Transferred from II C.M.D.S. 18 O.R. Disch'd re. 1 Off. 48 O.R. Rem.T 2 Off. 94 O.R. Weather fine, cold. Light fall of snow in morning. Under instruction of D.D.M.S. II Corps attempt + D.M.S. 39th Div.	
do.	4/1/18	8 a.m.	8 O.R. from 132 Fd. Amb. 8 O.R. from 134 Fd. Amb. will help 3 15 O.R. from 3 C.C.S. started work as 3 c.C.S. in dismantling + removing to Hospital Nissen huts To re-erection at GWALIA FARM. Lt. Col. C.M. DREW returned from leave & assumed command of unit. Fd. Amb. admitted. 2 Off. 19 O.R. Transfer from II C.M.D.S. 24 O.R. Discharged re. 2 Off. 30 O.R. Remaining. 2 Off. - 107 O.R. Weather fine cold.	

Original 2

Army Form C. 2118

WAR DIARY
or
INTELLIGENCE SUMMARY
(Erase heading not required.)

134th FIELD AMBULANCE R.A.M.C.

Instructions regarding War Diaries and Intelligence Summaries are contained in F.S. Regs., Part II. and the Staff Manual respectively. Title Pages will be prepared in manuscript.

Place	Date	Hour	Summary of Events and Information	Remarks and references to Appendices
WALIA FARM	5/1/18		Fd. Ambce Admitted 146 O.R. Arrich'd etc 44	Remaining 2 Off 149 OR.
	6/1/18	2.30 p.m. 3 p.m.	D.D.M.S. II Corps inspected the Hospital. Visited D.H.Q.A.D.Q.A. and saw bearers of the Ambulance. Fd. Ambce Adm'd 1 Off 39 OR Arch's etc 3 Off 36 OR	Rem's 112 OR
	7/1/18	11.15 a.m.	A.D.M.S. 39th Div inspected the hospital and made suggestions as to improvements. Fd. Ambce Adm'd 61 OR Arich'd etc 64 OR	Rem'g 109 OR
		9.30 p.m.	Capt C.D. COYLE, R.A.M.C., 132 Fd Ambce reported for duty and is taken on the strength of 134 Fd Ambce (Auth. A.D.M.S. 5/826 9/7-1-18.	
	8/1/18		Fd. Ambce Adm'd 1 Off 33 OR Dische's etc 1 Off 37 OR	Rem'g 105 OR
	9/1/18		Fd. Ambce Adm'd 48 OR Arich'd etc 25 OR	Rem'g 128 OR
	10/1/18		Fd. Ambce Adm'd 10ff 90 OR. Arch's etc 1 Off 77 OR Lieut C.S. VISGER R.A.M.C. is struck of strength of unit to day – evacuated sick – auth. A.D.M.S. 5/929 9/10-1-18	Rem'g 121 OR

WAR DIARY
INTELLIGENCE SUMMARY

Army Form C. 2118

134th FIELD AMBULANCE

Place	Date	Hour	Summary of Events and Information	Remarks and references to Appendices
GWALIA FARM	11/1/18	2.30 p.m	Fd Ambce admitted 16M 56 OR. Brack'd etc 10M 57 OR. Remg 120 OR. D.D.M.S. II Corps visited Hospital	
	12/1/18	2.15 p.m	Fd Ambce admitted 52 OR. Brack'd at 38 OR. Remg 134 OR. A.D.M.S. 39th Div visited Hospital. Lieut W. MICHEL M.O, R.C, U.S.A., & Lieut W. J. DALY, M.O, R.C, U.S.A taken on strength & sent to duty. Capt. R.F.K. WAY struck off strength & sent down to 3-day Fd Ambce admitted 55 OR. Brack'd 29 OR. Remg 159 OR.	
	13/1/18		Lieut W. H. HOWELL, M.O, R.C, U.S.A taken on strength & sent to duty. Lieut NOWISLL proceeded to II C.M.D.S for duty to-day. Capt C.D. COYLE & Capt C.W. MCCLANAHAN (U.S.A) proceeded to C.M.D.S for temporary duty.	
	14/1/18		Fd Ambce admitted 1 OM 53 OR. Brack'd 16M 580 R. Remg 1374 OR. Warning notice received from A.D.M.S. to be prepared to move South	

Original 4

Army Form C. 2118

WAR DIARY
or
INTELLIGENCE SUMMARY
(Erase heading not required.)

134th FIELD AMBULANCE

Instructions regarding War Diaries and Intelligence Summaries are contained in F.S. Regs., Part II. and the Staff Manual respectively. Title Pages will be prepared in manuscript.

Place	Date	Hour	Summary of Events and Information	Remarks and references to Appendices
GWALIA FARM	15/1/18		Ft Ambce admittes 3 OR Dischd etc 62 OR. Remaining 146 OR	
	16/1/18		Ft Ambce admitted 2 OR 84 OR. Dischd etc 2 OR 102 OR. Remg 128 OR. Arranged with new Commanding for about 1 acre to be cultivated. There are also several small plots between the huts which are available for cultivation. Began fencing etc	
	17/1/18		Ft Ambce Admittes 1 OR 119 OR Dischd etc 1 OR 62 OR Remg 185 OR. Orders received from A.D.M.S. to withdraw bed section from II Corps Main Dressing Station.	
		2.30 p.m.	A.D.M.S. inspected dental cases. Heavy snow and rain which impeded and delayed work.	
	18/1/18		Ft Ambce Admitted 2 OR 79 OR Trans of from CMDS. 24 OR. Taken over from 2/2 H.C.F.A 19 OR Dischd etc. 2 OR 76 OR Remg 231 OR	
		10-15 a	Captain C. B. COYLE and bed section from II Corps M.D.S reported for duty.	
		2 p.m.	Tent Section under command of Capt. C. D. COYLE proceeded to PROVEN to take over PROVEN School from the 1/2 Home Counties Ft. Ambce and function same. Lieut B.M. VANCE MORC USA so struck off strength of unit as from Hospital Nissen Hut completed taken into use from to-day	
	13/12/19			

Original 5

Army Form C. 2118
R.A.M.C.
1: 134th FIELD AMBULANCE

WAR DIARY
or
INTELLIGENCE SUMMARY
(Erase heading not required.)

Instructions regarding War Diaries and Intelligence Summaries are contained in F. S. Regs., Part II. and the Staff Manual respectively. Title Pages will be prepared in manuscript.

Place	Date	Hour	Summary of Events and Information	Remarks and references to Appendices
GWALIA FARM	19/1/18		Fd. Ambce. Admitted 16H 66 OR. Oracles etc 1 Off 74 OR. Remg 223 OR	
		9.30 a.m.	Examined & classified all ranks of N.T. 977.T. A.S.C. att'd to the Fd. Ambce.	
		5 p.m.	Lieut DALY M.O., R.C., U.S.A. proceeded to PROVEN school for duty, his Sanj. Dispenser also sent.	
		7 p.m.	Orders received for move of Ambce to PROVEN School on 21/1/18	
	20/1/18		Fd. Ambce. Admitted 3 Off & 9 OR. Transf'd from CMDS 9 OR. Dischd etc 3 M 62 OR. Remg 221 OR	
		9 a.m.	Capt. C.W. McCLANAHAN M.O., R.C., U.S.A. and Staff Sergeant CLEGG left to join II Corps Gas Course at MILLAIN	
	21/1/18		Fd. Ambce. Admitted 9 OR. Transf'd from CMDS md Dischd 6 OR. Handed over to 91st FA Y 6 OR. Remg 46 OR	
		12.15 p.m.	Fd. Ambce Bearer personnel detailed for special duty proceeded by route march to PROVEN.	
		12 noon	Musical Maidrhoina handed over to 91st Fd. Ambce. All extra-divisional parties reported unit.	
PROVEN		3 p.m.	Fd. Ambce arrived at PROVEN & proceeded to function the hospital Fd. Ambce.	
	22			

Original 6

WAR DIARY or INTELLIGENCE SUMMARY

Army Form C. 2118

134th FIELD AMBULANCE

Place	Date	Hour	Summary of Events and Information	Remarks and references to Appendices
PROVEN	22/1/18		Fd. Ambce Admits 1 Off 19 OR Arach's 1 Off 19 OR Remaining 46 OR. All the personnel employed to II Corps M.D.S. reported unit to-day. All N.C.O's N.C.O's been re-classified according to S.R.O. g 19.1.17. 9 Sunbeam Cars under Sgt Nesthefser proceeded to new location. Fd. Ambce Admits 33 OR Arach'd 79 OR Rem'g 8 orl	
	23/1/18	12 noon	A.D.M.S. visited.	
	24/1/18		Fd. Ambce Admits 36 OR. Transf'd to CRS 36 OR	
		8 a.m	1 Sunbeam & 2 Ford Cars reported A.D.M.S. 8 a.m in accordance with orders. Orders from Brigade received. Fd Ambce is moving to a new area under orders of 117 Bde. Named van Haepcot or School, PROVEN to holding parts of 90th Fd. Ambce. Patients sent to II C.R.S.	
	25/1/18	10 a.m	Transport arrived at PROVEN station & proceeded to entrain for MERICOURT L'ABBÉ.	
		2 p.m	Personnel arrived at station	
		4:30 pm	Entraining completed	
		4:40 pm	Train left PROVEN for MERICOURT L'ABBÉ	

Original 7

Army Form C. 2118
R.A.M.C.
134th FIELD AMBULANCE.

WAR DIARY
or
INTELLIGENCE SUMMARY
(Erase heading not required.)

Place	Date	Hour	Summary of Events and Information	Remarks and references to Appendices
On train from PROVEN to MERICOURT	25/1/18		Train journey completed without incident.	
		3.15 p.m	Train arrived MERICOURT L'ABBE. Met by guide.	
		4.15 p.m	Personnel marched M.T. sets for Fd. Ambce at SUZANNE — march 7½ Kilometres	
SUZANNE (AMIENS Sheet)		9 p.m	Personnel arrived	
		9.30 p.m	Transport arrived	
	26/1/18		Fd. Ambce. Admitted 19 O.R. Brsd 2 O.R. Rem'g 15 O.R. Proceeded to get site ready for reception of patients — 11.30 to CHARLET, patients in a hut; personnel in huts; stabling 8 vans.	
	27/1/18		Fd. Ambce. Admitted 14 O.R. Bvac'd 3 O.R. Rem'g 26 O.R.	
		9 a.m	Visited new location at HEUDECOURT and went round A.D.S. of 28th Fd. Ambce 9th Div Dvn whom I have to take over evacuation of the line held by 39 to Div Transport to DRS 34 OR	
	28/1/18		Fd. Ambce Admitted 14 O.R. Bvac'd etc 6 O.R. Transf to DRS 34 OR Rem'g 8 — nil.	
		9 a.m	Routes of Fd. Ambce closed	
		9 a.m	Captain C.D. COYLE & 2 O.R. proceeded to new location to take over Captain McNeill & 1 N.C.O proceeded as billeting parts to MONSLAINS.	

Original 8.

Army Form C. 2118

WAR DIARY
or
INTELLIGENCE SUMMARY

(Erase heading not required.)

134th FIELD AMBULANCE

Place	Date	Hour	Summary of Events and Information	Remarks and references to Appendices
SUZANNE	29/1/18	5-15 a.m.	Personnel moved off to rehearse at The PLATEAU near MARICOURT under Command of Lieut. W. H. DALY.	
		9.45 a.m.	Transport moved off by route march to new location	
		1.30 p.m.	Vacated the Chateau at SUZANNE & proceeded to HEUDECOURT.	
		3.30 p.m.	Evacuation of line. Arrived HEUDECOURT & thereafter visited REVELON FARM A.D.S. The Personnel & Transport spent the night at MOISLAINS (Sheet AMIENS) Advance party in occupation of A.D.S. at QUEEN's CROSS & REVELON FARM.	
HEUDECOURT Sheet 57C W.21.6.28	30/1/18	9.15 a.m.	Proceeded with O.C. 65th Fd. Ambce. to visit R.A.P.'s on right sector & Bearer posts.	
		11.30 a.m.	Personnel arrived – having come by railway from MOISLAINS.	
		2 p.m.	Transport arrived – having come by route march from MOISLAINS.	
		2.30 p.m.	A.D.M.S. visited & inspected A.D.S. at REVELON FARM.	
		Afternoon	Visited R.A.P.'s evacuating on REVELON FARM for middle hand & line. Captain R.A. MACNEILL visited A.D.S. at QUEEN's CROSS and Bearer posts in front thereof. Captain C.D. COYLE made complete reconnaissance of left sector & made complete reconnaissance of right sector.	
		4 p.m.	Posts taken over & manned by men of 134 Fd. Ambce. Relief completed. Wired A.D.M.S. 39th Div., 9th Div. & 21st Div. to this effect	

Army Form C. 2118

134th FIELD AMBULANCE

WAR DIARY
or
INTELLIGENCE SUMMARY
(Erase heading not required.)

Place	Date	Hour	Summary of Events and Information	Remarks and references to Appendices
HEUDECOURT	31/1/18		Fd Ambce now established with Headquarters at HEUDECOURT and running evacuation of line to be held by 39th Div. with a 2-Brigade front. Detailed report of situation of posts, evacuation arrangements &c. will be put in Diary to-morrow. Captain C.W. McCLANAHAN, M.O., R.C, USA & Staff Sergt. CLEGG reported from II Corps Gas Course. Captain J.H. PORTER reported and from duty with A.D.M.S. Captain C.D. COYLE in charge of medical arrangements Left Sector. Visited Trench foot Centre at HEUDECOURT, Area Commandant	
		6 p.m	Lieut DALY M.O, RC, USA & 26 men proceeded for duty with VII Corps Rest Station. Environs of HEUDECOURT heavily bombed by aircraft on night of 30-31st.	
				Andrews Lt Col Comdg 134 Fd Ambce 31/1/18

CONFIDENTIAL

WAR DIARY.

OF

134TH FIELD AMBULANCE

FROM 1ST FEB. 1918. TO 28TH FEB. 1918.

(VOLUME 24.)

Army Form C. 2118
R.A.M.C.
134th FIELD AMBULANCE

WAR DIARY
or
INTELLIGENCE SUMMARY
(Erase heading not required.)

Instructions regarding War Diaries and Intelligence Summaries are contained in F.S. Regs., Part II. and the Staff Manual respectively. Title Pages will be prepared in manuscript.

Place	Date	Hour	Summary of Events and Information	Remarks and references to Appendices
HEUDECOURT MAP 57c W21 & 82	1/2/18		134 Fd. Ambce is now evacuating line on a 6 battalion front. The scheme of evacuation is detailed in Appendix I. and shown on Sketch Map Appendix II. 2 S.S. Wagons from 132 Fd. Ambce & 2 from 133 Fd. Ambce taken on return strength of Fd. Ambce. These wegons with 2 from 134 Fd. Ambce are for duty with 148 Travelling Coy. Ford Car from 132 Fd. Ambce attached for duty.	Appendix I. Appendix II.
	2/2/18		Ford Car from 133 Fd. Ambce attached for duty. Visited A.D.S. at REVELON FARM and reconnoitred Decauville tracks converging on this point with a view to using them for evacuation purposes. 3 O.R. 132 Fd. Ambce attached for duty.	
	3/2/18		Visited all posts on left of line converging on QUEEN'S CROSS A.D.S. Found everything in order & personnel with knowledge of their duties. Following constructional work is being carried out at HEUDECOURT — building 2 dug-outs for shelter, repairing roads, building protection to entrance against bombing at A.D.S. REVELON FARM — shelter & protection from gas to ??(Fd.Ambce) A.D.S. QUEEN'S CROSS — 6th Divnl Pioneer work in hutments.	
	4/2/18	2.30 pm	Visited personnel at MOISLAINS (Corps Rest Station) who has visited posts on left of line this day. Thereafter interviewed A.D.M.S.	

Army Form C. 2118

134th FIELD AMBULANCE

WAR DIARY or **INTELLIGENCE SUMMARY**

(Erase heading not required.)

Place	Date	Hour	Summary of Events and Information	Remarks and references to Appendices
HEUDICOURT W21 b82 Map 57C	5/2/18		Constructional work at Headquarters and A.D.S.'s is being pushed forward. Interviewed Area Commandant with reference to selecting site of Dressing Station in event of HEUDICOURT being attacked. REVELON FARM A.D.S. is but 24 hours. 1 wounded & 8 sick passed thro' A.D.S. at QUEEN'S CROSS. Returned Ford Car to 133 F.A. 13 wounded & 4 sick treated at W19 & S2 is now completed. Car stand at W19 & S2. The Trench foot rooms are being fully taken advantage of by units of the Division.	
	6/2/18		Visited A.D.S. at REVELON FARM. Found constructional work going on and arrangements for evacuation working smoothly. Sick & C.M.D.S. from REVELON FARM 1 wounded 9 sick QUEEN'S CROSS 1 " 4 sick	
		7 p.m.	Elephant structure at REVELON FARM reported as erected. Reconnoitred roads from HEUDICOURT to NURLU – roads via LIERAMONT and FINS are the 2 best for transport. There are several cross country tracks. Captain C.W. McCLANAHAN M.O. R.C. U.S.A. relieves Lieut W.H. HOWELL at QUEEN'S X A.D.S. The latter then returned to 1st Q.rs for duty.	
	7/2/18		Interviewed Area Commandant re selecting a site for an R.A.P. should necessity arise in accordance with defence scheme. Inspected catacombs of HEUDICOURT and arranged that R.A.P. should be established there. Personnel 9/132 Fd Amber returned to their unit. 1 NCO & 29 O.R. 9/133 Fd Ambce returned to their unit. Completed dug-out behind the Camp.	

WAR DIARY
or
INTELLIGENCE SUMMARY
(Erase heading not required.)

Army Form C. 2118

Place	Date	Hour	Summary of Events and Information	Remarks and references to Appendices
HEUDICOURT W21 6 82 map 57C	8/2/18		Visited all posts on left of line with Capt. COYLE. 6th CHESHIRES are in line with RAP at R31 C 9 6 and there is no M.O. at RAP at R19 d 15. I have left the 4 RAMC bearers here to bring out cases that may come there via Relay Post "A". An N.C.O. is in charge. Selected site in GOUZEAUCOURT village as RAP for defence scheme. Reported this YVEDICOURT site to ADMS. Enemy shelled the immediate front of the Fd. Ambce. site & 20 casualties were evacuated. 3 men were killed – all belonged to 9th (Pioneer) Bn. Seaforth Hrs. Two men are on fire guard at night. All sleep in protected structures.	3
	9/2/18		Visited site of emergency RAP in HEUDICOURT and arranged with R.E. Officer to have a slide made for raising & lowering stretchers. Took over B.B. 117th Bde in relation to medical arrangements for Divisional Reserve. 46092 Pte W. KIRKHAM awarded Belgian Croix de Guerre (Ault m.S./H/4591 dated 27/1/18 and A.D.M.S. 1st Army No. F.D./12) Am. S. dated 30/1/18.) Wrote ADMS suggesting that the wagons used for Tunnelling Coy should be stabled at 132 Fd. Ambce. 15 men sent to each of the RDS's in relief of those in occupation. On return they are to return to H.Q.	
	10/2/18		46092 Pte S.W. KIRKHAM awarded Belgian Croix de Guerre (Ault – m.S./H/4591 dated 27/1/18. ADMS 1st Army No F.D./12/AMS dated 30/1/18.	

WAR DIARY or INTELLIGENCE SUMMARY

Army Form C. 2118

134th FIELD AMBULANCE R.A.M.C.

Place	Date	Hour	Summary of Events and Information	Remarks and references to Appendices
HEUDICOURT W.21.b.82 Map 57C	11/2/18		Visited A.D.S. at REVELON FARM and there met A.D.M.S. who made inspection of the line on the R.S. and inspected Headquarters 97th Amb in the afternoon. A.D.M.S. ordered that a post should be established at W.16.d.91 in a cellar so as to be ready for future requirements. Arranged with area Commandant for the place to be allotted to R.A.M.C. and wrote Engineers for a report as to what would be required to be done. A.D.M.S. ordered REVELON FARM to be maintained as an A.D.S. in the meantime. He also considered that cars should go further up the road to the R.A.P. at W.18.d.82. This has been arranged between O.C. A.D.S. and M.O. at the R.A.P.	
	12/2/18	3 p.m.	Visited A.D.S. to arrange about expected evacuations arising from a working party of 1/2 either bearers were sent out to strengthen the posts. The dugout at REVELON FARM is now completed. If this place is shelled the men will take refuge in the elephant and in a trench beside the farm. Another elephant is to be buried for personnel. No casualties occurred on R. Sector during night of 12-13 Feb. A.S.C. are engaged in digging trenches in their hut + building protection which as protection against bombing. Have secured some dug-outs close to 1ˢᵗ C.P. for personnel.	
	13/2/18	10 a.m.	Lieut W.H. HOWELL, M.O., R.C. U.S.A. relieved Capt. C.W. McCLANAHAN N.O., R.C. U.S.A. at QUEEN'S CROSS who returned to 1ˢᵗ Q⁽ᵈ⁾. R.E. report that they cannot spare anyone for work on proposed dressing station as they are employed on ……… Have asked for estimate of amount of men's labour to complete the work of material of ?	

Army Form C. 2118

R.A.M.O.
134th FIELD AMBULANCE
5.

WAR DIARY
or
INTELLIGENCE SUMMARY
(Erase heading not required.)

Army Form C. 2118

Instructions regarding War Diaries and Intelligence Summaries are contained in F. S. Regs., Part II. and the Staff Manual respectively. Title Pages will be prepared in manuscript.

Place	Date	Hour	Summary of Events and Information	Remarks and references to Appendices
HEUDICOURT W.21.b.82 Map 57c	13/2/18	2 p.m.	Lieut W. J. DALY, M.O., R.C., U.S.A. reported at H.Q'rs for duty from Corps Rest Station. Capt. C. W. McCLANAHAN, M.O., R.C., U.S.A., proceeded for duty to C.R.S.	
	14/2/18	10.30 a.m.	Attended conference at office of A.D.M.S. 39th Div.	
		2.30 p.m.	Capt'n R. A. MACNEILL went round part of the right sector.	
		2"	Reconnoitred FINS-GOUZEAUCOURT Road to find site for lorry stand. Also reconnoitred Reauville Trench in this neighbourhood with a view to utilizing them for evacuation of wounded. Sent report to A.D.M.S.	
	15/2/18	9.30 a.m.	Lieut W.J.DALY, M.O., R.C., U.S.A., posted for duty to A.D.S. REVELON FARM vice Lieut W. MICHEL, M.O., R.C., U.S.A., moved to 118th Rifle Brigade for temporary duty during absence on leave of Lieut BOGART, M.O., R.C., U.S.A..	
		10.30 a.m.	Inspected manure dump at HEUDICOURT & reported to Area Commandant necessity for having manure stacked in accordance with orders.	
		5.30 p.m.	Visited A.D.S. at REVELON FARM.	
	16/2/18	9 a.m.	Visited A.D.S. at QUEEN'S CROSS. Road to Courtaux near Queens Cross requires repair. This has been reported to A.D.M.S. Relieved 15 men on left sector. All men on return to Head quarters have a bath as a matter of routine. French method of foot treatment is discontinued from to-day except where supplies stocks of soap powder are still available. While at m now being used & so arrives from A.S.C. direct to units.	
			A case of measles occurred in 116 m.g. Co. at Q.29.a.80 (Sheet 57c) Army and has been transferred. Contacts are being isolated & inspected daily by an RAMC. Officer at QUEEN'S CROSS	

WAR DIARY or INTELLIGENCE SUMMARY

Army Form C. 2118
134th FIELD AMBULANCE

Place	Date	Hour	Summary of Events and Information	Remarks and references to Appendices
HEUDICOURT W21 & 82 Ref 57c.	16/3/18	2:30p	Rifles of M.T. A.S.C. inspected. Gas masks inspected.	
	17/3/18	9:30a.m	Inspected all R.A.M.C. foot: Rfts. in right sector. The R.A.P. in the tunnel at W18d34 has stretcher racks fitted & can accommodate 14 stretchers. An R.A.P. is being built at the tunnel at W18a6. All R.A.M.C. men were found to be adequately sheltered. Supplies arrive regularly & evacuation as far as the possible smoothly. 3 new trollys are now in use in this sector - making 6 in all. Tunnels for material required for the A.D.S. at W16d27 91 received last night & present 6" A.D.M.S. to day. Captain R.A. MACNEILL inspected materially 117 T.M.B. Arrangements complete for bathing R.A.M.C. personnel at A.D. Stations. Inspected A.D.S. at REVELON FARM. Began work on new A.D.S. at SUGAR REFINERY.	
	18/3/18			
	19/3/18		Small wind carried out last night by 30 men of 11th R. SUSSEX. 3 casualties all wounded.	
	20/3/18		Took over from 5/o/c 116 Inf. Bde. 2 incompletes dug-outs at REVELON FARM for use of R.A.M.C. personnel. Inspected A.D.S. at REVELON FARM & SUGAR REFINERY.	
	21/3/18		Took over command from Lt Col Drew. Withdrew from REVELON F.M. Lt MORALES MORC U3A sent to REVELON Fm to assist Rly Daly work. Inspected bearer & Relay Posts evacuating 117 Inf Bde.	

WAR DIARY or INTELLIGENCE SUMMARY

Army Form C. 2118

134th FIELD AMBULANCE

Place	Date	Hour	Summary of Events and Information	Remarks and references to Appendices
HEUDECOURT Sheet 57C West 1/4.	22/4/18	9:30 a	Visited A.D.M.S. and C.M.D.S. Proceeded to A.D.S. QUEENS Cross to relax site for emergency R.A.P. for left sector. Traced site of new A.D.S. on FINS-GOUZEAUCOURT road. Decided on. Visited Relay Post at GOUZEAUCOURT village.	
"	23/4/18	7 p.m.	Proceeded with D.A.D.M.S. to REVELON P.M. & visited all R.A.P.'s & Relay Posts & SUGAR Refinery. A/D.M.S. visited HEUDECOURT. Revised 4th Midlaw Horsed Ambulance stationed at METZ. 1 Sergt. (Sergt. McLEAN) & 6 men arrived at Relay Post "A" near GOUZEAUCOURT. Have seasonably Relief tents. Applied for open & 13th Fd. Amb. serving with their tents to be relieved.	
"	24/4/18	6 p.m.	Inspected sanitation of HEUDECOURT. & visited Battalion of Lonesian Regt. billeted in village. Arranged for evacuation of their sick & wounded in accordance with instructions from A.D.M.S. Inspected work at new A.D.S. which is proceeding satisfactorily; then to REVELON Fd. Amb. A.D.S. where work is in full swing. Also, their wounded yesterday reported to be doing well at No 55 C.C.S. D.A.D.M.S. visited own wounded here this afternoon, & advised in treatment locally.	
"	25/4/18		Showery, wet weather. Visited 117 Bde H.Q. Went round GOUZEAUCOURT Sector of front with D.A.D.M.S. Received warning of impending relief.	

Army Form C. 2118

134b FIELD AMBULANCE

WAR DIARY or INTELLIGENCE SUMMARY

(Erase heading not required.)

Place	Date	Hour	Summary of Events and Information	Remarks and references to Appendices
HEUDICOURT Sheet 57C W21 b & 2	26/2/18	6 p.m.	Fine, sunny. Tm Offrs from 27th Fld Amb arrived for preliminary inspection line. Cars taken to GOUZEAUCOURT & other to REVELON F.M. ADS & frown medical POP. Visited SUGAR REFINERY ADS & took preceding space. Some infantry now occupying R.E's in this work. Visited Queen's Cross ADS in evening & arranged transitions with Capt. Coyle during forthcoming minor operation. Received A.D.M.S. Op order No 29. This Fld Amb to be relieved by No 27 Fld Amb & to proceed to SAILLY LE SEC on 1/3/18, & grouped with 116 Inf Bde.	
	27/2/18 8 p.m.		Spent morning discussing & preparing for forthcoming relief. Arranged with Capt. Cook R.A.M.C to O/C A.D.S³ re handing over relief etc. Arranged with Capt. Cook R.A.M.C att. 17 KRRC re evacuation of wounded from 117 Inf Bde Sector in event to take place to night. Visited REVELON F.M. A.D.S. to arrange agency men. Capt. FLOYD R.A.M.C. to Queen's X ADS to arrange withdrawal of equipment.	
	28/2/18 6 p.m.		Arrangements completed regarding relief. Relief cancelled. Visited Queen's X A.D.S. in afternoon, and arranged relief of personnel procuring 117 Inf Bde sector which is being taken over by 21st Div. Offrs from 21st Div. shown over the forward posts & Revelon F.M. Broken to conference at A.D.M.S. Offices. Question regarding defence discussed.	
	11 p.m.			

J M Martin Capt
R.A.M.C
y/o.c. 134 F.Amb.

Copy No.4.

39th Division.

DEFENCE SCHEME.

MEDICAL ARRANGEMENTS APPENDIX NO.......

Ref. Map Sheet 57c.

MEDICAL INSTITUTIONS AND ACCOMMODATION.

A - LEFT SECTOR.

(a) ADVANCED DRESSING STATION, QUEEN'S CROSS (Q.28.d.2.3.)
Accommodation - 2 Officers,
                18 Other ranks,
                18 Stretcher cases.

(b) R. A. Ps.

Left R.A.P.	Right R.A.P.
(R.19.d.2.8.)	(R.31.c.8.8.)
Accommodation -	Accommodation -
8 Stretcher cases,	10 Stretcher cases,
M.O's staff,	Battalion M.O. and staff,
4 O.R., R.A.M.C. live	4 O.R., R.A.M.C.
in neighbouring	(This R.A.P. is in a
dugout.	tunnel in a quarry.)
M.O. lives in tunnel.	

(c) RELAY POSTS.
  (a) Q.30.b.8.0. Consists of a tunnel and elephant dugout. The elephant dugout can accommodate about 10 stretcher cases. 9 O.R., R.A.M.C. live here.
  (b) Q.35.b.8.9. Accommodation for 6 men and 6 stretcher cases.
  (c) Q.35.d.8.1. Three elephant dugouts. Accommodation for 16 stretcher cases and 7 O.R., R.A.M.C.
  Loading Post Stand for Ford car W.4.b.7.9. Accommodation for 4 O.R., R.AM.C. and 1 A.S.C. Driver. Two stretcher cases can be kept here if necessary.
  Loading Post and Car Stand, Q.28.c.6.6. Accommodation 4 O.R., R.A.M.C. and 1 A.S.C. Driver.
  (NOTE - A stand for the car is now under construction.)
  Horse Wagon Post, W.3.b.2.2. Accommodation for 2 O.R.

(B) - RIGHT SECTOR.

(a) ADVANCED DRESSING STATION - REVELON FARM (W.17.a.0.8.)
Accommodation - 2 R.A.M.C. Officers,
                10 O.R., R.A.M.C.
                20 Stretcher cases.
(An elephant dugout is in course of erection.)

(B) R. A. Ps.
  W.6.d.6.3. (Used by two Battalions.)
  Accommodation - 8 Stretcher cases, 8 O.R., R.A.M.C. living in neighbouring dugout.
  X.13.a.2.5. Accommodation - 3 Stretcher cases, 5 O.R., R.A.M.C. are accommodated in a neighbouring dugout. M.O. lives in a dugout.
  W.18.d.3.3. (underground tunnel) Accommodation for 8 stretcher cases. (There is also an elephant dugout on the surface which could accommodate 4 stretcher cases. M.O. lives in a tunnel. 9 O.R., R.A.M.C. are accommodated in a neighbouring tunnel.

W.18.c.8.5. (almost completed). At present unoccupied, but is being held by R.A.M.C. party from REVELON FARM; has accommodation for 8 stretcher cases when completed. W.23.b.1.1. (for support Battalion). Medical staff accommodated in dugouts. 1 O.R., R.A.M.C. attached as Runner.

(c) RELAY POSTS.
    (a) W.12.c.6.1. Accommodation - 5 O.R., R.A.M.C.
    (Car Stand, W.17.d.5.2. is in process of construction.)

TRENCH FOOT CENTRES.
Trench foot centres, each functioned by 5 O.R., R.A.M.C. are available at the undermentioned places -
1. REVELON FARM (W.17.a.0.8.)
2. HEUDICOURT (behind church).
3. QUEEN'S CROSS (Q.28.d.2.3.)
4. CAMP L.1. in the large Adrian hut (W.2.c.2.3.)

MEDICAL SUPPLIES.

Stretchers and blankets are maintained at the Relay Posts -

(a)	4 stretchers,	8 blankets.
(b)	3 "	6 "
(c)	6 "	12 "
W.12.c.6.1.	2 "	4 " and
at each R.A.P.	2 "	4 "
A.D.S. QUEEN'S CROSS	18 "	36 "
" REVELON FARM	10 "	20 "

DISTRIBUTION OF PERSONNEL.

A.D.S. QUEEN'S CROSS - 2 Officers and 18 O.R., R.A.M.C.
" REVELON FARM - 2 Officers and 10 O.R., R.A.M.C.
Forward Posts - 69 O.R. (in normal times).

EVACUATION.

A - LEFT SECTOR.
From R.A.P. R.19.d.2.8. by Decauville track to Relay Post (a), thence by Decauville track to Relay Post (b), thence by wheeled stretcher or hand carriage along road to QUEEN'S CROSS, thence by hand carriage to car stand at Q.28.c.6.6., thence by car through METZ to FINS. Alternatively, if the track is being shelled, Bearers from this R.A.P. carry stretchers along sunken road to (a) Post, thence along shelter of bank to (b) Post and thence to QUEEN'S CROSS. If the road between (b) Post and QUEEN'S CROSS is being shelled cases can be taken to (c) Post and thence by wheeled stretcher to stand for Ford car at W.4.b.7.9. thence to Main Dressing Station by FINS-GOUZEAUCOURT Road.
From R.A.P. at R.31.c.8.8. by hand carriage to a point at Q.36.b.2.1., thereafter by wheeled stretcher through GOUZEAUCOURT to Relay Post (b) or (c) according to the activity of the enemy, and thence to Main Dressing Station as before. The road from the R.A.P. is not at present suitable for wheeled stretchers.

B - RIGHT SECTOR.
From R.A.P. W.6.d.6.3. by trolley carriage on Decauville track to REVELON FARM, thence by car to Main Dressing Station.
From R.A.P. X.13.a.2.5. by hand carriage to sunken road at W.18.d.9.1. thence by hand carriage and wheeled stretcher

to REVELON FARM.
From R.A.P. W.18.d.3.3. along sunken road by hand carriage and wheeled stretcher to REVELON FARM.
A car stand is being constructed at W.17.d.5.2. which will facilitate evacuation from this point.
The Decauville track runs between REVELON FARM through W.18 towards VAUCELLET FARM. It is intended to make use of this for evacuations from this sector and trollies have been indented for.
From R.A.P. W.23.b.1.1. cases are evacuated by wheeled stretcher along road to Headquarters at HEUDICOURT, thence by car to Main Dressing Station.

METHOD OF RELIEF. As no particular enemy activity is at present going on I intend to relieve the Posts once every 14 days.

WATER. Water is supplied by petrol tins from Headquarters at HEUDICOURT to A.D.S. at QUEEN'S CROSS as the tank there is at present out of order.
A water cart is stationed at REVELON FARM.

ALTERNATIVE ROUTES OF EVACUATION. Alternative routes can be used as shown on the accompanying map.

ESSENTIAL REQUIREMENTS IN CONSTRUCTIONAL WORK. Completion of tunnel at QUEEN'S CROSS A.D.S.
Provision of apparatus for raising and lowering stretcher cases into tunnels.
Provision of elephant shelters at A.D.S. REVELON FARM.
Construction of Car Stands at W.17.d.5.2. and Q.28.c.6.6.
Provision of extra trollies.
Repair of Decauville track between (a) Post and (c) Post.
Repair of Water Tank at QUEEN'S CROSS.

H.Q. OF UNIT EVACUATING THE LINE. Located at HEUDICOURT (W.21.b.9.1.) Accommodation - 4 Officers, 230 Other Ranks, 45 Horses.

COPIES TO -

1. A.D.M.S.
2. O. i/c A.D.S. REVELON FARM.
3. " QUEEN'S CROSS.
4. War Diary.
5. File.

ORIGINAL

T.I

CONFIDENTIAL

140/284/9.

Vol 25

WAR DIARY

OF

134 FIELD AMBULANCE

FROM MARCH 1st 1918 TO MARCH 31st 1918

(VOLUME 25.)

Army Form C. 2118

134th FIELD AMBULANCE

WAR DIARY
or
INTELLIGENCE SUMMARY
(Erase heading not required.)

Place	Date	Hour	Summary of Events and Information	Remarks and references to Appendices
HEUDICOURT Sh. 62.8 Sheet 57.	1/3/18	8 p.m.	Rough stormy day. Visited Queen's Cross A.D.S. and discussed the theoretical tactics of the Defence Scheme. Reconnaissance of alternative route for walking wounded round METZ, in order to avoid the shelling of patients through METZ, which may possibly be shelled. Capt. Hoyle interviewed ADMS regarding the transfer from HEUDICOURT to a point near NURLU of a certain amount of Ambulance Transport.	
"	2/3/18	9 a.m.	Very cold, with fine snow, windy. Completed Defence Scheme as regards new forward posts, both on Right + Left sectors. Route for walking wounded almost completely pegged out. Arranged for reserve of rations, dressings, splints etc to be held at A.D. Stations various. Reliefs from ADS, and 225 Fd.Amb. R.E. One Corporal and eleven men unimprovement reported. Changed relief of remainder of unrelieved personnel at Queen's Crm ADS & posts forward of them from S.B's of 132 Fld. Amb.	
"	3/3/18	8 p.m.	Cold. Relief carried out in GOUZEAUCOURT Sector. Returned men taken & given clean change, & then sent to 132 F.Amb. Inspected sanitation of HEUDICOURT, which is in satisfactory as can be considering that Inhabitants are not to be used. Arranged for largest strokes of dressings at A.D. Stations & also reserves of dressings at the posts	

WAR DIARY or INTELLIGENCE SUMMARY

Army Form C. 2118

134th FIELD AMBULANCE.

Place	Date	Hour	Summary of Events and Information	Remarks and references to Appendices
HONECOURT Sheet 57 N31 d 2.8	4/3/18	8pm	Weather improving & brighter. Interviewed Salvage Officer near Fins to make enquiries regarding tank. Visited 39 Div Baths officer re salvage thereof small Primus & men from the line boiled at Sugar Refinery & charged at our intervals. Inspected route at Sugar Refinery, and discussed forward evacuation with Lt DALY - M.O.R.C. who I think has a very thorough knowledge of it.	
"	5/3/18	8pm	Weather fine. Selected site for A.D.M.S. at W.8. a.1.9. (sheet 57) for establishment of a new Relay Post on the FINS—GOUZEAUCOURT Road. This site is excellent & unreel also the road is a car stand is situated this road just excellent protection. Elephant shelters to be erected stage & party detailed for occupation. Visited REVELON FARM the afternoon. Guns very active in the evening.	
"	6/3/18	8pm	Fine clear weather. Heavy enemy damage on our front line. Early this morning, resulted in some casualties. Visited Bussu. Our A.D.S. and made a reconnaissance for new route for walking wounded. One selected is Queen's X. - just S of DESSART wood. - New Post at W.8. a.1.9. - M.D.S. working party detailed for Post at W.8. a.1.9. & freezing party commenced. Application for leave to England from Capt FLOYD forwarded.	

Army Form C. 2118

134th FIELD AMBULANCE

WAR DIARY
or
INTELLIGENCE SUMMARY
(Erase heading not required.)

Place	Date	Hour	Summary of Events and Information	Remarks and references to Appendices
HEUDICOURT W.21 & 28 Sheet 57	7/3/18	8p-	Cool & breezy. Visit by A.D.M.S. in morning. Proceeded to work being carried out at W.8.a.1.9, and W.3 Central, where prob are being established in connection with Defence Scheme. Parties detailed for this work, billeted close by, where they can act on Raids Stretcher Bearers of necessity on GOUZEAUCOURT Sector. Capt Coyle & A.D.S. QUEEN'S CROSS informed of this. Received A.D.M.S. medicine arrangements in connection with Defence Scheme.	
	8/3/18	8p-	Bright & Sunny. Clouded Sky. Route for walking wounded (left sector) completed & work proceeding on new prob. Capt McCLANAGHAN MORC reported must arrive from VII Corps R.S. yesterday & posted to REVELON F.M. to take charge there. Lt. MICHEL MORC also reported back yesterday, on relief by Lt. BOGART MORC on M/o/C 16th Rifle Bde. Lt. MICHEL remains at H.Q. T mile west Queen's X A.D.S. for instruction. Visited REVELON F.M. A.D.S. Sugar Refinery, where much work is being done. Queries A.D.M's with regard to area in which Sugar Refinery is. He upton 39 & 61 A.B.B's Visited 11th R. Sussex Regt. Capt FLOYD's leave allotment cancelled.	
	9/3/18	8p-	Sunny & Clear sky. Proceeded to Queen's X A.D.S. with Lt. MICHEL MORC & inspected work at TYKE DUMP, T.W.8.a.1.9, also walking wounded route. Received word of proposed raid by 11/3 R. Sussex tonight in front of GOUZEAUCOURT. Adequate arrangement for evacuation made. Seventeen time in force today. Inspected Sanitorium of HEUDICOURT, - Satisfactory. Some officers went to a lecture on AFRICA this afternoon by Sir HARRY JOHNSTON. Wrote to A.D.M.S. Wareting allocation of Medical Defence Scheme.	

WAR DIARY or INTELLIGENCE SUMMARY

Army Form C. 2118

134th FIELD AMBULANCE

Place	Date	Hour	Summary of Events and Information	Remarks and references to Appendices
HEUDICOURT W21 b 7.8 Sher 57	9/3/18	4 p.m.	Continued — Lieut BOGART MORC reported for duty from 16th Rifle Brigade and Lieut. MICHEL MORC detailed to replace him. Visited ADMS and 133 Fld Amb.	
	10/3/18		Fine thirteen day; hazy. Visited SUGAR REFINERY ADS where work is almost completed. Visited REVELON FM ADS and 11th R. Sussex Regt. Inspected work being carried out at TYKE DUMP and Sunken Rd WB a.1.9 men at these places were called upon last night as reserve Bearers by O.C. Queen's Own ADS so as nothing this morning. Shewed amount of shelling last night since this morning. A few dropped close to SUGAR REFINERY ADS Received warning notice of impending relief by 9th Division (21 Fld Amb) handed over to 2 Lt Brew on his return from A/ADMS 5.50 pm. Wrote Major Raine, Lt Col. R.A.M.C. Taken over C/Drews.	
		8.30 p.m.	Warning notice received from A.D.M.S. that the ambulance would probably be relieved on the 12th by 27th Ambce 9th Div.	
	11/3/18	9 a.m.	Orders received from A.D.M.S. that 7th Ambce is to be relieved to-day by 27th Fd Ambce	
		12 noon	Advance party of 27 Fd Ambce arrived	

WAR DIARY or INTELLIGENCE SUMMARY

(Erase heading not required.)

Army Form C. 2118

134th FIELD AMBULANCE

Instructions regarding War Diaries and Intelligence Summaries are contained in F.S. Regs., Part II. and the Staff Manual respectively. Title Pages will be prepared in manuscript.

Place	Date	Hour	Summary of Events and Information	Remarks and references to Appendices
HEUDICOURT	11/3/18	12 noon	Advance party proceeded to new site at GURLU WOOD (Sheet 62c).	
		3 p.m.	Transport proceeded to new site.	
		5:30 p.m.	Personnel proceeded to new site (Entraining at Queens Cross) all patients having by 23 Fd Ambce having taking over certificates passed	
GURLU WOOD Sheet 62c D28c86	12/3/18	8:30 a.	All details of unit now encamped at GURLU WOOD.	
	13/3/18.		All personnel employed in camp fatigues generally during morning. In the afternoon, church & football.	
	13/3/18	9 a.m.	Physical drill for all ranks (RAMC & ASC)	
		10:15 a.	Kit Inspection.	
		3 p.m.	Equipment checked & all ranks drilled in wagon loading.	
		5:30 p.m.	Football.	
			Reconnoitres routes to entraining point at La Capelette (Sheet 62c). Captain C.W. MACLATVATHAN, M.O. R.C., U.S.A. proceeded for temporary duty to Vth Army Convalescent Depot.	
	14/3/18	9 a.m.	Physical drill.	
		10:15 a.	Fatigue parties employed on cleaning equipment & making huts bombproof.	
			from 10-15 a.m. to 12 n.	
		Afternoon	Recreation for all ranks. We are now in B.H.Q. Reserve under orders to move at 12 hours' notice.	

1875 Wt. W 593/826 1,000,000 4/15 J.B.C. & A. A.D.S.S./Forms/C.2118.

Army Form C. 2118

134th FIELD AMBULANCE

WAR DIARY
or
INTELLIGENCE SUMMARY
(Erase heading not required.)

Place	Date	Hour	Summary of Events and Information	Remarks and references to Appendices
GURLU WOOD. Sheet 62c. D.28.c.8.6.	15/3/18	9 a.m.	Physical drill for all ranks. Thereafter action drill & ambulance drill. Recreational training in the afternoon. Weather fine. A.D.M.S. 39th Divn visited the camp.	
	16/3/18	9 a.m.	Fine bright day. Drill as on 15th. In the afternoon fatigue parties employed on company barricades round the huts and in the horse lines. Captain C.W. McCLANAHAN M.O. R.C. U.S.A. returned from 5th Army Convalescent Depot and in orders from to-day as M.O. i/c 39 Divn Machine Gun Bn. Lieut W.J. DALY, M.O. R.C. U.S.A proceeded to Corps HQrs. to relieve Captain McClanahan. 39th Divn Routine Orders no 6/664 of 16/3/18.	
	17/3/18	9 a.m.	Fine bright day. Received Copy no 12 17 RAMC Routine Orders.	
		10 a.m.	Church Parade for nonconformists. All ranks continued completion of defences. Captain C.D. COYLE and 3 OR proceeded to 5th Army School of instruction at HAM for the course commencing on 18/3/18.	
		3.30 p.m.	Football match 7th Ambce V. A.S.C. Resent F.A. 2 A.S.C. 0.	
	18/3/18	9 a.m.	Fine bright morning. Bathing parade in the morning at MOYSLAINS. Recreational training for all ranks in the afternoon.	

Army Form C. 2118.

WAR DIARY
or
INTELLIGENCE SUMMARY.
(Erase heading not required.)

134th FIELD AMBULANCE R.A.M.C.

Place	Date	Hour	Summary of Events and Information	Remarks and references to Appendices
GURLU WOOD D28c86 Sheet 62c	19/3/18	9 a.m.	Rain which continued all day. Lieut W.H. HOWELL, M.O, R.C, U.S.A, proceeded to 5th Army Convalescent Depot at CERISY (Amiens 17) to relieve Lieut W.T. DALY who proceeded on 6 days' leave to PARIS.	
	20/3/18	9 a.m.	Dull morning with some rain. Physical drill for all ranks.	
		9:20 a.m.	Proceeded to Peronne with 2 O.R. to attend funeral of Brig. Gen Cape a/Commander 39th Div Killed in action on 18/3/18	
		10:15 a.m	Route march	
		4 p.m	Recreational training	
	21/3/18		Heavy bombardment before stand 5 a.m.	
		7:45 a.m	Order received to send H. Sunbeam cars to report to OC 3 MAC. PERONNE. 3 canopies sent immediately. The other 2 are in workshop.	
		8 a.m	Orders issued for all ranks to stand to & transport to be prepared to move at short notice	
		8:45 a.m.	Sent Lieut BOGART to 116 Adv N²Q'rs for information as to events. He reported the Brigade is standing to and there has been a gas-shell bombardment before the	
		9 a.m.	by the Boche	
		10:15 a.m	Thick mist morning Received replied from OC 132 Fd Ambce for 1 bearer sub division & 3 horsed ambces to proceed to D.A.C.G. to assist him	
		10:30 a.m	Party marched off under command of Lieut C.S. BOGART, M.O, R.C USA

Army Form C. 2118.

134th FIELD AMBULANCE R.A.M.C.

WAR DIARY
or
INTELLIGENCE SUMMARY.
(Erase heading not required.)

Instructions regarding War Diaries and Intelligence Summaries are contained in F.S. Regs., Part II. and the Staff Manual respectively. Title pages will be prepared in manuscript.

Place	Date	Hour	Summary of Events and Information	Remarks and references to Appendices
GURLU WOOD	9/3/18	10.45 a.m	Vicinity of camp is being shelled with H.V. shells. Mist is now clearing & sun is coming through.	
		11 a.m	Bombardment now intense.	
		9.30 a	Sent Major J.H PORTER RAMC to 116 Bde H.Q.rs to ascertain if any move	
			ever to take place	
		2.15 p	Major PORTER returned, reported that 116 Bde were about to move to reinforce 16th Division and that we were not running any orders to 134 Fd Ambce	
		3.00 p	Reported this to ADMS	
		5 p.m	Orders from A.D.M.S. that I am now to take orders for move from him	
		5 p.m	Details at order of A.D.M.S. Captain R.A MACNEILL to examine G.I.W. at the Gap TEMPLEUX-LA-FOSSE.	
		9 p.m	Thick mist Bombardment not so intense.	
		10.30 p	Order from A.D.M.S. that Fd Ambce is at disposal of A.D.M.S. 16th Divn. Informed A.D.M.S. that my horsed ambulances are with 132 Fd Ambce & that I have at present 8 F.O.R. available for duty	
		10.45 p	2/Lieut R. STEEL i/c CHESHIRE with 20 bearers from 118 Bde reported here awaiting orders from 132 Fd Ambce of remarks	
		11.30 p	Informed by A.D.M.S. that clothing & equipment from D.A.D.O.S. and kept to be held "B" until further orders.	

WAR DIARY or INTELLIGENCE SUMMARY.

Army Form C. 2118.

134th FIELD AMBULANCE R.A.M.C.

Place	Date	Hour	Summary of Events and Information	Remarks and references to Appendices
GURLU WOOD Sheet 62c D28c86	22/3/18	12 n. 9 a.m.	Casting & equipment arrived. All ranks still standing to. Thick misty morning.	
		10 a.m.	Enemy began to shell TEMPLEUX - LA FOSSE and vicinity. 1 camp. Several shells fell in the camp in the course of the day. One shell landed on hut and killed 41 men of 13th Bloskers & wounded 30. Bearers sent out from Fd. Ambce. to collect.	
		11 a.m.	Casualties are now coming in and I am establishing a collecting post here & evacuating to 133 Fd. Ambce at MOISLAINS.	
		12 noon	As shelling continues I have decided to move transport to point on NURLU - PERONNE road. Transport moved off. A.D.M.S. informed. Transport parked at St Denis Corner on PERONNE road.	
		1 p.m.	Stretcher bearers of Fd. Ambce & of the CHESHIRES sent out to collect wounded in direction of LONGAVESNES.	
		3.30 p.m.	1 N.C.O. & 16 men R.A.M.C. sent to assist M.O. I/Cambs. R. in evacuation. All the cars of the Fd. Ambce. & 2 horsed ambces of 133 Fd. Ambce. are evacuating wounded as fast as they can. But necessary dressings and collecting wounded are being done here as shelling continues & it is necessary to get wounded down.	

WAR DIARY or INTELLIGENCE SUMMARY.

Army Form C. 2118.

134th FIELD AMBULANCE

Place	Date	Hour	Summary of Events and Information	Remarks and references to Appendices
GURLU WOOD	2/3/18	5 p.m.	As quickly as possible. Reported that 63rd Fd Ambce is established at BUSSU.	
		6.15 p.m.	All wounded now cleared. Reported this to A.D.M.S. Over 100 stretcher cases have been evacuated & a large number of walking wounded.	
		7 p.m.	Main body of 7d Ambce proceeded to join transport at ST DENIS Corner. I proceeded to report situation to A.D.M.S.	
		8 p.m.	1 N.C.O. & 10 men left to evacuate any wounded that may arrive. Ordered verbally by A.D.M.S. to proceed to HAUT ALLAINES. Visited Area commandant who allotted me a site on the ALLAINES - CLERY road at the X in FEUILLACOURT (Amiens 19)	
		9 p.m.	Major COYLE proceeded to GURLU WOOD to get in touch with the Brigades.	
		10 p.m.	The holding party at GURLU WOOD joined main body, reports no wounded coming in.	
		10.30 p.m.	The 7d Ambce set out for site on the ALLAINES - CLERY Road.	
		11.30 p.m.	Arrived at camping place & all ranks bivouaced in a field.	
		11.45 p.m.	Reported to A.D.M.S. at HAUT ALLAINES.	

Army Form C. 2118.

134th FIELD AMBULANCE

WAR DIARY
or
INTELLIGENCE SUMMARY.
(Erase heading not required.)

Instructions regarding War Diaries and Intelligence Summaries are contained in F. S. Regs., Part II. and the Staff Manual respectively. Title pages will be prepared in manuscript.

Place	Date	Hour	Summary of Events and Information	Remarks and references to Appendices
On the ALLAINES CLERY road at a rendezvous (Annex 1?)	23/3/18	4.15am	Sent off 1 Ford and 1 Sunbeam car to O.C. 132 Fd Ambce. Verbal order received from A.D.M.S. to proceed to CLERY forthwith	
		4.45am	Set out for CLERY	
CLERY		8.20am	Arrived CLERY and parked in a field in the village	
		9am	Major COY LE returned & reported he had been in touch with Brigade 132 Fd Ambce. Also reported that Ford Car No. 20 WD 24998 broke down at 4a.m. about 1 kilometre in front of BUSSU. The back axle had broken through about 4 inches from right hand wheel. Impossible to salve it. Car rendered useless & burned.	
		9.45am	Reports to A.D.M.S. I ordered to stand by to await further orders	
		10.20am	Capt. R.A. MacNEILL left for England on expiry of contract.	
		1p.m.	Left CLERY & order of A.D.M.S. and proceeded via HEM to point on FEUILLERES—HERBECOURT road between H20 Y4 26 (Sheet 62b)	
On road bet. HZ6B. H2Z6 Sheet 62b		2.45pm	Arrived a transport of 132 Fd. Ambce. joined my unit.	
		3.15pm	Reported position to A.D.M.S. at FRISE.	
		5pm	Major PORTER proceeded to get in touch with 132 Fd Ambce at H.2.b sheet 62.C. My Ambce is now acting as reserve for 132 Fd Ambce	

Army Form C. 2118.

R.A.M.C.
134th FIELD AMBULANCE.
12

WAR DIARY
or
~~INTELLIGENCE~~ SUMMARY.
(Erase heading not required.)

Instructions regarding War Diaries and Intelligence
Summaries are contained in F.S. Regs., Part II.
and the Staff Manual respectively. Title pages
will be prepared in manuscript.

Place	Date	Hour	Summary of Events and Information	Remarks and references to Appendices
On road Somme between H30 & H26 c88 (Sheet 62c)	22/3/18	6.30.a.	Major PORTER returned from 132 Fd Ambce having reported my location	
		6.35.a.	After consultation with D.A.Q.M.G. 39 Div I ordered my transport to move to a point on HERBECOURT - CAPPY road at H 30.6.8 as the present site is on the sky-line under direct observation by enemy. All find line transport has left this district. Officers & personnel with stretchers & knapsacks remain to reinforce 132 Fd Ambce as required.	
		10.p.	Ordered by A.D.M.S. to move to site on HERBECOURT - CAPPY road. H30 b (Sheet 62c) Evacuated many wounded who had been brought down by lorries	
H30.c8.8 #30 b		11.10.p	Arrived with personnel and transport. 132 Fd Ambce informed	
Sheet 6c 30 c 88 #30 b (War)	24/3/18	3.46.a.	also A.D.M.S. of new site. Sent 4 men and 2 stretchers to 14 K.R.R.C. at FEUILLERES	
		6.a.	Sent all available cars to 132 Fd Ambce who are now parked on HERBECOURT - CAPPY road about 1½ miles W of HERBECOURT and 1 mile E of my Ambce.	
		4.30.p.	Ordered transport to proceed to S.27.b. (Sheet 62c) in view of 132 Fd. Ambce proximity. Officers & bearers remain to reinforce 132 as required. Visited 132 Fd Ambce & informed by O.C. that he does not think he will require bearers from 134 Fd Ambce.	

6 APR 1918
134th FIELD AMB[ULANCE]

Army Form C. 2118.
R.A.M.O.
134th FIELD AMBULANCE

WAR DIARY
or
INTELLIGENCE SUMMARY.
(Erase heading not required.)

Place	Date	Hour	Summary of Events and Information	Remarks and references to Appendices
630 c8P #20.6 Sheet 62C.	24/3/18		Intermittent shelling all morning	
		10.35 p.m	O.C. 132 Fd Ambce delivered my withdrawal. Proceeded to point on CAPPY BRAY road about midway between three villages. Transport went on ahead	
Point midway between CAPPY BRAY & CAPPY (and Point			Major COYLE reports EADMS. Major PORTER kept in touch with 132 Fd Ambce	
		11.55 p/m	Parked & prepared to move as ordered	
		3.30 a.m	Bombs dropped round camp.	
	25/3/18	1 6.i.m	Major COYLE proceeded to reconnoitre & get in touch with 132 Fd Ambce	
		9.40 a.m	Sent car to pick up 3 Stretcher Cases at SUZANNE.	
		9.10 a.m	1 Off & 30 O.R. auxiliary stretcher bearers from 1/6 CHESHIRES proceeded to reinforce 132 Fd Ambce.	
		12 mn	Major COYLE returned reports he had been in touch with 132 Fd Ambce & that A.D.M.S. had ordered the unit to move to CHUIGNES	
in CHUIGNES about 800am 17		1.25 p/m	Arrived at "L" in CHUIGNES. Thanks here. Reports arrival to A.D.M.S.	
		7p.m	Orders received from A.D.M.S. to proceed at 12 midnight to MERICOURT-sur-SOMME.	

WAR DIARY or INTELLIGENCE SUMMARY

Army Form C. 2118.

134th FIELD AMBULANCE

Place	Date	Hour	Summary of Events and Information	Remarks and references to Appendices
"D" in CHUIGNES	24/3/18	8.10 p.m.	Transport of 132 Fd Ambce & 3 Ambce weapons of 134 arrived & placed under my orders.	
by road along the M1 in MERICOURT SOMME	26/3/18	12 midnight	Left CHUIGNES with all transport for ride at MERICOURT – SM. SOMME	
		1.50 a.m.	Arrived thereat. Major COYLE reported to A.D.M.S.	
		11.30 a.m.	Proceeded to MORCOURT & saw A.D.M.S.	
		12.30 p.m.	Orders received from A.D.M.S. to take over evacuation of the Line from 132 Fd Ambce. Line is now PROYART – RAINECOURT. Major COYLE proceeded to get in touch with O.C. 132 Fd Ambce.	
		12.30 p.m.	Bearer Officer of 132 Fd Ambce. Wounded are being evacuated along MORCOURT – CERISY road.	
		1.30 p.m.	Took over evacuation of line.	
		2 p.m.	1 Officer & 1 bearer sub division of 132 Fd Ambce reported for duty. The position now is Major COYLE is forward with cars clearing No 2 Q of Fd Ambce are at MORCOURT evacuation is by lorry & MAC Car from MORCOURT back & by Fd Ambce cars from line to collecting post in MORCOURT.	

Army Form C. 2118.

R.A.M.C.
134th FIELD AMBULANCE
13

WAR DIARY
or
INTELLIGENCE SUMMARY.
(Erase heading not required.)

Instructions regarding War Diaries and Intelligence Summaries are contained in F.S. Regs., Part II. and the Staff Manual respectively. Title pages will be prepared in manuscript.

Place	Date	Hour	Summary of Events and Information	Remarks and references to Appendices
MORCOURT	26/3/18	3¹ a.	Major COYLE reported line now running between PROYART YANNECOURT. I therefore decided to establish N² Q⁰ of Fd. Ambce at LA MOTTE with a forward post at about half-way between LA MOTTE & the PROYART–RAINECOURT road.	
		4 p.m.	Marched to LA MOTTE via CERISY	
LA MOTTE		7 p.m.	Arrived LA MOTTE. Yesterday established Dressing station in the School. Major COYLE is at the Forward Post Somewhere in by-car down the LA MOTTE – FOUCAUCOURT road. All is quiet at present.	
		8.30 p.m.	Major PORTER returned from reconnaissance & reported that Major COYLE is in touch with 116, 117, 118 Bdes & had a ambulance car & 1 lorry with him.	
LA MOTTE	27/3/18	9 a.m.	Visited Forward Post. Line is quiet at present. Arranged details of evacuation with Major COYLE	
		10 a.m.	Wounded are coming in.	
		12 noon	Position now is Dressing Station & N² Q⁰ of Fd. Ambce in LA MOTTE Advanced Dressing Station & N² Q⁰ of H. Ambce at 132 Fd. Ambce Transport on outskirts of VILLERS–BRETONNEUX with 132 Fd. Ambce at Xroads to MORCOURT on LA MOTTE – FAUCOURT road.	

Army Form C. 2118.

RAMC
134th FIELD AMBULANCE

WAR DIARY
or
INTELLIGENCE SUMMARY.
(Erase heading not required.)

Instructions regarding War Diaries and Intelligence Summaries are contained in F.S. Regs., Part II. and the Staff Manual respectively. Title pages will be prepared in manuscript.

Place	Date	Hour	Summary of Events and Information	Remarks and references to Appendices
LA MOTTE	27/3/18	12 nn	Fd. Amb. Cars are evacuating from forward to LA MOTTE Fd. MAC clean from there	
		12.30 pm	Send 2 extra cars 9,12 bearers to Major COYLE. Many wounded are coming in. Enemy is shelling the road. Wounded are being cleared.	
		3.30 pm	No.Q's of Fd. Amber hampered to VILLERS-BRETONNEUX with advanced post at LA MOTTE – Major COYLE in charge.	
		10.50 pm	Wounded are coming in & being evacuated. Cars, bearers wheeled stretchers are all going as hard as they can. Captain COYLE reported that there are no wounded on the road & that the enemy is patrolling LA MOTTE. The line now held is behind LA MOTTE. All wounded behind our lines are now collected.	
VILLERS BRETONNEUX		6.30 pm	Send 6 wheeled stretchers to collect some wounded at HAMEL. All wounded cleared from No Q's of Ambce.	
		11 pm	Reported to ADMS	
CACHY	30/3/18	11.45 pm 9.30 am	Arrived with main body of ambce at CACHY. Major PORTER Major Warwick at forward post at VILLERS-BRETONNEUX. I visited post at Villers-Bretonneux & was ordered by ADMS to establish an ADS at MARCELCAVE with HQrs at AUBERCOURT.	

WAR DIARY
or
INTELLIGENCE SUMMARY.

(Erase heading not required.)

Army Form C. 2118.

R.A.M.C.
134th FIELD AMBULANCE.

Place	Date	Hour	Summary of Events and Information	Remarks and references to Appendices
AUBERCOURT	27/3/18	11 a.m.	Main body arrived at Aubercourt. Line is now MARCELCAVE – WIENCOURT. Evacuation is by bearers along Marcelcave – Aubercourt road. Major PORTER established post in MARCELCAVE but was shelled out. I proceed to establish at MARCELCAVE, found the town being heavily shelled.	
		2 p.m.	Withdrew headquarters to a house at the 5 roads below the "S" in Aubercourt as a more suitable collecting post.	
		4 p.m.	Major PORTER attempted to get into MARCELCAVE but was stopped by the heavy shell fire. Cavalry have been coming in all day. have being got away satisfactorily	
DOMART		11.30 p.m.	Am now established with No 2 Q at DOMART 4 advances post at AUBERCOURT vide order of A.D.M.S. Forward post reported that wounded are being cleared almost as they arrive	
	28/3/18	9 a.m.	Line now runs from C in Marcelcave to the "S" in Corveilles Forward post retired during night from AUBERCOURT to School in HANGARD	

Army Form C. 2118.

134th FIELD AMBULANCE
R.A.M.C.
18

WAR DIARY
or
INTELLIGENCE SUMMARY.
(Erase heading not required.)

Instructions regarding War Diaries and Intelligence Summaries are contained in F.S. Regs., Part II. and the Staff Manual respectively. Title pages will be prepared in manuscript.

Place	Date	Hour	Summary of Events and Information	Remarks and references to Appendices
DOMART	29/3/18	11.25 a.m.	Bde HQrs in wood east of Villers-Bretonneux. Continued RAP in Quarry at junction of 5 roads at DEMIUM. Can evacuate from RAP DEMIUM road. DEMIUM is being heavily shelled. Major General FEETHAM killed. Casualties are now coming in.	
		11.30 a.m.	DOMART is being shelled with shrapnel. Several casualties including Major Gen Malcolm Comdg 66th Divn wounded	
BERTEAUCOURT		2 p.m.	Withdrew No QR to BERTEAUCOURT. Advanced post at HANGARD. Many wounded. Flick evacuated including 60 French soldiers. Cars constantly at work. Evacuation appears to go smoothly.	
BERTEAUCOURT	30/3/18	8 a.m.	Major Porter reports enemy entering DEMIUM. He is withdrawing to BERTEAUCOURT which is now the advanced post.	
		9 a.m.	Sent an Officer to BOVES to establish dressing station at BOVES	
		11.30 a.m.	No QR established at BOVES in the school next to the Church. Sent up 8 cars to GENTELLES & CACHY.	

6 - APR 1918
134th FIELD AMBULANCE

Army Form C. 2118.

WAR DIARY
or
INTELLIGENCE SUMMARY.
(Erase heading not required.)

134th FIELD AMBULANCE

Place	Date	Hour	Summary of Events and Information	Remarks and references to Appendices
BOVES	28/3/18		H.Q. 9 Brigade at CACHY.	
		11.30 a.m.	Capt Cooke established a post at CACHY. Major PORTER now at the X roads where the THEZY road meets the Berteaucourt-Boves road.	
			Cars are working the BOVES-BERTEAUCOURT & the BOVES-GENTELLES roads.	
		3 p.m.	Sent up the horsed Ambulances under Lieut HOWELL to CACHY. They made two journeys brought back many wounded	
			Wounded from all divisions are now coming in. Have arranged with a Ft Amber of 61st Div. to send overflow there & vice versa according as we are cleared. Wounded are brought by roads evacuated as occasion offers.	
		8 p.m.	Maj. PORTER now at GENTELLES. 39th Div line is just in front of CACNY	
		9 p.m.	Heavy rain all day. Sir J. 9.8.55.30 fell into a hole which was being prepared by William Coy no 9 & 5.30 to be abandoned as before help could come for blowing up a bridge & had enemy had taken town	

Army Form C. 2118.

R.A.M.C.
134th FIELD AMB.   20

WAR DIARY
or
INTELLIGENCE SUMMARY.
(Erase heading not required.)

134th FIELD AMBULANCE
6 – APR 1918

Instructions regarding War Diaries and Intelligence Summaries are contained in F. S. Regs., Part II. and the Staff Manual respectively. Title pages will be prepared in manuscript.

Place	Date	Hour	Summary of Events and Information	Remarks and references to Appendices
BOVES	2/3/18	9 a.m.	The 39th Div. is being relieved in the line. Ordered advance pacts to report to N.Q. 39 Div. that I am going out of the line. Reports to A.D.M.S. 61st Div.	
		10 a.m.	All wounded now cleared. Handed over premises to 61st Div.	
GUIGNEMICOURT		11 a.m.	Marched to GUIGHA GUIGNEMICOURT. Arrived there at 5 p.m. Spent day here. Very wet day.	
			Casualties of personnel = 2 men wounded 1 man missing 1 Ford car } abandoned 1 Sunbeam car }	

6/4/18

M. Drew, Lt Col
Comdg 134 Fd Amb.

CONFIDENTIAL

WAR DIARY
OF
134th Field Ambulance

FROM 1ST APRIL 1918 TO 30TH APRIL 1918

(VOLUME 26.)

COMMITTEE FOR THE
MEDICAL HISTORY OF THE WAR
Date

Army Form C. 2118.

WAR DIARY
or
INTELLIGENCE SUMMARY.
(Erase heading not required.)

Instructions regarding War Diaries and Intelligence Summaries are contained in F.S. Regs., Part II. and the Staff Manual respectively. Title pages will be prepared in manuscript.

134th FIELD AMBULANCE

Place	Date	Hour	Summary of Events and Information	Remarks and references to Appendices
GUIGNEMICOURT	1/4/18	9 a.m.	Bright morning. Dull later. Unit stood by waiting for orders for further move.	
		5 p.m.	Funeral of Maj.-Gen. FEETHAM. 16ff & 20 OR attended to represent RAMC.	
HALLIVILLIERS	2/4/18	9.20 a.m.	Passed starting point en route to HALLIVILLIERS.	
		4 p.m.	Tea ambers arrived & in billetes for night here.	
	3/4/18	10 a.m.	Left HALLIVILLIERS by route march for FRESNOY-ANDAINVILLE.	
		4 p.m.	Arrived FRESNOY-ANDAINVILLE and in billets.	
FRESNOY- ANDAINVILLE	4/4/18		Reported arrival to ADMS. Cheery wire from 116 Bde group.	
		8 p.m.	Maj.-Gen. BLACKLOCK CMG DSO, visited the unit.	
	5/4/18		Personnel employed in cleaning up generally.	
		10 a.m.	Orders received from Bde for move to St OMER.	
		5 p.m.	Order received cancelling above order until further notice.	

T2134. Wt. W708—776. 500000. 4/15. Sir J. C. & B.

Army Form C. 2118.

134th FIELD AMBULANCE

WAR DIARY
or
INTELLIGENCE SUMMARY.
(Erase heading not required.)

Instructions regarding War Diaries and Intelligence Summaries are contained in F.S. Regs., Part II. and the Staff Manual respectively. Title pages will be prepared in manuscript.

Place	Date	Hour	Summary of Events and Information	Remarks and references to Appendices
FRESNOY-ANDAINVILLE	6/4/18	9 a.m.	Dull morning.	
			Orders received from Brigade to proceed on 7/4/18 by route march to DARGNIES	
FRESNOY-ANDAINVILLE	7/4/18	9.30 a.m.	Left for DARGNIES. Passed Starting point at OISEMONT at 11.30 a.m.	
DARGNIES	7/4/18	4-15 p.m.	Unit arrived & billeted. March for the day = 19 miles.	
DARGNIES	8/4/18	9 a.m.	Dull morning. Reconnoitred road to EU. Reported to A.D.M.S. at GAMMACHES.	
		5.30 p.m.	Transport proceeded to EU to entrain for ARQUES.	
		8.20 p.m.	Personnel proceeded to EU to entrain for ARQUES. March = 6 miles.	
EU	8/4/18	11.30 p.m.	Train left for ARQUES.	
ARQUES	9/4/18	9.30 a.m.	Train arrived at ARQUES. All unit entrained trained.	
		11.30 a.m.	Unit proceeded by route march to LONGUENESS	
LONGUENESS	9/4/18	12.45 p.m.	Unit arrived LONGUENESS & were billeted there. March = 3½ miles	
LONGUENESS	10/4/18	9 a.m.	Dull damp day. Unit spend day here cleaning up generally	
		6 p.m.	Orders received from 116 Bde to proceed by road on 11/4/18 to BERTHEM	
	11/4/18	8.10 a.m.	Dull morning. Unit proceeded by route march from LONGUENESS to BERTHEM.	
BERTHEM	11/4/18	11.20 a.m.	Starting point passed by time	
		3.30 p.m.	Arrived at BERTHEM on billets	

Army Form C. 2118.

134th FIELD AMBULANCE

WAR DIARY
or
INTELLIGENCE SUMMARY.
(Erase heading not required.)

Date	Hour	Summary of Events and Information	Remarks and references to Appendices
BERTHEM 12/4/18	9 a.m.	Clear sunny morning. Men employed in cleaning up & arranging billets.	
	4 p.m.	Sent Lieut. BOGART with box of dressings & stretchers, augmented howitzer medical companion to meet M.O. of a composite battalion assembling at the Church of St Martins - an - ZAERT.	
13.4.18	9 a.m.	Cold morning with N.E. wind	
	12 noon	A.D.M.S. visited the Fd Ambce.	
	5 p.m.	Lieut BOGART returned having handed over dressings to 6th Composite Battalion. Day spent in cleaning up.	
14.4.18	9 a.m.	Cold windy morning. Duel Major J.A. PORTER returned to duty from Hospital. Lieut W.H. DALY met advance party of 75th Div of American forces at AUDRUICQ and offered any assistance regimental to the medical authorities.	
15.4.18	9 a.m.	Dull cold windy morning.	

WAR DIARY
or
INTELLIGENCE SUMMARY

Army Form C. 2118.

R.A.M.C.
134th FIELD AMBULANCE

Place	Date	Hour	Summary of Events and Information	Remarks and references to Appendices
BERTHEM	16/4/18	9pm	Mill: temporarily ctd. Lt. Col Drew handed over to Major Potts. Reins in his Keep granted 14 days special leave to G. 30/4/18. Applied for return. motor cycle from ADMS. New Talbot Ambulance received from 132 ignored. Visited H.K. 77 Division U.S.A. & met Lt. Colonel Field Ambulance. REYNOLDS. Unit inspection of the Division, Arranged evacuation + collection of American Sick. Provided 2 G.S. wagons for transference of their baggage. Conducted Lt. Col Reynolds to ADMS 39th Divn where various points of interest were discussed. Detailed Ambulance Cars to report to 77 USA Divn in accordance with orders of ADMS. 70 Nos & men of this unit were inoculated today at 5·30pm with T.A.B. Vaccine.	MP
BERTHEM	17/4/18	9pm	Syphilis day. One more sick in tilet out of 70 men inoculated yesterday. All remainder excused duty for today. Others doing general fatigue work. Recommendation for "Card of Recognition" by M.G.C. 39 Divn Ambulance C.O. ADMS in case of Sergt. NUTTER, Sergt. CRADDUCK & Pte THOMPSON DSC	MP

Army Form C. 2118.

R.A.M.C.
134th FIELD AMBULANCE

WAR DIARY
or
INTELLIGENCE SUMMARY.
(Erase heading not required.)

Instructions regarding War Diaries and Intelligence Summaries are contained in F.S. Regs., Part II. and the Staff Manual respectively. Title pages will be prepared in manuscript.

Place	Date	Hour	Summary of Events and Information	Remarks and references to Appendices
BERTHEN	Cont. 17/5/16	9pm	Instructed all officers today as to the duties of Orderly Medical Officer. Our Advice to report to A.D.M.S. 39 Divn. Visited by Lt. Col. REYNOLDS 77 USA Divn M.C. who gave list of locations of American Units.	
BERTHEN	18/5/16	9pm	Dull wet day. 4/0 Blankets sent to Fumigation, & inquiries re: not regaining both for men. Both arranged with Major Frising at RECEIVES transws & for two days later. Interviewed asked for M. Officer for 77 USA Divn by A.D.M.S. — not approved. Lt Col REYNOLDS 77 Divn USA & Major GRIFFIN of same Divn visited thw Ambulance & remained for dinner.	
BERTHEN	19/5/16	9pm	Cold & Boggy. Routine Work. Attended lunch (from Canteen Funds) for convalescents of our men in next Cook house. Later Sir Omer and Aliern Incident Show for 77 Divn USA on return approved incident.	

Army Form C. 2118.

R.A.M.C.
134th FIELD AMBULANCE

WAR DIARY
or
INTELLIGENCE SUMMARY.
(Erase heading not required.)

Instructions regarding War Diaries and Intelligence
Summaries are contained in F. S. Regs., Part II.
and the Staff Manual respectively. Title pages
will be prepared in manuscript.

Place	Date	Hour	Summary of Events and Information	Remarks and references to Appendices
BERTHEM	27/4/18	9p	Cold & cloudy. Unit went on Route march after morning inspection under Major COYLE R.A.M.C. Visited by Major OWEN D.A.D. R.A.M.C. 39th Divn. and Area Commandant who suggested improvements in the billeting in this area. No. 10108 Q.M.S. HINDE. W. remove & reported for duty viz. Sergt Major TUSTAIN. Sent to care. Arranged under orders of A.D.M.S. for one 1 sick etc for 1 361 Infantry Company ARDRES.	JMP
BERTHEM	28/4/18	9a	Bright clear day. Sunday service C of E. 11am-00 E & R.C. arranged for today. Men went to y'known.	JMP
BERTHEM	29/4/18	9p	Fine sunny day, but chilly. Routine parades & inspections for those who did not attend on 19th inst. at 9:30am Remainder went on route march. Transport being painted.	JMP
BERTHEM	30/4/18	9p	Weather finer & warmer than yesterday. Routine morning parades. Unit paid at 10.30 am. Received news this another American	JMP

Army Form C. 2118.

R.A.M.C.
134th FIELD AMBULANCE

WAR DIARY
or
INTELLIGENCE SUMMARY.
(Erase heading not required.)

Instructions regarding War Diaries and Intelligence Summaries are contained in F. S. Regs., Part II. and the Staff Manual respectively. Title pages will be prepared in manuscript.

Place	Date	Hour	Summary of Events and Information	Remarks and references to Appendices
	23/4/18	9pm	Battalion was due to arrive, & detailed necessary transport. Men, horses being closely arranged transport ASC. Visited ARDRES and No 2 Coy. Enquiries into loss of ASC (MT) rifles en route.	WD
BERTHEM	24/4/18	9pm	Dull day with a little rain. Parade, route march, & fatigues in the forenoon. Received instructions from ADMS to prepare lectures on "Duties of Bearer Officer" for American medical Officers to be given at an early date. Lt. Daly R.A.M.C. detailed to give lecture on "Duties" and Major COPE R.A.M.C. to act as referee for field training of American medical units.	WD
BERTHEM	25/4/18	9pm	Bright day & 21/4/18 warmer. Routine parades. 21/4/18 - six men posted from 77th Ameri can Divi for instruction in water duties. Lecture & demonstration given by Lieut DALY M.O.R.C.	WD
BERTHEM	26/4/18	9pm	Dull & warm day with slight rain. Usual parades & fatigues. Visited ARDRES to arrange for demonstration in the lorries to be given to American Officers on the transport plant that Detailed Sergeant J. H. NUTTER M.M. R.A.M.C. for attachment to an	WD

(A8504) Wt W17711/M2031 750,000 5/17 Sch. 53 Forms/C2118/14
D. D. & L., London, E.C.

Army Form C. 2118.

R.A.M.C.
134th FIELD AMBULANCE

WAR DIARY
or
INTELLIGENCE SUMMARY.
(Erase heading not required.)

Instructions regarding War Diaries and Intelligence Summaries are contained in F.S. Regs., Part II. and the Staff Manual respectively. Title pages will be prepared in manuscript.

Place	Date	Hour	Summary of Events and Information	Remarks and references to Appendices
BERTHEN	21/4/18	9p.m.	American Sanitary Train. Adjusted non-commissioned ranks in accordance with establishment in this unit — two acting corporals + two lance/corporals being named. One private ranks.	JAP
BERTHEN	27/4/18	9p.m.	Dull misty day. Route march & a short route march for those not otherwise employed. Forwarded proceedings of a Court of Enquiry regarding loss of A.S.C.(M.T.) rifles to A.D.M.S.	JAP
		10 p.m.	Received orders from A.D.M.S. to detach Major C.D. COYLE R.A.M.C. to report to D.D.M.S. TROUVILLE.	JAP
BERTHEN	28/4/18	9a.m.	Dull rainy day. Church service & parade. Major COYLE R.A.M.C. proceeded to CALAIS en route to TROUVILLE in accordance with instructions. Visited ADMS & was definite for lecture on water duties to the junior American Medical Officers.	JAP
BERTHEN	29/4/18	9p.m.	Dull cloudy day with lightning. Hand parade and inspection of men. About twenty Americans including one Press reporter for instruction in "water duties". Three cases of measles (illness) from 77 to USA Ann today. There have now been daily for the past few days. Attended lecture & demonstration	JAP

-2 MAY 1918
134th FIELD AMBULANCE

WAR DIARY
INTELLIGENCE SUMMARY

Army Form C. 2118.

134th FIELD AMBULANCE

Place	Date	Hour	Summary of Events and Information	Remarks and references to Appendices
BERTHEM	29/4/18	2/pm	An "Delousing" at AUDRICQ given by Major Martin Ravne to American Medical Officer. 30th men of this unit entertained from 6 to 8.30 pm at AUDRICQ by the W.A.A.C.	4HP
BERTHEM	30/4/18	4/m	Bull slight rain. Usual morning parade & short route march & drill. Capt. O'Connor M.O.R.C and Lt Wagner M.O.C. Lt.Lt. 77th Divn. U.S.A. reported for instruction & attached at BERTHEM. Under orders of A.D.M.S No 6/970 of 20th April Lt BOGART M.O.R.C and Lieut W F TISDALE R.A.M.C were detailed & report to A.D.M.S 25th Division Chateau Contour for duty. Detailed to give lecture on 8th May at POLINCOVE Lt Colonel C. M. DREW. Ravne returned from leave & Major M. Porter to report on handing over command to A.D.M.S Bde. Divn.	4HP

Handed over 1/5/18 J Porter Major RAMC
9 am
Taken over J C S Crichton Major RAMC
1/5/18

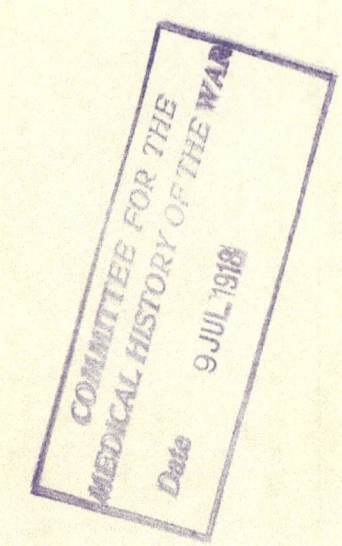

WAR DIARY

OF

No. 134 FIELD AMBULANCE.

FROM :- May 1st, 1918. TO :- May 31st, 1918.

(VOLUME V)

Army Form C. 2118.

134th FIELD AMBULANCE

WAR DIARY
or
INTELLIGENCE SUMMARY.
(Erase heading not required.)

Instructions regarding War Diaries and Intelligence Summaries are contained in F. S. Regs., Part II. and the Staff Manual respectively. Title pages will be prepared in manuscript.

Place	Date	Hour	Summary of Events and Information	Remarks and references to Appendices
BERTHEM (then) HAZEBROUCK (SA)	1.5.18	9 a.m.	Drill morning with bad wind. Personnel received in drills & fatigues.	Adm. 10 O.R. Evac. 9 O.R. 1 O.R. to D.R.S. Remaining nil.
		10.30 am	Reported to A.D.M.S. 39 Div.	
	2.5.18	9 a.m.	Drill morning. Bright later. Lieut Valentine AAMC attached temporarily for duty. Adm 9 O.R. Evac 9 O.R. Remaining nil	
	3.5.18	9 a.m.	Bright sunny morning. Personnel were bathed and had change of underclothing at Spulaques	
		2 p.m.	Demonstration of Fd Ambce equipment given to medical officers of 44 & Div. U.S.A. Adm. 1 Off 2 O.R. (U.S.A) Evac. 1 Off. 9 2 O.R. (U.S.A).	
	4.5.18	9 a.m.	Still morning. Rain during night. Minimum Staff Captain 7, 116 & 119 Brigades arranges to collect any sick of injured and to send on M.O. from 3:5:18 to see the sick of the Brigades	
		11.30 am	6 Sergeants from 305 Fd Ambce U.S.A reported for instruction in the different branches of Fd Ambce work. Adm 1 Off 4 O.R. & 5 O.R. (American army). Evac. & transferred 1 Off 4 O.R. 4 O.R. (U.S.A). 1 O.R (USA) remaining.	

Army Form C. 2118.

2

134th FIELD AMBULANCE
R.A.M.C.

WAR DIARY
or
INTELLIGENCE SUMMARY.
(Erase heading not required.)

Instructions regarding War Diaries and Intelligence Summaries are contained in F. S. Regs., Part II. and the Staff Manual respectively. Title pages will be prepared in manuscript.

Place	Date	Hour	Summary of Events and Information	Remarks and references to Appendices
BERTHEN	3/5/18	9 a.m.	Rain. Dry & dull later. Rain in the afternoon	
		9.15 a.m.	M.O. proceeded to see sick 9/116 Bgde. & 9/117 Bgde.	
			One genito-urinal nephritis admitted (evacuated) from U.S. Army.	
		3 p.m.	Baynes hoff Cr S.M.E. R.C. & Nonconformist Chaplains atten 6/17 Bgde & 117 Bgde arriving arrived 9/116 & 117	
	4/5/18	10 a.m.	All available transport sent out.	
			2nd Board QUDREICQ. Transport returned on completion of duty.	
		7 a.m.	Bright morning.	
		9 a.m.	Instruction given to personnel to proceed with 9/77th Divn. U.S.A. on	
		10.30 a.m.	go-to-nowhere duties. Formed Water Club.	
		2.30 p.m.	A.D.M.S. 39 Div. visited the unit	
			1 section of the ambulance less personnel & 1 S.S. waggon were attached to Brenain Brigam 77th Divn American E.F. Tr movement purposes Tr G. clery.	
			Adm 1.O.R. Evac 1.O.R. & 9.O.R. Rem 9 2 O.R	
	5/5/18	8 a.m.	Heavy rain. Passed W. T. DAVY, M.R.C. U.S.A. proceeds to 25th Divn for duty (Capt A.D.M.S 3 9/26/9/70 9 6/5/18.	

134th FIELD AMBULANCE
1 JUN 1918

Army Form C. 2118.

WAR DIARY
or
INTELLIGENCE SUMMARY
(Erase heading not required.)

134th FIELD AMBULANCE

Place	Date	Hour	Summary of Events and Information	Remarks and references to Appendices
BERTHEM Vaglrived S(A)	7/5/18		Lecture on water duties given to personnel of 97th Div. U.S.A. Admitted 2, O.R. Evac 11 O.R. Transferred to D.R.S. 9. Remg 3 O.R.	
	8/5/18	9 a.m.	Bright sunny morning. Routine all day. All personnel of unit paid. Sent transport & equipment of 1 section to Ameron. Surgeon 97 Div. U.S.A. for use in instruction of Medical Officers. Adm. 12 O.R. Evac. 11 O.R. Remg 4 O.R.	
	9/5/18	9 a.m.	Bright morning. Transport of 1 section occupied as on 8/5/18. Routine all day. Admitted 12 O.R. Evacuated 10 M 9 O.R. To duty 1 O.R. Remg 6 O.R.	
		4 p.m.	C.O.'s drill morning.	
	10/5/18	9 a.m.	Transferred 1 O/Sgt 1 Cpl 9/16 men R.A.M.C. to 133 Fd. Ambce —	
		1 3 p.m.	Dull A.D.M.S. 7/89 9 9 5-18	
	11/5/18	9 a.m.	Dull. Bright later. Division Surgeon 97 Div. visited the unit.	
		9.5 a.m.	Personnel of 305th Amb. Co 9 Fd. Hosp. U.S.A. arrived	
		3 p.m.	for instruction in Ambulance purposes.	

Army Form C. 2118.

134th FIELD AMBULANCE

WAR DIARY
or
INTELLIGENCE SUMMARY.
(Erase heading not required.)

Instructions regarding War Diaries and Intelligence Summaries are contained in F. S. Regs., Part II. and the Staff Manual respectively. Title pages will be prepared in manuscript.

Place	Date	Hour	Summary of Events and Information	Remarks and references to Appendices
SERTHEM	12/5/18	9 a.m.	Dull. Bright later. The 134 Fd. Ambce. is from to-day reduced to the training Cadre laid down by D.D.M.S. in S. & concerts of O.C. Q.M. Sgt. Major & 21 Sgts. & O.R. The remaining personnel proceeded at 3.20 p.m. to ROUEN base depot, marching on strength 129 O.R.	
	13/5/18	9 a.m.	Rain. Bright later. All equipment medical & ordnance checked prior to handing over to the 305 American Fd. Ambce.	
	14/5/18	10 a.m.	Fine bright morning. Proceeded to A.D.M.S.	
		2 p.m.	305 A. Fd. Ambce.	
		5 p.m.	All personnel transport regrouped of 305 A Fd Ambce with training cadre of 134 Fd. Ambce entrained at ALDRUICQ & proceeded to MONDICOURT.	
PA.5. (8bed LENS)	15/5/18	5 a.m.	Train arrived MONDICOURT. Detraining marched to PA.5. and were under Canvas.	
		9.30 a.m.	Reported to A.D.M.S. 42 Div. to which Div. I am now attached.	
			All equipment & stores despatched handed over to O.R. 305 U.S. Fd Ambce now consists of Training Cadre only.	

Army Form C. 2118.

R.A.M.C.
134th FIELD AMBULANCE

WAR DIARY
or
INTELLIGENCE SUMMARY.
(Erase heading not required.)

1 JUN 1918

Place	Date	Hour	Summary of Events and Information	Remarks and references to Appendices
PK5 (Bai LENS 4)	14/5/18	9 a.m.	Bright morning. All ranks of the training cadre are instructing Officers & ranks of 305 A.Fd. Ambce. in the methods of the British Fd. Ambce. as far as work in the field is concerned. Col. MATTHEWS, A.S.O., A.D.M.S. 42 Divn. & Brig.-Genl. JOHNSON, U.S.A. visited camp.	
	17/5/18	9 a.m.	Bright morning. Vicinity of Camp bombed during night.	
	18/5/18	9 a.m.	Bright morning. Thunderstorm in the afternoon. Col. POLLOCK, DSO, DDMS IVth Corps visited the camp.	
	19/5/18	9 a.m.	Bright day. Interviewed Brig.-Gen. JOHNSON, U.S.A., comdg. American troops in this district, re sending further 2 Lt 305 Fd Ambce into the line for instruction. He Ken. agreed to this.	
	20/5/18	9 a.m.	Bright day. Maj.-Gen. Sir MURRAY IRWIN, DMS. 3rd Army visited the Camp.	
	21/5/18	9 a.m.	Dull day. Nothing unusual to record.	
	22/5/18	9 a.m.	Bright weather	
	23/5/18	9 a.m.		

Army Form C. 2118.

R.A.M.C.
134th FIELD AMBULANCE

WAR DIARY
or
INTELLIGENCE SUMMARY.
(Erase heading not required.)

Instructions regarding War Diaries and Intelligence Summaries are contained in F. S. Regs., Part II. and the Staff Manual respectively. Title pages will be prepared in manuscript.

Place	Date	Hour	Summary of Events and Information	Remarks and references to Appendices
P.A.S. (Sheet LENS 11)	24/5/18	9 a.m	Rain all day	
		11 a.m	Col. POLLOCK DDMS IVth Corps lectures American Officers on evacuation of wounded	
		2 p.m	Reconnoitred area between B.H.Q. line between MARIEUX & PAS in reference to evacuation in event of the enemy to ambce being called on to evacuate the line	
	25/5/18	9 a.m	Fine morning	
		9.30 a.m	Reconnaissance as above continued	
			Battery manual to record	
	26/5/18		Bright day	
	27/5/18	9 a.m	Bright day	
			Visited with American Officers the 4th Corps Gas Centre	
		2 p.m	Bright day	
	28/5/18	9 a.m	O.C. 305 Fd Ambce & myself attended conference ADCs M.S.	
		11 a.m	5 Divisions at IVth Corps H.Q.s.	
	29/5/18	9 a.m	Bright day	Appendix I
			Sent in report on having 9 30s American Fd Ambces from 14-29 May	
			Bright morning	
	30/5/18	9 a.m		
		9.30 a.m	Lent 1st Echelon of Car filled with 5 different kinds of splints	

134th FIELD AMBULANCE
1 JUN 1918

Army Form C. 2118.

134th FIELD AMBULANCE. R.A.M.C.

WAR DIARY
or
INTELLIGENCE SUMMARY.
(Erase heading not required.)

Place	Date	Hour	Summary of Events and Information	Remarks and references to Appendices
P.A.S. (Sheet LENS 11)	30/5/18	11 a.m	Lecture by Col GRAY, C.B., consulting surgeon to 3rd Army, on use of Splints	
	31/5/18	9 a.m	Bright morning. All the unit inoculated to-day with T.A.B. vaccine	

Andrew, Lt. Col.,
Comdg 134 Fd. Ambce.

1/6/18.

Appendix I

CONFIDENTIAL.   Copy No. 3

REPORT ON TRAINING OF 305th FIELD AMBULANCE, U. S. ARMY,

- by -

Lieut. Colonel C.M. DREW, Commanding 134th Field Amb. B. E. F.

        The training of this Field Ambulance, which began on the 14th May, has steadily progressed.

    The 134th Field Ambulance was reduced to the training cadre laid down by D.G.M.S., B.E.F., and attached in an advisory capacity.

    All the equipment of the 134th Field Ambulance, B.E.F., was taken over by the American unit on the 14th inst. so that this Ambulance is organised on the same basis as a corresponding British unit.

    The main object has been to instruct all ranks in British methods of evacuation, treatment of wounded and recording same, and use of equipment.

    Prior to the actual taking over, two Officers and six N.C.Os had been attached for ten days to 134th Field Amb. and had been distributed amongst the various Departments to learn the general routine.

    Lectures have been delivered on the following, amongst other subjects :- the system of evacuation; equipment of A.D.S's and forward posts and of Main Dressing Stations; equipment of Field Ambulance; duties of bearer officers and bearers; water duties; camp sanitation; horse management.

    Col. C.E. Pollock, D.S.O., D.D.M.S., IVth Corps, delivered a lecture to Officers on the 24th May on the subject of evacuation of wounded.

    Demonstrations and exercises have also been given in Ordnance and Medical equipment; loading of patients; loading of equipment; the establishment of A.D.S's and collection of wounded from R.A.P's; use of Field Medical Cards; A. & D. Books; Pack Stores; Gas Defence and treatment of Gas cases; Tent pitching; the use of water carts and component parts thereof; construction of latrines, soakage pits, incinerators &c. Riding and Driving, wagon drill, picketing &c. and horsemastership have been fully dealt with; shoeing in the field; details of harness and saddlery, shaft draught, lead and wheel sets and N.C.O's harness; wagon construction and maintenance; feeding and grooming and treatment and observation of sick horses explained; billetting of troops, entraining of Field Ambulance, defence against hostile aircraft, use of distinguishing sign posts and precautions against fire have been practically dealt with.

    Drills and exercises have also been carried out with all ranks wearing the Gas respirator.

    Every effort has been made to familiarise Officers, N.C.Os and men concerned with the use of British Army Forms and for some days past American personnel have completed these forms and performed all necessary services in connection therewith with only slight supervision. This applies to drawing of rations, Ordnance, Medical and Engineers stores &c.

It was considered that the best way of imparting practical knowledge to N.C.Os and men strange to British Army methods, was to arrange that every man having special duties to perform should be set to work with British personnel having corresponding duties - Thus, American water duty men assisted British water duty men; dispensers, pack store men, wagon orderlies, nursing orderlies, drivers &c. did likewise, and in this way a practical knowledge of work in the field has been swiftly obtained.

Officers have been instructed in the making of reconnaissances, and have made actual reconnaissances on the ground with a view to establishment of A.D.S's and Main Dressing Stations in the event of hostile attack, or of an advance.

Arrangements were made with Col. W.R. MATTHEWS, D.S.O., A.D.M.S., 42nd Div., for the Officers, N.C.Os and men to be attached to a Field Ambulance evacuating the line. This was done and valuable instruction was received at the A.D.S. and M.D.S. of the 57th Div. After three days experience, the first detachment was withdrawn and relieved by a similar number of Officers, N.C.Os and men. These detachments have now had actual experience of line work and it is proposed to continue these reliefs until the whole Field Ambulance has first hand knowledge of line work.

The Officers have visited the Vth Corps Gas Centre where a demonstration was given of the treatment and administration of gassed cases and the method of organising a Gas Centre explained.

At the invitation of Col. C.E. POLLOCK, D.S.O., D.D.M.S. Vth Corps, the Commanding Officer attended a Conference of A.Ds.M.S. of Divisions on 28th May.

Col. GRAY, Consulting Surgeon IIIrd Army, is to give a demonstration on the use of splints on the 30th May.

The discipline of the unit is good and considerable keenness has been displayed by all ranks in adapting themselves to conditions of active service in the field with British organisations.

The 305th American Field Ambulance is now completely organised on the basis of a British Field Ambulance.

C M Drew
Lieut. Col., R.A.M.C.
Commanding 134 Field Ambulance.

29/5/18

COPIES TO:-

1. A.D.M.S., 30th Div.
2. A.D.M.S., 42nd Div.
3. War Diary.
4. File.

ORIGINAL

4

Yue qu8

CONFIDENTIAL.

Vol 28

160/3046,

WAR DIARY

OF

134th FIELD AMBULANCE

From 1st June 1918 To 30th June 1918

(VOLUME 28.)

COMMITTEE
MEDICAL HISTORY
Date 7 AUG 1918

Army Form C. 2118.

134th FIELD AMBULANCE

WAR DIARY
INTELLIGENCE SUMMARY.
(Erase heading not required.)

Instructions regarding War Diaries and Intelligence Summaries are contained in F. S. Regs., Part II. and the Staff Manual respectively. Title pages will be prepared in manuscript.

Place	Date	Hour	Summary of Events and Information	Remarks and references to Appendices
PAS. (Sheet LENS 11)	1/6/18	9 a.m.	Fine Bright day. Lecture on Sanitation by DADMS (Sanitation) III Army. Reconnoitred positions behind for S. It. Q'mastmath of P.A.S.	
	2/6/18	2.30 p.m. 9 a.m.	Parade of Transport by American Unit. Fine day. Routine all day.	
	3/6/18	9 a.m.	Bright weather.	
	4/6/18	9 a.m.	Dull & cloudy. Arrived Surgeon 77th Divn. U.S. Army visited the Camp.	
	5/6/18	9 a.m.	Routine all day.	
	6/6/18	9 a.m. 6.45 p.m.	Bright morning. 305 7d Amber American E.F. proceeded by route march to LONG PRE to entrain for unknown destination. All equipped and transport 9/134 7d. Ambers handed over and work them. All available motor transport less 1 Ford car of 134 7d Amber proceeded as far as entraining point to duty on the train of march.	
	7/6/18	9 a.m. 11 a.m.	Bright morning. All the Horse Transport A S C personnel attached 9/134 7d. Amber. proceeded to entrain at HANDICOURT for LOSTRAT to report 50 to Co. 39 gen. Train. Cadre now only remain in camp and are expressed on F.G. 118 to 39 Divn	

Army Form C. 2118.

WAR DIARY
or
INTELLIGENCE SUMMARY.
(Erase heading not required.)

134th FIELD AMBULANCE R.A.M.C.

Instructions regarding War Diaries and Intelligence Summaries are contained in F. S. Regs., Part II. and the Staff Manual respectively. Title pages will be prepared in manuscript.

Place	Date	Hour	Summary of Events and Information	Remarks and references to Appendices
PAS	10/6/18	9 a.m	Bright morning. Rain during night	
Nr LENS II		10.45 a.m	Cars returned from duty with 77th Div American E.F.	
		11.45 a.m	Left PAS with Cars and all personnel and proceeded by road to BERTEHEM.	
BERTEHEM		7 p.m	Arrived BERTEHEM & reported to ADMS. 39 Div	
HAREBROUCK Sh	12/6/15	6 a.m	Capt. & Q.M. E. G. FLOYD proceeded on leave to ENGLAND.	
	13/6/15	9 a.m	Bright morning. Personnel paid.	
			Evacs 3 marquees for detachm'g army sick regiment. Bivouac bedding	
	14/6/18	9 a.m	Bright morning	
		8 p.m	Full orders read out on parade by the Sergeant Major	
	19/6/18	9 a.m	Bright morning	
			Training cadre proceeded to VIEIL MOUTIER and took over 7th amber aid here. Awaiting arrival 9 American E.F.	
VIEIL MOUTIER	20/6/18		Employed in collecting sick 7 & 8 Div American E.F.	
(N'd Calais 18)	21/6/18		Collecting American sick.	

Army Form C. 2118.

WAR DIARY
or
INTELLIGENCE SUMMARY.
(Erase heading not required.)

134th FIELD AMBULANCE

Place	Date	Hour	Summary of Events and Information	Remarks and references to Appendices
VIEIL MOUTIER	22/6/18	2 p.m.	312 Ft Ambce U.S.A arrived and are billeted in surrounding farms	
	23/6/18	9.30 a.m	Training of Americans began	
			Bural Scheme – 6.30 a.m	
			7.30 a.m Breakfast	
			9-10 a.m – Parade 10-12-1.5 p.m Lecture Demonstrations 2-4 p.m Lectures & demonstrations	
	24/6/18	9 a.m	Heavy rain Training continued	
	25/6/18	9.30 a.m	Fine morning Training continued	
	26/6/18	9.0 a.m	Fine morning Training continued Capt FLOYD returned from leave	
		6 p.m	Training Cadre marched to DESVRES to entrain for ABBEVILLE where ambulance is to re-equip	
27/6/18		7.00 a.m	and arrived at BOULOGNE 9 were billeted at No 3 rest camp.	
		2.15 p.m	Left BOULOGNE	
ABBEVILLE		9.30 p.m	Arrived ABBEVILLE	
	28/6/18	10.30 a.m	Took over wagons, horses & 372 Ambce. Personnel found awaiting. Complete according to having come from ROUEN	
		4 p.m	Drew medical & surgical equipment from No 13 Base Depot Medical Stores.	
	29/6/18	8 a.m	Drew Ordnance equipment	
		9 p.m	Transport entrained by route march to Headquarters 39 Divn at WOLPHUS Sheet 1A.26.B.B.BUCK.5A).	

Army Form C. 2118.

134th FIELD AMBULANCE

WAR DIARY
or
INTELLIGENCE SUMMARY.
(Erase heading not required.)

Place	Date	Hour	Summary of Events and Information	Remarks and references to Appendices
ABBEVILLE	30/6/18		Personnel standing by awaiting orders to proceed to HQ 39 Div. by train. Orders received to proceed at 9 a.m. on 19/1/18.	
	3/6/18.		Andrews, Lt. Col., Comdg 134th Fd Ambce	

CONFIDENTIAL

WAR DIARY

of

134 FIELD AMBULANCE

FROM, 1st JULY, 1918. TO 31st JULY, 1918.

(VOLUME 29.)

Army Form C. 2118.

WAR DIARY
or
INTELLIGENCE SUMMARY.
(Erase heading not required.)

134th FIELD AMBULANCE

Place	Date	Hour	Summary of Events and Information	Remarks and references to Appendices
ABBEVILLE	1/4/18	10 a.m.	Personnel (RAMC) left by train for AUDRUICQ. Arrived ETAPLES. Spent night here in rest camp.	
ETAPLES	2/4/18	12:30 p.m.	Left ETAPLES by train for AUDRUICQ	
		7-10 a.m.	Arrived AUDRUICQ and marched LOBERTEHEM	
BERTEHEM (Sheet HAZEBROUCK S/A)	3/4/18	1 p.m.	Personnel arrived at BERTEHEM and are billetted in the village.	
		3 p.m.	Transport arrived.	
		6 p.m.	Inspection of unit by Commanding Officer.	
	3/4/18	9 a.m.	All personnel employed all day on fatigues. Unit ordered to remain closed until further orders.	
	4/4/18		A.D.M.S. visited the Unit. Received orders to proceed on 7th to join 30th Div. Am E.F. Divisional Amm. E.F.	
	5/7/18		Routine.	
	7/4/18	8:20 a.m.	H. Ambre left BERTEHEM by route march to join 30th Div 14 21E BROUCK S/A)	
		1 p.m.	Halt on outskirts of HATTEN (Sheet HAZEBROUCK S/A)	
		3 p.m.	Marched to point on road between MERRIS GHEM & FRUCKINGHOVE	
		4:30 p.m.	Arrived and messages here tonight. Men marched well.	
	8/4/18	8:30 a.m.	Left camp by route march for Ambre. Halt at Sheet 27 L10 E34	
		1 p.m.	Halted at HERTZEELE (Sheet HAZEBROUCK S/A)	
		3 p.m.	Left HERTZEELE	
		6:30 p.m.	Arrived at L16 E34 Sheet 27 Work over side.	

Army Form C. 2118.

R.A.M.C.
134th FIELD AMBULANCE

WAR DIARY
or
INTELLIGENCE SUMMARY.
(Erase heading not required.)

Instructions regarding War Diaries and Intelligence Summaries are contained in F. S. Regs., Part II. and the Staff Manual respectively. Title pages will be prepared in manuscript.

Place	Date	Hour	Summary of Events and Information	Remarks and references to Appendices
NINE ELMS (Shed 2) L.10.6.34	9/7/18	9 a.m.	Div. Surg. 30th Div. Am. E.F. visited the camp. RAIN most of the day.	
	10/7/18	9 a.m.	Rain. Showery day. Obtained some stores for R.R.C.S. and prepared a ward for reception of light cases. Collecting sick from 119th & 118th Inf. Reg. Am. E.F. and transferring them to 131 Ft Ambce at ROUSBRUGGE (Field Nº 21 BROCK STAJ)	
	11/7/18	9 a.m.	Rain. Routine	
	12/7/18	9 a.m.	Rain. Showers later. Routine	
	13/7/18	9 a.m.	Rain. Showers later. Visited the posts (medical) to be used in event of 30th Div. Am E.F. occupying BLUE LINE in front of POPERINGHE.	
		2 p.m.	Attended conference at Div. Surg's office — question of evacuation discussed.	
	14/7/18	8 a.m.	Visited all posts as on 13/7/18 with Div. Surg	
		9 a.m.	Rain. Showers.	
		2.30 p.m.	Reconnoitred HERTZEELE WATOU road with Div. Surg. to find Ambce site.	

Army Form C. 2118.

WAR DIARY
or
INTELLIGENCE SUMMARY.
(Erase heading not required.)

134th FIELD AMBULANCE

Place	Date	Hour	Summary of Events and Information	Remarks and references to Appendices
Sheet 27 L10 & 34	13/7/18	9 a.m. 8.45 a.m.	Fair but cloudy. A.D.S. visited the Ambce. Artillery active during afternoon & evening. A.D.M.S. II Corps inspected Ambce.	
	14/7/18	9 a.m.	Fair. Heavy rain and thunder during night. Reconnoitred roads and Fd. Ambce sites in WATOU and HOUTKERQUE areas.	
	17/7/18	9 a.m.	Fair. Routine all day. Rain about 8 p.m. D.S. visited the camp at 6.30 p.m.	
	18/7/18	9 a.m.	Fine morning. Heavy bombardment by our guns. Sick and wounded of 30th Divn. Am. E.F. are being collected from the units now occupying the trenches in the neighbourhood of POPERINGHE.	
	19/7/18	9 a.m.	Fine morning. Fairly quiet night. Reconnoitred roads and positions to be taken up in event of Blue line being occupied by 30 Divn. Am E.F.	
	20/7/18	9 a.m. 11 a.m.	Fine morning. Thunderstorm in the afternoon. D.v. Surg. 30 Divn. Am.E.F. visited the unit.	

Army Form C. 2118.

134th FIELD AMBULANCE

WAR DIARY
or
INTELLIGENCE SUMMARY.
(Erase heading not required.)

Instructions regarding War Diaries and Intelligence Summaries are contained in F. S. Regs., Part II. and the Staff Manual respectively. Title pages will be prepared in manuscript.

Place	Date	Hour	Summary of Events and Information	Remarks and references to Appendices
MOYNIHAM Camp 27/L10 B.34	24/7/18	9 a.m. 11 a.m.	Bright morning. Visited M.O. of VOGELTGE (Sh.I.27) and found that an A.D.S. is being prepared here. This will be used by 134 Fd. Ambce. in event of Blue Zone being occupied by 30th Div. Am. E.F.	
	22/7/18	9 a.m. 7 p.m.	Bright morning. Major J.H. PORTER reported for duty.	
	23/7/18	9 a.m.	Rain all day. Holding half of BERTEIHEM reopened vacant. Bethune given by Col. Sickland, V.S.A. to American Officers on "B an".	
	24/7/18	9 a.m.	Bright morning. Rain later. Routine all day.	
	25/7/18	9 a.m.	Rain. Pers. moved to units. Routine. Major PORTER proceeded on leave.	
	26/7/18	9 a.m.	Rain. Routine all day. Hand gave concert to patients at 6 p.m.	
	27/7/18	9 a.m.	Rain. Personnel of bands of 3.9th & 960th Brigade Am. E.F. reported for instruction in Field Medical Work.	

Army Form C. 2118.

WAR DIARY
or
INTELLIGENCE SUMMARY.
(Erase heading not required.)

134th FIELD AMBULANCE

Place	Date	Hour	Summary of Events and Information	Remarks and references to Appendices
MOYNIHAN Camp L.10 b 3.4	28/7/18	9 a.m.	Rain. Band of 117 Inf. Reg. attended for instruction and tried out.	
		9 a.m.		
		5.30 p.m.	Transport Ers/section proceeded to WENDINGHEM and are to remain for this time — Gen. of Div. Insp.	
	29/7/18	9 a.m.	Fine weather. Routine all day. The unit played a cricket match with 133 Fd. Amb — Result 134 Fd. Amb 92 runs 133 Fd. Amb 84 runs.	
	30/7/18	9 a.m.	Fine weather. Routine.	
	31/7/18	9 a.m.	Fine weather. Nothing unusual to report.	

Chateau, Lt. Col.
Comdg 134 Fd. Amb.

31/7/18

CONFIDENTIAL

Vol 30
40/3200.

WAR DIARY.

OF

134 FIELD AMBULANCE

FROM 1st Aug. 1918 TO 31st Aug. 1918

(VOLUME 30)

ORIGINAL
Aug. 1918

COMMITTEE FOR THE
MEDICAL HISTORY OF THE WAR
Date 5 OCT 1918

Army Form C. 2118.

R.A.M.C.
134th FIELD AMBULANCE

WAR DIARY
or
INTELLIGENCE SUMMARY
(Erase heading not required.)

Place	Date	Hour	Summary of Events and Information	Remarks and references to Appendices
NINE ELMS	1/8/18	9 a.m.	Fine weather.	
		3 p.m.	M Officers & 209 enlisted men of Sanitary train of 30th Am. Div. arrived in adjoining camp and are attached to 134 Fd Amb. for training purposes.	
	2/8/18	9 a.m.	Heavy rain all day. Conference of officers and selected (American Sanitary train) personnel in execution of line.	
		9.30 a.m.	3 Officers & 41 O.R. (American Sanitary train) proceeded to report to O.C. 99 Fd. Amb. for first hand instruction in execution of line. Div Surgeon 30th Am. E.F. visited Camp. Remainder of Am. Sanitary train employed in specialist duties attached to corresponding personnel of 134 Fd. Amb. for instruction.	
	3/8/18	9 a.m.	Rain. Lectures given on Evacuation of wounded, names of medical establishments and water carts & water duties. Practical demonstrations in Bandaging and application of Splints.	
	4/8/18	9 a.m.	Fine morning. Officers instructed in making reconnaissance in the field. Visit to R.A.P's. A.D.S. and Relay Posts in connection with Blue line defence. Other ranks continued First aid work. Organization of Fd. Ambce explained. Demonstration of medical, surgical and ordnance equipment.	
		3 p.m.	D.D.M.S. "Corps visited Camp. 44 Reinforcements arrived from Rene. Enemy artillery active in neighbourhood of camp - shelling balloons	

Army Form C. 2118.

134th FIELD AMBULANCE

WAR DIARY
or
INTELLIGENCE SUMMARY.
(Erase heading not required.)

Place	Date	Hour	Summary of Events and Information	Remarks and references to Appendices
Sheet 27 L10 6 84 NINE ELMS	5/9/18	9 a.m.	Fair. Lecture on gas protection and orders to all Amn. Sanitary personnel. Practical demonstration on working of Fd. Ambee and its interior economy. Methods of dealing with patients, sanitation etc. to all ranks.	
		2 p.m.	Lectures to Officers on how to man and equip A.D.S. & relay posts, Evacuation of line in trench warfare and during a withdrawal, how to maintain discipline and punctuals in the field. O.R.'s occupied in the afternoon with instruction in knots and D.S. visits the Ambee. Began work in making a large Red Cross (7×4 ft) to designate unit to enemy air craft.	
	6/9/18	9 a.m.	Dull. Much rain during night. O.R.'s (Am Fd Ambee) made him of A.D.S. R. Posts & R.A.P.'s and were shown practically how to choose routes & evacuation explained on the spot. Lectures to Officers on Thomas Splint, evacuation grounds in an advance, organisation of British Fd. Ambee personnel. All ranks of Am. Fd. Ambee ordered to wear gas mask for 1 hour by day for 4 days then 1 hour by night for 4 nights. Officers of Am. Fd. Ambee employed & instructed in duties of orderly officer.	
		4 p.m.	Officers & men drilled in loading stretchers & trenching with loaded stretchers.	

Army Form C. 2118.

134th FIELD AMBULANCE

WAR DIARY
or
INTELLIGENCE SUMMARY.
(Erase heading not required.)

Place	Date	Hour	Summary of Events and Information	Remarks and references to Appendices
Sheet 27 L10 b34 NINE ELMS	7/8/18	9 a.m.	Dull cloudy morning. Enemy aeroplanes active during night. A few bombs dropped near camp. Officers 9 a.m. Ft. Ambce. made reconnaissance gas posts in Lgt of line & submitted schemes for evacuation of wounded. Men instructed in stretcher drill & first aid.	
	8/8/18	9 a.m.	Bright morning. Instruction of Americans continued - First aid, gas drill, carrying, loaded stretchers, anatomy and reconnaissance work. D.S. visited the Camp.	
	9/8/18	9 a.m.	Bright morning. Instruction of Americans in First aid & stretcher drill.	
	10/8/18	9 a.m.	Dull morning. Enemy shelled vicinity of Camp. D.S. 30th Am. Bn. visited. Instruction 9 a.m. Ft. Ambce. continued. Routine all day.	
	11/8/18			
	12/8/18	9 a.m.	Fine morning. Major J.H. PORTER, RAMC. returns from leave. Bandaging and stretcher drill practice for men 9 a.m. F.F.	

Army Form C. 2118.

R.A.M.C. 4
134th FIELD AMBULANCE

WAR DIARY
or
INTELLIGENCE SUMMARY.
(Erase heading not required.)

Instructions regarding War Diaries and Intelligence Summaries are contained in F. S. Regs., Part II. and the Staff Manual respectively. Title pages will be prepared in manuscript.

Place	Date	Hour	Summary of Events and Information	Remarks and references to Appendices
MOYNIHAN CAMP 27/L10 & 34	13/8/18	9 a.m.	Fine morning. Officers attended lecture at HOOGSTANDE Belgian Hospital on treatment of "wound 9. jambe".	
	14/8/18	9 a.m.	Fine morning. D.S. visited the camp. Otherwise routine.	
	15/8/18	9 a.m.	Fine morning.	
		1.30 p.m.	Ordered to take over evacuation Pt. for 30th Am. Div.	
		3 p.m.	Visited MOORE PARK (H.Q.) 101 Fd Amb, & taking over here.	
	16/8/18	9 a.m.	Fine morning.	
		10 a.m.	Went round Ambce posts on the sector immediately South of YPRES he taking over. Advance parties proceeded to the various posts in the line - Major Cooke, M.C. in Command.	
		3 p.m.	Again went round the posts with Div Surgeon. Found advance parties established.	
	17/8/18	9 a.m.	Fine morning. Main body of Fd Ambce left MOYNIHAN CAMP for MOORE PARK (New 28).	
MOORE PARK 29/S 4 & 47		4 p.m.	All fd hands handed over and 134 Fd. Amb. established with H.Q. at MOORE PARK and now functioning the sector South of YPRES the 30th Am. Div.	

Army Form C. 2118.

134th FIELD AMBULANCE

WAR DIARY
or
INTELLIGENCE SUMMARY.
(Erase heading not required.)

Place	Date	Hour	Summary of Events and Information	Remarks and references to Appendices
PEOPLE- RINGE Rd 28/ B d 9.7	18/8/18		Scheme of Evacuation transferred shown in Appendix I	Appendix I
		3 p.m.	Major PORTER visited all the posts and reported that everyone was settled down and that Evacuation was proceeding smoothly	
	19/8/18	9 a.m.	Fine day. Visited all R.A.P's and Fd Ambce posts and Mr Q y Scott Infantry appoints with Col WHALEY DS 30th Am Div. It is intended gradually to replace British personnel by personnel of 119 Fd Ambce Am. E.F.	
	19/8/18	9 a.m.	Fine day. Inspected Transport at MENDINGHEM. Visited 119° & 110 & 119 Fd Ambce Am E.F. to arrange about shifts. Met D.M.S. II ARMY then.	
		3 p.m.	Inspected sites for Camp for Fd Ambce and returned decided to send British personnel on relief to MOYNIHAN Camp 27/L.10634	
	20/8/18	10 a.m.	Fine morning. American reported for duty and are distributed through the various posts.	
		2.30 p.m.	Went round the lines and visited all posts. Going relieved family accident in neighbourhood of Belgian Battery Corner A.D.S.	
	21/8/18			

WAR DIARY
or
INTELLIGENCE SUMMARY.
(Erase heading not required.)

Army Form C. 2118.

R.A.M.C.
134th FIELD AMBULANCE

Place	Date	Hour	Summary of Events and Information	Remarks and references to Appendices
MOORE PARK Sheet 28 54 d 77	20/8/18	5.30 pm	D.D.M.S. II Corps visited H.Q & 7d. Ambce	
	21/8/18	9a to 10a.m	Fine morning. Americans reported for duty and posted to the various posts. The state now is 25/o Bonhak & 75/o American personnel in the line. Major Cooke on relief by Lieut JOHNSTON 119 7d Ambce returned to H.Q. and thereafter proceeded to MOYVIHAIN CAMP with details of 134 7d Ambce not required for the line. Now forms a bearer reserve pool. One water cart and one horsed Ambce from 119 7d Ambce (Am. S.B.) and relieved corresponding Bonhak movement at VLAMERTINGHE MILL. Strength 12 O/R need draft until over 15 months service without leave have now gone on leave. Inspected post at POPERINGHE TOWN HALL and the reserve A.D.S. at the Brewery in the outskirts of POPERINGHE at	

Army Form C. 2118.

R.A.M.C.
134th FIELD AMBULANCE

WAR DIARY
or
INTELLIGENCE SUMMARY.
(Erase heading not required.)

Place	Date	Hour	Summary of Events and Information	Remarks and references to Appendices
MOORE PARK 28/5 & 29/7	28/8/18	9 a.m.	Fine morning. Visited all posts in the line. Found the work satisfactory and settling down to the work satisfactorily. 2/Lt. O.T.R. of 119 Am. Fd. Ambce. relieved corresponding number of British personnel in the line. The state now is 13% British and 87% American personnel. Friendship of the line very few casualties are being dealt with.	
	29/8/18	9 a.m.	Fine morning. Inspected camp ad. 27/L10.b.3.4 and found everything satisfactory. Visited pool in POPERINGHE and on the POPERINGHE-VLAMERTINGHE road, condition entirely satisfactory. 11 men from T.M.B. in neighbourhood reports sick this morning — doubting Investigation showed that the illness was caused by eating meat which had become bad on account of the heat. All except one were put in 24 hours.	
	30/8/18	9 a.m.	Fine morning. Inspected all posts in the line. Impressed with confidence shown by the American personnel. Both Officers and men are working well, are keen on the job and show aptitude for the work. A.D.M.S. II Corps visited VLAMERTINGHE MILL MOORE PARK.	

WAR DIARY
or
INTELLIGENCE SUMMARY.
(Erase heading not required.)

Army Form C. 2118.

R.A.M.C.
134th FIELD AMBULANCE

Place	Date	Hour	Summary of Events and Information	Remarks and references to Appendices
MOORE PARK	25/8/18	9 a.m.	Fine morning. Rain in the evening. Visited all the Fd. Ambce posts and the R.A.P. at 28/H24c1015 with Major Gen. LEWIS comdg 30 Div. Am. E.F. and Col. WHITLEY Div. Surg. The General expressed his satisfaction with all he had seen. Thereafter visited the detachment of 134 Fd. Ambce and H.Q. no. 2 of 119 Fd Ambce (Am. E.F.) at 28/L10 e34. The General again was satisfied with what he saw. During the night the enemy had gas shelled some of the forward area. All casualties were quickly evacuated.	
	26/8/18	9 a.m.	Dull & cloudy. Rain later.	
		4 p.m.	One of the Ambulance cars collided with Light Railway train. Car had to be evacuated.	
	27/8/18	9 a.m.	Dull morning. Slight showers during the day.	
		9 a.m.	Visited Fd. Ambce posts in the line with Div. Surg. 30th Am. Div. 27 gassed cases had been dealt with during night at the A.D.S. and evacuated to M. D.S. (Am. E.F.)	
		11:10 a.m.	1 Officer 38 O.R. of 116 Fd. Ambce reported and were detailed for duty at the various posts in the line relieving a corresponding number of posts, personnel of 119 Fd. Ambce (Am. E.F.)	
		5:30 p.m.	Major J.A. PORTER M.C. visited the Fd. Ambce posts and reported that the relief had been carried out.	

Army Form C. 2118.

134th FIELD AMBULANCE

WAR DIARY
or
INTELLIGENCE SUMMARY.
(Erase heading not required.)

Place	Date	Hour	Summary of Events and Information	Remarks and references to Appendices
MOORE PARK	28/8/18	9 a.m.	Dull, Rain later.	
		9.30 a.m.	Personnel of 118 Fd. Ambce. Ocr. E.F. relieved remainder of 119 Fd. Ambce. 1/2 Lt. BRANDAU in command of 9 A.D.S. & forward posts.	
		4.30 p.m.	Visited A.D.S. at Belgian Battery Corner with Div. Surg. Relief had been carried out and 118 Fd Ambce personnel established in the posts.	
	29/8/18	9 a.m.	Bright morning. Major PORTER visited the posts in the forward area.	
	30/8/18	9 a.m.	Bright morning. Found everything satisfactory.	
		9.30 a.m.	Proceeded to the A.D.S. and inspected the Fd. Ambce. posts. Thereafter with Major PORTER reconnoitred the area between Belgian Battery Corner and VLAMERTINGHE MILL with a view to establishing relay posts on the Decauville track and road in the event of an attack and the A.D.S. became untenable.	
	31/8/18	9 a.m.	Bright morning.	
		9 a.m.	It is reported that the enemy has retired from KEMMEL HILL. Went round the Fd. Ambce posts with Div. Surgeon.	
		11 a.m.	Visited transport at MENDINGHEM and warned W.O. i/c to be prepared to move at short notice.	
		2.30 p.m.	Visited the A.D.S. with Div. Surg. Found that the 30th Div. has sent out reconnoitring patrols. Casualties began to come in.	
		3.53 p.m.	Ordered Major Cooke to take over command of A.D.S., extra bearers to come to A.D.S. and extra cars for duty.	
		5.35 p.m.	Major Cooke took over command 9 A.D.S. 11 cars are now on the road. Wounded being brought to MENDINGHEM without delay.	

Cunden, Lt. Col.
Comdg. 134 Fd. Ambce.

COPY.   ADMINISTRATIVE ORDER NO.5 - 30th AMERICAN DIVISION.

SECRET.   APPENDIX III. *Appendix I*

MEDICAL ARRANGEMENTS.

1. REGIMENTAL AID POSTS.

   Left Regiment.
   (a) I.19.b.2.5.   DOLL'S HOUSE.   Front Line Left.
   (b) I.19.c.3.7.   SWAN CHATEAU.   "   "   Right.
   (c) H.15.b.9.4.   Support.

   Right Regiment.
   (a) H.30.a.5.9.   Front Line Left.
   (B) H.24.c.4.0.   "   "   Right.
   (c) H.23.b.5.2.   Support.

   Reserve Regiment.
   (a) G.11.d.4.3.
   (b) G.11.d.1.2.
   (c) H.7.c.7.0.

2. RELAY POSTS.
   AMBULANCE FARM,   H.14.b.8.2.
   BRANDHOEK,   G.12.b.8.8.

3. ADVANCED DRESSING STATION,
   AND CAR LOADING POST.   BELGIAN BATTERY CORNER.   H.24.a.5.8.

4. BEARER POST & D.W.W.C.P.   Mill, VLAMERTINGHE.   H.18.a.9.8.

5. RESERVE A.D.S. &
   "A" FLD.AMB.HDQRS.   MOORE PARK.   G.4.a.7.7.

6. ADVANCE DRESSING STATION &
   FOR GREEN LINE.   HARBISON POST.   G.3.c.5.3.

7. MAIN DRESSING STATION &
   GAS CENTRE ("B" F.A.HQRS)   MENDINGHEM.   27/E.6.d.central.

8. CORPS W.W.C.P. & DIVISION
   REST STATION ("C" F.A.HQRS) BANDAGHEM.   19/W.28.d.4.0.

9. MEDICAL INSPECTION ROOM FOR
   MINIMUM RESERVE & TRANSPORT LINES.   27/L.14.b.2.5.

10. SCHEME OF EVACUATION.

   "A" Field Ambulance is responsible for the evacuation of casualties from the 2 Regiments in the Line and the Regiments in Reserve, also sick in the forward area.

   Cases are conveyed from the Regimental Aid Stations by Light Railway, hand carriage, or wheeled stretchers to Advance Dressing Station, BELGIAN BATTERY CORNER; thence by Division Ambulance cars to the Main Dressing Station, MENDINGHEM.

   Uregtn cases will be sent to Casualty Clearing Station from Advance Dressing Station direct.

   From AMBULANCE FARM, local sick are evacuated by Division cars to MILL, VLAMERTINGHE.

   Walking Wounded are directed to the Division Station for Walking Wounded at the MILL, VLAMERTINGHE. Cases are loaded on the Light Railway at ORILLA (28/H.1.b.9.3.) and unloaded at PUGWASH SIDING (27/E.6.b.1.5.), 300 yards from the M.D.S. MENDINGHEM.

   Trains are obtained by M.O.i/c Mill, VLAMERTINGHE, by application to O.C., No.12 Light Railway Operating Coy, Headquarters, at CORNISH CROSS (28/A.16.a.central).

ORIGINAL.
BOX 19/8

CONFIDENTIAL.

WO 31
140/3327.

WAR DIARY.

of

134TH FIELD AMBULANCE.

From :- 1st September 1918. To 30th September 1918.

(VOLUME 31.)

Army Form C. 2118.

R.A.M.C.
134th FIELD AMBULANCE

WAR DIARY
or
INTELLIGENCE SUMMARY
(Erase heading not required.)

Instructions regarding War Diaries and Intelligence Summaries are contained in F. S. Regs., Part II. and the Staff Manual respectively. Title pages will be prepared in manuscript.

Place	Date	Hour	Summary of Events and Information	Remarks and references to Appendices
MOORE PARK 28/S4 d 4.7	1/9/18	9 a.m.	Fine morning. From 9 a.m. 29/8/18 to 9 a.m. 1/9/18 2 officers and 70 wounded were passed through the A.D.S. There was no hitch in the evacuation. During the night 31/8/1/9/18 the R.A.P. at 14/I 19 6 2 5 was moved forward to 28/I 20 c 3 3 (WOODCOT E HOUSE) and the post at 28/I 19 6 2 5 became a Relay post.	
		9.30 a.m.	38 O.R. 9 118 Fd Amb. proceeded to forward posts to relieve corresponding number 9/118 Fd Amb. who returned on relief to MENDINGHEM.	
		10 a.n.	Visited the posts and found evacuation going satisfactorily. Ordered 1/R.C. BRANDAU 119 Fd Amb. On E.F. to return to his unit - tour of duty at A.D.S. expired. 1/Friend SMITH (118 Fd Amb.) relieved him.	Wounded shell
		2.15 p.m.	Again visited the forward posts with Div. Surgeon coming in. Evacuation going well.	
		3 p.m.	As the R.A.P.s at 28/I 19 C 37 and 28/H 15 6 94 are expected to be moved forward to night. Ordered 24 extra bearers to proceed to the MILL and remain there until required for duty, at the new Relay Posts forward of regiment.	
		9 p.m.	Visited the MILL and found all in readiness for the bearers to move forward if required. Warning notice received to day to hand over all posts to a Fd Amber 9 35 Div. which is relieving the 30th Div. (Am E.F.)	
MOORE PARK 28/S4 d 4.7	2/9/18	9 a.m.	Bright morning. Quiet night.	
		9.30 a.m.	Visited forward posts with O.C. 105 Fd Amber. re handing over	

(A8704) Wt. W.771/M3031 750,000 5/17 Sch. 52 D. & Co., Ltd. London, E.C. Forms/C218/14

Army Form C. 2118.

134th FIELD AMBULANCE
R.A.M.C.

WAR DIARY
or
INTELLIGENCE SUMMARY.
(Erase heading not required.)

Instructions regarding War Diaries and Intelligence Summaries are contained in F.S. Regs., Part II. and the Staff Manual respectively. Title pages will be prepared in manuscript.

Place	Date	Hour	Summary of Events and Information	Remarks and references to Appendices
Moore Park 20/54 d 4.7	2/9/18		Found all RAP's had been cleared. The Battalions in front appear now to be consolidating positions. Front line appears to run from VOORMEZEELE to LOCK 8 and then in front of WOODCOTE HOUSE.	
		12p.m.	Orders received to hand over line to 105 Fd Amb and move to 9 Elms camp 27/L.6.34 - relief to be completed by 12 midnight on night of 3/4 Sept 1918.	
		12.30p.m.	Received the 4 extra cars from 118 to return to their unit.	
	3/9/18	9 a.m.	Bright morning.	
		9.30a.m.	The 105 Fd Amb arrived at MOORE PARK and proceeded to take over the line.	
		11 a.m.	D.S. 30th Div. visited the camp.	
		4.30p.m.	All reliefs completed and 105 Fd Amb now responsible for the evacuation of the line.	
			All details 2/118 & 119 Fd Ambces (Am. E.F.) returned to their units.	
27/L10 6.34		5p.m.	Arrived 9 Elms and took over the camp.	
			Received orders to-day to be prepared to move with 30th Div. Am. E.F. to III (British) Army.	
	4/9/18	9 a.m.	Bright morning.	
		4 p.m.	Cleared by men of Ambce. Preparing for move by rail. Nothing unusual to record.	

Army Form C. 2118.

WAR DIARY
or
INTELLIGENCE SUMMARY.
(Erase heading not required.)

Place	Date	Hour	Summary of Events and Information	Remarks and references to Appendices
17/L10 d 34	5/9/18	9 a.m.	Bright morning. Reconnoitred route to entraining station.	
		10 a.m.	Preparing for train journey to IIIrd (British) Army	
	6/9/18	9 a.m.	Bright morning. Fd Ambce paraded & proceeded by route march to MENDINGHEM (BALLANCE CAMP) 27/E 6 d 42.	
27/E 6 d 42		2 p.m.	Arrived at BALLANCE CAMP (27/E 6 d 42) and billeted for night.	
		3.45 p.m.		
	7/9/18	4.20 a.m.	Reveille.	
		5.20 a.m.	Fd Ambce proceeded by route march to HEIDEBEEK (19/x 27 a 2.4) entraining station. The horse transport proceeded to station at 3 p.m.	
		6.15 a.m.	Arrived at entraining station (19 x 27 a 2 4) and breakfasted.	
		6.30 a.m.	The whole Fd Ambce is entrained.	
		7.30 a.m.	Train left for PETIT HOUVIN (Sheet LENS 11)	
		6 p.m.	Train arrived at PETIT HOUVIN – journey uneventful. Unit detrained & proceeded for billet area at MESNIL St POL (Sheet LENS 11)	
MESNIL St POL Sheet LENS 11		8 p.m.	Unit arrived and are billeted in an old farm in the village of MESNIL St POL.	
			It rained most of the day with occasional thunder.	
	8/9/18	9 a.m.	Rain. Unit is engaged in general fatigues in the camp. Sick are being collected for units in the neighbourhood and are then sent to 119 Fd Ambce at FRAMECOURT (Sheet Lens 11).	

Army Form C. 2118.

134th FIELD AMBULANCE

WAR DIARY
or
INTELLIGENCE SUMMARY.
(Erase heading not required.)

Place	Date	Hour	Summary of Events and Information	Remarks and references to Appendices
M/SMIL S^tPOL blw PENS II	9/9/18	9 a.m.	Heavy rain which continued nearly all day. The personnel are occupied in fatigues and trying to get the site to appear habitable. As it continues to rain, mud is everywhere.	
	10/9/18	9 a.m.	Rain.	
			Reported D.D.M.S. I Corps. Routine.	
	11/9/18	9 a.m.	Rain. Routine.	
	12/9/18	9 a.m.	Rain. Routine.	
	13/9/18	9 a.m.	Fair with showers. Routine.	
	14/9/18	9 a.m.	Showery. Routine.	
	15/9/18	9 a.m.	Dry fine day.	
			Orders received to be prepared for a move in next 48 hours.	
	16/9/18	9 a.m.	Fair. Collecting local sick and awaiting detailed orders to move on 19th which arrived at 3 p.m.	
	17/9/18	4.30 a.m.	Reveille.	
		5.15 a.m.	Breakfast. Thereafter finishing breaks & packing the wagons.	
		6 a.m.	Parade ready to march off to entraining station.	
		6.15 a.m.	Personnel under command of Major PORTER marches to entraining station at PETIT HOUVAIN (Sheet LENS 11)	
		6.45 a.m.	Transport marched off under command of Lieut TISDALE to proceed by road to new location	

WAR DIARY
or
INTELLIGENCE SUMMARY.

Army Form C. 2118.

Place	Date	Hour	Summary of Events and Information	Remarks and references to Appendices
MESNIL S:POL	17/9/18	8:45 a.m.	Motor transport proceeded to new location	
SWD LENS 11		10:30 a.m.	Motor transport arrived. All ranks billeted in the village of LEALVILLERS	
LEALVILLERS		5 p.m.	Personnel arrived on lorries in trains	
SWD LENS 11	18/9/18	9 a.m.	Joined Collecting sect'n 7 Division	
		3:30 p.m.	Transport arrived	
			Visited 59 CCS to arrange for evacuation of sick	
	19/9/18	9 a.m.	Personnel on route march and doing corps drills & exercises	
			Have prepared a house for reception of sick – to be used if required	
		5 p.m.	A.D.S. visited	
		9 a.m.	True. Rondin	
	20/9/18	9 p.m.	Warning order received for unit to be prepared to move by bus	
			Showery	
	21/9/18	9 a.m.	Orders received to new billeting heads	
		9:50 a.m.	Billeting party proceeded to new site at present unknown	
		9:40 a.m.	Transport under command of Lieut W.F. TISDALE proceeded by road to new site	
		4 p.m.	Route march to new site	
		9 p.m.	Attended Conference at Office of Div. Supp. 30th Am. Div.	
			Capt R.L. MORRIS reported for duty with Fd. Ambce – orders of Div. Surg.	

WAR DIARY
or
INTELLIGENCE SUMMARY.

Army Form C. 2118.

(Erase heading not required.)

Instructions regarding War Diaries and Intelligence Summaries are contained in F. S. Regs., Part II. and the Staff Manual respectively. Title pages will be prepared in manuscript.

Place	Date	Hour	Summary of Events and Information	Remarks and references to Appendices
LEALVILLERS Sheet LENS 11	22/9/18	9 a.m.	Showery.	
	23/9/18	11 a.m.	Motor transport proceeded by road to new area.	
		9 a.m.	Fair.	
		10/-	Personnel entrained & proceeded to new area.	
	24/9/18	9 a.m.	Fine morning.	
		9.0 a.m.	Personnel arrived in new area and found transport & motor ambulance had arrived. Billeting officer had taken over site	
BRUSLE 62c/T34 b24			at BRUSLE 62c/T34 b24	
		9 a.m.	All unit now established at above site & standing by to take the line when called on.	
	25/9/18	9 a.m.	Fine morning. Cleaning up & necessary structures prepared. Camp is being cleared up.	
	26/9/18	9 a.m.	Fair.	
		11 a.m.	4 motor ambulance cars sent to 189 Fd. Ambce. (Am.) for duty in the line.	
		4.45 p.m.	One Ford car sent for duty to the line.	
			Personnel are doing physical drill & route marching with view to having them for open warfare.	
			The Ambce. is standing by as reserve to take over line	
	27/9/18	9 a.m.	Fair.	
		10 a.m.	Drills exercised for the personnel. Lieut. I.C.M. & 2 Men to act as helping hands. 1 Fd. Ambce. ads at BRIE	

Army Form C. 2118.

WAR DIARY
~~INTELLIGENCE SUMMARY.~~

(Erase heading not required.)

134th FIELD AMBULANCE

Place	Date	Hour	Summary of Events and Information	Remarks and references to Appendices
BRUSLE 62c I.34.b.2.4	25/9/18	noon	Orders received to move to HERVILLY (62c K.25 d.10.6) take over the ADS at JEANCOURT (62c L.26 d.1.1) & the forward posts. Ready for the afternoon.	
HERVILLY 62c K.23 d.10.6		4 pm	Arrived in HERVILLY. Bearers with Major R.C. COOKE proceeded to the forward post at L.23 d.2.5 Sheet 62c & took over the working of the line from 118 American Field Ambulance. Major PORTER with the Tent Subdivision proceeded to JEANCOURT & took over the A.D.S. from 118 American F.A.	
		6 pm	All bearers of 134 F.A. and reporters, were dispatched to the forward post at L.23 d.2.5.	
JEANCOURT	29/9/18	5 AM	H.Q. & Transport moved to JEANCOURT	
		5.50 AM	Zero hour. Weather appalling. Wounded poured through all day without a hitch conveying the cast on by the roads the difficulty being found in moving over the roads.	
		10 AM	One hundred American Infantry reporters for duty as bearers; 50 of these were used by Major COOKE	

Army Form C. 2118.

WAR DIARY
or
INTELLIGENCE SUMMARY.
(Erase heading not required.)

Place	Date	Hour	Summary of Events and Information	Remarks and references to Appendices
JEANCOURT 6" L26 d.1.1	29/9/18	3 p.	Major Porter reconnoitres the forward posts.	
	30/9/18	3 p.	Weather cleared & roads became better. Wounded still coming through. I reconnoitres the forward posts. Owing to a further attack by the Australians through this Division, we were found our position well behind the line.	
	30/9/18			

Andrews Lt Col
Comdg 134 Fd Ambce.

ORIGINAL.
Oct 1914 –

WO 32
16/332/

CONFIDENTIAL.

WAR DIARY

of

134TH FIELD AMBULANCE.

From:- 1st October 1918. To 31st October 1918.

(VOLUME 32.)

COMMITTEE FOR THE
MEDICAL HISTORY OF THE WAR
4 DEC. 1918
Date

Army Form C. 2118.

WAR DIARY
or
INTELLIGENCE SUMMARY
(Erase heading not required.)

Place	Date	Hour	Summary of Events and Information	Remarks and references to Appendices
JEANCOURT b.26.d.1.1	1/10/18	5p.m.	Things quietened down.	
		7p.m.	Stretchers of the 13th F.A. were withdrawn. Major COOKE & remainder of bearers were withdrawn to T.Q.	
"	2/10/18	2 Am	The unit ceased to receive patients. We received orders to pull out during the morning.	
		6 Am	All surplus equipment was handed over to the Australian 3rd A.D.S. was not handed over, being 3 too far in the rear.	
		8.30 Am	Unit marched out.	
		noon	Thermit halts to midday meal, at a kilometer East of PERONNE.	
		2p.m	March continues	
ASSEVILLERS 62.c N.13 central		5p.m	Arrived at destination. Billets good.	

Army Form C. 2118.

WAR DIARY
or
INTELLIGENCE SUMMARY
(Erase heading not required.)

Place	Date	Hour	Summary of Events and Information	Remarks and references to Appendices
ASSEVILLERS Sheet 62c N 13 b Central	Oct 3rd	10 a.m.	Lt Col Drew left on 14 days leave to England. Major J H Poher M.C. left to join the 51st Wing RA.7 more others of the Strength of the Unit.	
			Unit settled into billets. A Hospital has taken out to receive all patients from the 130th Infantry. Cap't Morris 泡 D.C. (50) (Found for Surgeon Sgt. Burgess's Office, ref. a move back into the Conference at Bri. Surgeon's Office.	
	4/10/18	from 3 p.m.	Reconnoitred the A.D.S., M.D.S. – Walking Wounded Center, at BELLICOURT TEMPLEUX & HARGICOURT Infectively. L't FERRAN M.R.C. & Lieut WYMAN joined the Unit for temporary duty.	
		5 p.m.	Receive movement orders at 5 p.m.	
HAMEL 62c/K13c Central	5/10/18 9 Am		Unit moved by road to HAMEL, less Bearer Divisions, which entrained at H+d, detrained at RONSSOY, there came under orders of 132 Field Ambulance. Lieut FERRAN was in charge of this party.	
		Midnight	The Winter time came into use.	

Army Form C. 2118.

WAR DIARY
or
INTELLIGENCE SUMMARY.
(Erase heading not required.)

Place	Date	Hour	Summary of Events and Information	Remarks and references to Appendices
HAMEL	5/10/18	7 A.m.	The unit, less Bearers, moved by road to TEMPLEUX (L.1.d.6.c.) where a portion of the Transport were parked; the remainder moved to HARGICOURT & took over the walking wounded centre (6.f.c.2.5.d.1.8.) from the 7th Australian Field Ambulance.	
		7.15 A.m.	OC Motor Transport less one Sunbeam, came under orders of OC 132 Fields Amb. & proceeded to the ADS. at 6.2.b/G.22.6.8.10. The remaining Sunbeam Car moved with the unit.	
		3 p.m.	Divisional Surgeon visited the camp. Wounded came in steadily throughout the day.	
		5 p.m.	Notified Capt. MORRIS D.C. received orders to go to 118 Field Amb (American). Evacuation carried out by light railway from HARGICOURT Station.	
HARGICOURT 6/f.c.25.d.1.8	7/10/18	4 p.m.	The unit moved forward to another site at BELLICOURT	
BELLICOURT 62.B/G.10.a.2.3		10 p.m.	(62.B.G.10.a.2.3) under Canvas. Train load of civilian refugees to TINCOURT.	
	8/10/18	2 p.m.	Lts HAMILTON, WHITE, RANGLEY D.C. joined the unit for temporary Duty.	
		5.10 p.m.	Zero.	

WAR DIARY
or
INTELLIGENCE SUMMARY.

(Erase heading not required.)

Army Form C. 2118.

134th FIELD AMB...

Place	Date	Hour	Summary of Events and Information	Remarks and references to Appendices
BELLICOURT 62B/G10a23	8/10/18	3 p.m.	Wounded came through all day, were evacuated by light railway & by lorries. G.O.C. 4th Army visited camp.	
JONCOURT 62cf/H8d9.10	9/10/18	4 A.m. 8 A.m.	Reveille. Unit moved to JONCOURT (62B H8 d 9.10) & establishes a W.W. Centre there at 8 A.m. Cases evacuated by light Railway thence. Forward lorries placed at BRANCOURT (62B c27 central) & PRÉMONT (62BC 4 6 central)) for collecting walking wounded.	
JONCOURT 62c/H8d9.10	10/10/18	8 A.m.	Reconnaissance made as far as BUSIGNY (57B/V.16) & forward lorry post establishes at V27 6 8 9/57 B. Relay lorry post placed at PRÉMONT 62B/C4 6 central. Evacuation carried out by light Railway & lorry.	62B/C4 6 central
JONCOURT 6f H8dg10	11/10/18	8 A.m.	Capt HALL M.R.C. & party 106 Field Amb (17th American Div) arrived to take over. No orders from the 30th American Div received. Weather bad & terrain for walking wounded westward beyond PRÉMONT	62B/C4 6 central

WAR DIARY or INTELLIGENCE SUMMARY

Army Form C. 2118.

Place	Date	Hour	Summary of Events and Information	Remarks and references to Appendices
JONCOURT 28/H8 d 9.10	11/10/18	7 pm	3 Horse Ambulances detailed to clear Roads 57B/V16 to clear the walking wounded.	
	12/10/18	8 Am	The walking wounded site was handed over to the 27th Dist. (American)	
		12 Am	The unit proceeded by Road to its new site at BRANCOURT 62B/C22 C14	
BRANCOURT 62B/C22 C14		2 pm	Arrives in billets. Bearers returned from 132 Fols Amb.	
	13/10/18	10 am	Divisional Surgeon visited the unit.	
		5 pm	Visited Div. Surgeon's Office. The unit is now acting as a Collecting Station for sick of the 120th Infantry.	
BRANCOURT	14/10/18		Thin. Cleaning billets. Kit inspection.	
do	15/10/18	10 Am	Conference at Div. Surgeon's Office - The will proceed into the line tonight & established a walking wounded Centre Reconnoitred BUSIGNY - VAUX ANDIGNY Road & picked a site at 57B V17 C 5.6.	
		11 Am		

Army Form C. 2118.

WAR DIARY
or
INTELLIGENCE SUMMARY.
(Erase heading not required.)

Place	Date	Hour	Summary of Events and Information	Remarks and references to Appendices
BRANCOURT b2B/C22c44		3 pm	Unit moves by road with half the transport to the new site at V17 c 5.6 Sheet 57B. Getting in at 5 pm. The remainder of the transport, & the 2 m. stores remain at BRANCOURT. 2 N.C.O's & 8 men were detailed to run the loading post at MONTBREHAIN Rail head: they have two operating tents & 2 Bell Tents as a camp.	
57B V17 c 5.6		5 pm	A walking wounded post was established.	
do	16/10/18	9 am	All bearers & all the wheel stretcher carriers, under Lieut FERRAN proceeded to 57B V9 c 6.6, & came under orders of O.C. 115 Field Amb (American). The motor transport has 1 Ford proceeded to the same place for duty with 118 Field Amb.	
		10 am	Various Divl Surgeons Office & loading post at Mont'brehain. Several N.C.O.s there are down with influenza.	
		11 am	Capt. GROOVER M.C. U.S.A. reports for duty with the unit. Lieut TISDALE reports back from leave.	

WAR DIARY or INTELLIGENCE SUMMARY

Army Form C. 2118.

Place	Date	Hour	Summary of Events and Information	Remarks and references to Appendices
BUSIGNY V.17.c.6.6 BUSIGNY	17/10/18	5.20 A.M.	Zero hour. Four lorries had reported during the night. One of these was sent forward to LA HAIE MENNERESSE at 5.40 A.M. (W.13.b./57B).	
			Wounded came in continually that forward, including a convoy of 16 G.S. waggons.	
		6 A.M.	I reconnoitred Vaux ANDIGNY (W.19.c.20) & found 8 horse ambulances into the village.	
		Noon	I reconnoitred MOLAIN (W.16.a. + c./57B) through - the lorry up to there from LA HAIE MENNERESSE; it could go no further as the bridges over the SELLE were blown up. Front line uncertain. So I did not move forward.	
		3 p.m.		
BUSIGNY V.17.c.6.6 /57B	18/10/18	5 A.M.	Reconnoitred a place in VAUX ANDIGNY & moved the unit & walking station there.	
VAUX ANDIGNY 57B/W.20 central		7.30 A.M.	Wounded, especially gassed cases, poured in.	
		9 A.M.	The village was shelled, so I moved about 200 cases to the outskirts of the village on the BOHAIN Road (V.19.d.8.2/57B).	
		10 A.M.	Reconnoitred St MARTIN RIVIERE (57B/W.10 & 10.9) & found the lorry from MOLAIN into this village. Front line still uncertain.	
		1.30 p.m.	Motored to Montbrehain to see if the loading party at the light Railway were getting on all right - everything satisfactory.	

WAR DIARY
or
INTELLIGENCE SUMMARY.

Army Form C. 2118.

134th FIELD AMBULANCE

Place	Date	Hour	Summary of Events and Information	Remarks and references to Appendices
VAUX ANDIGNY 57B/V20 central	18/10/18	Noon	I moved the transport lines from BRANCOURT 62B/C22c14 to BUSIGNY 57B/V7c56.	
	19/10/18		Very few wounded came through. I was preparing to move into St MARTIN RIVIÈRE (W10 a), when I was advised of a disproportionate S of a relief.	
		10 pm	The walking wounded were taken on by the 2nd Field Amb.	
Do	20/10/18	9 Am	Visited Divl Surgeon's Office, who gave me orders to move to BUSIGNY (V7c56)	
BUSIGNY 57B/V7c56		11 Am	Unit arrived at old site. All came through from O.C. 118 Field Amb. (American).	
		3 pm	Lt. Col. Glen Drew reports back from leave.	
BUSIGNY 57B/V7c56	21/10/18	Noon	Unit proceeded by road to ESTREES 62B/H20 6.5. Billets were found in old ruins.	
ESTREES 62B/H20 6.5		5 pm	Arrival in billets.	
	22/10/18	8 Am	Unit proceeded by road to billets at MARQUAIX 62°/K14 c05	
MARQUAIX 62°/K14 c05		12 Am	Arrival in billets	

WAR DIARY
or
INTELLIGENCE SUMMARY.
(Erase heading not required.)

Army Form C. 2118.

Place	Date	Hour	Summary of Events and Information	Remarks and references to Appendices
MARQUAIX 62c/K14.c.0.5.	23/10/18	9am	The Transport less 1 water cart, 2 G.S. waggons & Cooks limber under Sgt Redworth, joins the 126th Infantry Transport & proceeds by road to staging area at SUZANNE.	
		3pm	Troops moves to TINCOURT Station for entraining.	
		5pm	The remaining transport moves to ROISEL Station for entraining.	
WARLOY 57D U 24 d 3.10	24/10/18	9am	The troops detrains at HEILLY (Amiens 17) & marches to the new site at WARLOY	
		3pm	Orders received to form the Divisional Skin Depot at the hospital.	
	25/10/18	9am	Parade. Routine work. Cleaning up the hospital. Fine weather. All ranks carrying out prophylactic against influenza.	
	26/10/18	10am	Capt. CHIPMAN M.C. USA, the Divisional virologist, reports for duty. To take over all Skin Cases. Skin department in full swing.	
	27/10/18		Routine work. Fine weather.	
	28/10/18		Fine weather. Normal routine	

Army Form C. 2118.

WAR DIARY
or
INTELLIGENCE SUMMARY.
(Erase heading not required.)

Place	Date	Hour	Summary of Events and Information	Remarks and references to Appendices
WARLOY 57d/U24 d 3.10	29/10/18	9 am	Usual Routine. I visited 41 Stationary Hospital at the ASYLUM AMIENS to enquire for our evacuated men.	
	30/10/15	9 am 4 pm	Usual Routine. Weather fine. Lieut- BRANDAU M.C, U.S.A. reports for temporary duty.	
	31/10/16	9 am 11 am noon	Usual Routine. Sr. Surgeon visited the Hospital. Orders received to turn the Hospital into a General Hospital as well as a skin Hospital.	
		7 pm	Lieuts W. FOREMAN, H.W. STRAUS, W.L. ATKINS reported for temporary duty.	

31/10/18.

G.F. Moore
Major RAMC
o/c 134 Field Ambulance

Original
w/11/18

Vol 33
14/3401

CONFIDENTIAL.

WAR DIARY

OF

134 Field Ambulance

from 1st Nov. 1918 to 30th Nov. 1918

(Volume 33.)

Army Form C. 2118.

R.A.M.C.
134th FIELD AMBULANCE

WAR DIARY
or
INTELLIGENCE SUMMARY
(Erase heading not required.)

Place	Date	Hour	Summary of Events and Information	Remarks and references to Appendices
WARLOY 57d U24 d 3.10.	1/11/18	9 am.	It was billetted in the Hospital grounds have been allotted in the village, & the Hospital outbuildings made ready for patients. Weather fine.	
	2/11/18	9 am	Usual routine work. Many Sick admitted.	
	3/11/18	9 am	Usual routine.	
	4/11/18	11.30 am	Sgt HEATHFIELD A.S.C.(MT) who has died at 41st Stationary Hospital was fetched & buried with full military honour. A convalescent hospital has been opened in the village for the convalescents of this hospital.	
		3 pm	The Divl Surgeon visited the Hospital. Six international Officers, NCOs &men were cited in the American Divisional Order, dated 2/11/18. for meritorious conduct in the	

action from 29.9.18 - 19.10.18.
The Capt A.hario R.C.COOKE MC 7:1270 Sgt. F.W.UNWIN T4/065479 Dr G. BOWERS 41524 PG A.R SIM
Capt. & 2L EG FLOYD R.A.MC(TF) M/074752 Cpl(A/Sgt) S HEATHFIELD M/021134 PG T.H.BAYLISS
                                    72277 Cpl(A Sgt) E.A GRADDUCK 1237 PG W.HELLIER
                                    72165 Cpl. W.C. DANIELLS M.M. 72248 PG W.J GALLAGHER
                                                                        M/08743 PG T.H.THOMPSON

Army Form C. 2118.

R.A.M.C.
134th FIELD AMBULANCE

WAR DIARY
or
INTELLIGENCE SUMMARY

(Erase heading not required.)

Place	Date	Hour	Summary of Events and Information	Remarks and references to Appendices
WARLOY 57d U24 d 3.10	5/12/18	9 A.m. 10 A.m.	Usual routine. Capt. McBRAYER R.A. & Lieut HAMILTON E.S. D.C.USA reported for temporary duty.	
	6/12/18	9 A.m. 9.30 A.m. 3 P.m.	Usual routine. Lieut. ATKINS M.C.USA returns to this unit. Col. WHALEY visited the unit	
	7/12/18	9 A.m. 11 A.m.	Usual routine. Col. WHALEY visited the unit. Influenza epidemic is now on the wane.	
	8/12/18	9 A.m. 2 P.m.	Usual routine. Col. WHALEY visited the unit.	
	9/12/18	9 A.m. 4 P.m.	Usual routine. Weather fine. I visited workshops of the M.T. Col. WHALEY visited the hospital	
	10/12/18	9 A.m.	Usual routine. One reinforcement for A.S.C (MT) arrives. Capt Chipman M.C.USA. proceeded to II Corps (American) for duty	

Army Form C. 2118.

134th FIELD AMBULANCE

WAR DIARY
or
INTELLIGENCE SUMMARY.
(Erase heading not required.)

Place	Date	Hour	Summary of Events and Information	Remarks and references to Appendices
WARLOY 57d U24 d 3.10	11/11/18	5 A.m. 9 A.m.	The Armistice was signed. Normal routine. There is a marked decrease in the influenza admissions	
	12/11/18	9 A.m.	Normal Routine. Weather fine	
	13/11/18	9 A.m.	Normal Routine	
	14/11/18	6 10 A.m. noon 2 p.m.	Routine Reveille 5 A.m. Breakfast 5.30 A.m. Parade 6.40 A.m. Moved off 7 A.m. to LA HOUSSOYE Sheet 57d I 3 d Position on parade ground taken up at 9.30 A.m. Regt Review by C.G. 30th American Division at 10 A.m. Arrived back in billets Lieut STRAUS M.C. U.S.A. proceeded to 113 M.G.C. for temporary duty.	
	15/11/18	9 A.m.	Normal Routine weather fine	
	16/11/18	9 A.m. 1 p.m. 5 p.m.	Orders received to evacuate the Hospital. Hospital clear of patients. All surplus stores & equipment handed over to American Div. Lieuts FOREMAN & BRANDAU M.C. U.S.A & Lieut HAMILTON D.C. U.S.A. were recalled to their units. Orders received to proceed by road to QUINEVILLE	

Army Form C. 2118.

134th FIELD AMBULANCE

WAR DIARY
or
INTELLIGENCE SUMMARY.
(Erase heading not required.)

Instructions regarding War Diaries and Intelligence Summaries are contained in F.S. Regs., Part II. and the Staff Manual respectively. Title pages will be prepared in manuscript.

Place	Date	Hour	Summary of Events and Information	Remarks and references to Appendices
PICQUIGNY (Amiens No.17)	17/11/18	4 A.M.	Reveille	
		6.40 A.M.	Unit marched off, halting for lunch on the outskirts of AMIENS	
		1 p.m.	march continued to PICQUIGNY, where the unit rested for the night	
	18/11/16	4 A.M.	Reveille	
		6.15 A.M.	Unit marched 6½M. halting for lunch at FONTAINE sur SOMME	
		11.30	Unit continued the march to ABBEVILLE, reporting to O.C. A.H.T.D.	
		4 p.m.	All horses handed over to A.H.T.D.	
ABBEVILLE	19/11/16	9 A.M.	All stores equipment handed in	
		9 A.M.	Orders received to proceed to ETAPLES tomorrow	
		1 p.m.	Orders received to stand fast	
	20/11/16	9 A.M.	Military medals have been awarded to 145297 Sgt. F.M. UNWIN, R.A.M.C., 412840 Q.M.S. A.R. SIM, R.A.M.C., 92242 Ptn. J. GALLAGHER, R.A.M.C., M2/074762 Cpl. S. HEATHFIELD M.T. A.S.C., 9 M1/08743 Pte. T.H. THOMPSON M.T. A.S.C.	
		9 A.M.	Route march. Unit still awaits movement orders.	
	21/11/16	9 A.M.	Route march	
	22/11/18 9 A.M. to 30/11/18		Route march. Unit remained in camp at ABBEVILLE, standing by awaiting further orders as to disposal	

C.M. Andrew, Lt Col
Comdg 134 Fd Ambulance

Wrapper Indorsement.

Hq. 30th Division, Division Surgeon's Office, Am.E.F., November 10, 1918 –
To The D.A.G., G.H.Q., 3rd Echelon, Rouen, France.

Forwarded.

A. M. Whaley,
Colonel, Medical Corps, U.S.A.
Division Surgeon.

Wrapper Indorsement.

Hq. 30th Division, Division Surgeon's Office, Am. E. F., November 10, 1918 –
To The D.A.G., G.H.Q., 3rd Echelon, Rouen, France.

Forwarded.

A. M. Whaley,
Colonel, Medical Corps, U.S.A.
Division Surgeon.

CONFIDENTIAL WAR DIARY.

134th FIELD AMBULANCE.

From:- DECEMBER 1st TO DECEMBER 12th

VOLUME 34.

Army Form C. 2118.

134th FIELD AMBULANCE

WAR DIARY
or
INTELLIGENCE SUMMARY.
(Erase heading not required.)

Place	Date	Hour	Summary of Events and Information	Remarks and references to Appendices
ABBEVILLE	2/4/19	4 pm	All motor transport proceeded to Reserve Park at WISSANT (Pas de Calais / S).	
	3/4/19 to 8/4/19		Awaiting orders.	
ETAPLES	9/4/19	1.15 pm	Unit proceeded to R.A.M.C. Base Depot ETAPLES. Personnel transferred to command. 1 Commander on disbandment. All books, records, accounts finally closed. 9 sent to respective destinations. Unit disbanded finally.	
	12/4/19			

19/4/19

Christopher, Lt Col
Comdg 134 Fd Ambce.

www.ingramcontent.com/pod-product-compliance
Lightning Source LLC
Chambersburg PA
CBHW080911230426
43667CB00015B/2653